The Economist's Oath

Advance praise for *The Economist's Oath*

"Economists matter. They have influence and power; what they do affects people's lives. With influence comes responsibility. All too often economists don't even consider those responsibilities. They should, and this book will help them do so."

—David Colander,
CAJ Distinguished Professor of Economics,
Department of Economics, Middlebury College

"Economists rarely seem to think about the ethics of their profession. This book makes a powerful case as to why they should and what professional ethics would mean."

—Dean Baker,
Co-Director, Center for Economic and Policy Research

"The economics profession today faces a crisis of confidence and identity. This partly stems from a blindness to ethical factors in economic policy advising and making. *The Economist's Oath* is a major contribution to the necessary rethinking of professional economic conduct."

—Robert H. Nelson,
University of Maryland

"It is remarkable that the economics profession has failed to produce a code of ethics. *The Economist's Oath* is a wake-up call not only to professional economists but to everyone who relies upon their judgment and advice—in short, to all of us."

—James K. Boyce,
University of Massachusetts, Amherst

The Economist's Oath
On the Need for and Content of Professional Economic Ethics

George F. DeMartino

OXFORD
UNIVERSITY PRESS

Oxford University Press, Inc., publishes works that further Oxford University's objective of excellence in research, scholarship, and education.

Oxford   New York
Auckland   Cape Town   Dar es Salaam   Hong Kong   Karachi   Kuala Lumpur   Madrid   Melbourne
Mexico City   Nairobi   New Delhi   Shanghai   Taipei   Toronto

With offices in
Argentina   Austria   Brazil   Chile   Czech Republic   France   Greece   Guatemala   Hungary   Italy
Japan   Poland   Portugal   Singapore   South Korea   Switzerland   Thailand   Turkey   Ukraine
Vietnam

Library of Congress Cataloging-in-Publication Data
DeMartino, George.
 The economist's oath : on the need for and content of professional economic ethics/George F. DeMartino.
    p. cm.
 Includes bibliographical references and index.
 ISBN 978-0-19-973056-8 (cloth : alk. paper)
 1. Economics—Moral and ethical aspects. 2. Business ethics. 3. Social ethics. I. Title.
 HB72.D36 2010
 174—dc22
                                                    2010012669

1 2 3 4 5 6 7 8 9
Printed in the United States of America on acid-free paper

Note to Readers
This publication is designed to provide accurate and authoritative information in regard to the subject matter covered. It is based upon sources believed to be accurate and reliable and is intended to be current as of the time it was written. It is sold with the understanding that the publisher is not engaged in rendering legal, accounting, or other professional services. If legal advice or other expert assistance is required, the services of a competent professional person should be sought. Also, to confirm that the information has not been affected or changed by recent developments, traditional legal research techniques should be used, including checking primary sources where appropriate.

(Based on the Declaration of Principles jointly adopted by a Committee of the American Bar Association and a Committee of Publishers and Associations.)

For Ilene and my extended family,
who have shared with me the excitement of this project,
and for Julie Graham, in memoriam

Contents

Acknowledgments

Over the years that I have worked on this project, I have received support from a number of people. First and foremost, I benefited enormously from the research assistance of a wonderful cohort of students at the Josef Korbel School of International Studies of the University of Denver, including Erica Bouris, Blaire Davis, Kate Drexler, Alex Karklins, Kamelia Kirilova, Hanna Parakhnevich, Raphael Reinke and, in particular, Emma Ekdahl, Galen Smith, Rod Thompson, and Kate Watkins. Emma and Galen provided outstanding assistance over the past two years when the demands of the work were most acute and deadlines most pressing. Without their contributions, this book would remain a work-in-progress for a long time to come. I have received suggestions and guidance for this project and/or comments on various parts of the manuscript and related papers from William Black, James Boyce, David Ciepley, Jim Crotty, Jack Donnelly, Rachel Epstein, Jamie Galbraith, Rob Garnett, John Harvey, Barry Herman, Michael Joffe, Thomas Mayer, Deirdre McCloskey, Steve Payson, Steve Pepper, Yvon Pho, Martin Rhodes, Charlie Sawyer, John Siegfried, Martha Starr, Rob Williams, Steve Ziliak, and many subscribers to the History of Economics Society listserv. I am particularly indebted to Ilene Grabel, who read the full manuscript and provided invaluable advice.

Thanks to Joan Dubinsky, Ethics Officer of the IMF, and to the many economists whom I interviewed during the course of my research (most of whom will remain anonymous, owing to the nature of our discussions)— and to the members of the Association for Integrity and Responsible Leadership in Economics and Associated Professions (AIRLEAP) and the Association for Economic and Social Analysis (AESA); both provided insight, encouragement, and other assistance. I also received financial support from the PINS program at the University of Denver and from a sabbatical enhancement from the university. I am also grateful to the Political Economy Research Institute and the Department of Economics at the University of Massachusetts for providing me with the opportunity to work intensively on this project during a sabbatical in the fall of 2008 and to Julie Graham, who opened her home to me during my stay in Massachusetts and encouraged me in many ways at an important stage in the project. Her sudden passing this spring leaves so many of us with terrible sadness but also with enduring inspiration. Elizabeth Dunn, Zachary Elder, and the other librarians at the Special Collections Library at Duke

University were most helpful to me as I explored the American Economic Association archives that are housed there. I benefited from the anonymous reviews for Oxford University Press (OUP) and from the consistent support of OUP Executive Editor Terry Vaughn and Assistant Editor Joe Jackson. Finally, I received helpful suggestions and criticisms during many university seminars and conference presentations where I tried out the ideas that appear in this book.

Preface

I began thinking about the idea of professional economic ethics in 2004 when I was invited to give a plenary talk on the future of economics at the first meeting of the International Confederation of Associations for Pluralism in Economics (ICAPE). At the time, I was teaching a graduate seminar on the normative foundations of economics, and a discussion with my students on the maxi-max decision rule that appears in Robert Nozick's *Anarchy, State and Utopia* provoked me to think about the practice of economic policy making. It struck me immediately that the maxi-max principle that Nozick identifies and derides in this text was in fact the guiding decision rule in the market liberalization project in the global South from the 1980s onward and in the transition economies during the 1990s. I then began to wonder about whether the use of this decision rule is not just unwise (as Nozick rightly claims) but also unethical when applied by a profession that enjoys influence over the lives of others. How could the profession employ a decision rule of this sort that is so terribly dangerous? This, in turn, led me to investigate what kind of professional ethics the economics profession had come to embrace—and I learned then that, in fact, unlike most every other profession of consequence, economics had rejected consistently over the past century any sort of professional ethics to guide the behavior of its members in the course of their practice. I came to conclude that this allergy to professional ethics was damaging for the profession and for the communities that economists purport to serve. This became the focus of my ICAPE talk, and when the resulting paper appeared the next year in *Challenge*, I presumed that I was finished with the topic.

Over the next year or so, however, I found my thoughts returning to the matter of professional economic ethics. By then I was teaching a course on professional ethics and international affairs, and as I delved more deeply into the literature on professional ethics, I came to be convinced that the lack of professional economic ethics represented a grave problem. Indeed, I have come to believe that the disregard of professional economic ethics itself entails a professional ethical failure. And so I decided to explore the matter in a book-length treatment that would provide me with the space necessary to accomplish two goals. The primary objective of this book is to make the case for professional economic ethics. This case has many steps, and it constitutes Part I of the book. Here I provide a provisional mapping of the economics profession, identifying where economists work and what they do. I then draw on the results of dozens of interviews with applied economists that I conducted to tease out the kinds of mundane, everyday ethical dilemmas that they face as they try to do good work. Next, I present a brief historical account of the economics profession in the United States and present what I take to be the most plausible reasons for the failure of the profession to examine the ethical entailments of its practice when all around it other professions were taking that step. I explore what are the strongest arguments against the idea of professional economic ethics, drawing on both what economists have had to say and what mainstream economic theory would lead us to infer about the relative worthlessness and dangers associated with the adoption of professional ethics. This is followed by a two-step argument that comprises a rebuttal of the economist's case against—and a positive case for—professional economic ethics.

The second goal of the book is advanced in Part II and is of necessity more tentative. It begins to examine the content of professional economic ethics. Chapter 8 explores the lessons that economics can learn from other professions that have wrestled with the daunting difficulties that arise in the context of professional practice. There I consider several ethical principles and questions that have emerged within other professions that are relevant for economics. I then ask whether economists and the economics profession have performed their duties in ways that are consistent with these principles, even if the profession recognizes no explicit professional responsibilities. If that is the case, then we might conclude that economics does not need a formal body of professional ethics since economists have intuited the relevant principles and applied them in their work. Chapters 9 and 10 present two case studies that examine the role of the profession in epoch-making interventions—the market liberalization project in the global South and transition economies (the case that first attracted me to the subject) and the campaign to resist government regulation of financial markets in the United States and beyond during a period of rapid financial innovation (from the 1990s to the present). I attempt to show that in both cases, the profession failed to honor principles that are widely regarded across the professions as fundamental to ethical professional practice. In Chapter 11, I explore the content and contours of the yet-to-be established field of professional economic ethics. The subsequent chapter then explores how undergraduate and graduate economic training might be reformed were the profession to take seriously its obligation to engage professional economic ethics. I conclude this book with a proposed oath—the *Economist's Oath*—which gathers together many of the central ideas that arise throughout the book.

In the first instance, at least, the establishment of the field of professional economic ethics requires no blue-ribbon committees, white papers, or other formal initiatives. It requires instead only the contributions of individual scholars and practitioners within economics and beyond: contributions that take the form of posing and exploring questions pertaining to the ethical obligations of the profession and its individual members to the communities they serve. *What does it mean to be an ethical economist—and what does it mean for economics to be an ethical profession?* My hope is that this book will provoke others who share some of my concerns about our profession to begin work in this area—to investigate the content of economic practice (within and beyond academia), to examine the ethical entailments of this work, and to begin to pose for consideration how economists and their professional institutions might alter their behavior and governance to ensure that well-meaning economists do right while trying to do good.

Part I

THE CASE FOR PROFESSIONAL
ECONOMIC ETHICS

Chapter 1

"I Do Solemnly Swear"

I do solemnly swear:

That I will be loyal to the Profession of Economics and just and generous to its members. That I will practice the art of economics in uprightness and honor.

That into whatever community I shall enter, it shall be for the good of the community to the utmost of my power, holding myself aloof from wrong, from corruption, from the tempting of others to vice.

That I will recognize and keep always in view that the community I serve is never a means for my ends, but always an end unto itself. It, and not I, is the rightful architect of its future. . .

UNIVERSITY COMMENCEMENT, 2015

Imagine that we are attending the graduation ceremony at a leading United States university not too many years from now—say, 2015. At the appropriate moment in the proceedings, those receiving the PhD in economics stand up, raise their right hands, and recite the *Economist's Oath*. The *Oath* commits the initiates to respect the autonomy and agency of the communities they will serve. It demands that they try to anticipate the potential harm that their policy interventions and advising might cause to others and take steps to mitigate it. It urges them to maintain an attitude of humility—to keep in view their own fallibility and the likelihood of consequential error that resides in the methods of their profession. The *Oath* emphasizes the value of pluralism and open inquiry. These principles appear in a new body of professional economic ethics which these students have studied carefully and debated vigorously during their graduate studies—both in the classroom and in apprenticeships outside the university.

We economists find this scenario a bit absurd. We tend to think that the exercise, were it to occur, would be pointless. We know that professional ethics without enforcement mechanisms amounts to little more than window dressing intended to give the appearance of virtue where it may be entirely absent. Economists know that all of us are rational individualists who value, above all else, our own interests. We are not likely to be distracted from our egoistic pursuits by a collection of pieties politely called professional ethics. Inducements would be necessary to make the oath effective. And this would require a binding code which is backed by state-sanctioned professional licensing so that the economist who runs afoul of the rules can be punished and perhaps even "disbarred." But don't we economists know better than anyone that licensing interferes with market competition? Isn't licensing a barrier to entry that restricts supply and garners monopoly rents? This is precisely what we teach our students in Econ 101, after all. How could the economics profession, which celebrates the competition emanating from free markets, possibly countenance something like that? Even worse, ethical matters are irreducibly subjective and irresolvable via the kind of rational methods and empirical techniques with which economists are equipped. The pursuit of professional ethics surely would generate endless debate that would inspire cynicism rather than useful guidance. Why, then, should we expend the precious intellectual resources necessary to pursue professional ethics when the likely benefits are so meager and when there is so much other important work to be done?

ECONOMISTS' INFLUENCE OVER OTHERS

Later on, I will explore and refute these claims against professional economic ethics. I will argue that there is an urgent need for professional economic ethics. Why? The central claim can be put simply. The economics profession today has an enormous impact on the life chances of people across the globe: one that is far greater than that of most other professions. It is not always the impact that economists hope to have, to be sure, not least since economists' prescriptions are often distorted in the political arena, but it is considerable nonetheless. This was not always the case: the profession's influence is the result of its enhanced status over the postwar period to which the profession consciously aspired (Bernstein 2001). Economists' influence has been amplified by the emergence of important multilateral economic institutions and by institutional changes in developed and developing countries that place economists in positions with substantial decision-making authority. Despite the long-standing celebration among economists of the free market as the best means for directing social affairs, the fact is that the economists who guide the world's leading economic departments and ministries, central and development banks, multilateral agencies, global consulting firms, and related institutions engage in practices that influence economic flows and outcomes, sometimes decisively. In the extreme, economists sometimes undertake "social engineering," helping to design institutions that are fundamental to economic affairs.[1] Their interventions introduce and restrict liberties and freedoms, incentives, rewards, punishments, and risk; they affect incomes, careers, entitlements and all the other factors that contribute to economic security. Today, economists work not just as detached academic scientists describing the world but as mechanics and engineers, purposively seeking to change it.

Economic interventions of the sort undertaken by economists today entail a responsibility that is, in a word, awesome. Unfortunately, in this work, the profession exhibits a mixture of naïveté and hubris (McCloskey 1990). Too often, economists view their applied work as the straightforward application of objective principles without taking into account the value judgments that economic interventions necessarily entail (DeMartino 2000). Moreover, economists often speak as if they have in hand the uniquely correct understanding of economic affairs; they tend to act as if they know which interventions are optimal and as if they are warranted in using the levers of influence at their disposal to enact them. In this way, economists see themselves as fulfilling their ethical obligations—to their science, their professional colleagues and clients, and the communities that will presumably benefit from their interventions.

Naïveté and hubris regarding economic science and the capacities of the economics profession are dangerous. Economics treats matters that are not amenable to complete modeling or dependable prediction. Successful economic interventions require as much art, judgment, practical wisdom, and luck as scientific expertise. Unintended consequences are sometimes more powerful than intended consequences; unanticipated costs and benefits can overwhelm anticipated costs and benefits; events that are predicted to be extraordinarily rare occur with surprising frequency; and more confounding, the presumed beneficiaries of economic policy sometimes oppose and take steps to subvert the interventions taken by economists on their behalf.

Consequential Errors

These features help to explain why economists have made extraordinary errors over the past several decades. One of the most stunning of these occurred in the private sector and involved the implosion of Long Term Capital Management (LTCM) in the fall of 1998, which threatened to destabilize U.S. and international financial markets. LTCM had been a star of the financial world since its creation in 1994 because of the involvement of a group of extraordinary financial economists—including two—Robert C. Merton and Myron Scholes, who would go on to win the 1997 Nobel Memorial Prize in economics. LTCM economists acted as if market instability and uncertainty could be reduced to calculable risk. Committed to the idea of efficient markets, the LTCM economists constructed models for establishing the appropriate spread between various kinds of linked assets. When their models flagged a diversion from these spreads, the firm invested heavily to capture the anticipated future corrections in market valuations.

LTCM funded its arbitrage activities by leveraging its capital to extraordinary levels. So long as LTCM models correctly anticipated market trends (which they did with reassuring consistency for the better part of three years), aggressive leveraging allowed LTCM to profit enormously even when price movements were miniscule. But just as leverage provided the basis for impressive returns on the way up, it ensured LTCM's implosion when events unfolded in ways that contradicted the economists' predictions. During the late summer and fall of 1998, LTCM began to hemorrhage tens to hundreds of millions of dollars per day. When Russia declared a debt repayment moratorium in August, LTCM lost $535 million in one trading session. As a consequence of the erosion of its capital and its stubborn refusal to sell depreciating assets, the firm's leveraging rose from 30:1 to 100:1 in just five weeks. Suddenly, major Wall Street banks and other financial institutions around the world faced the prospect of devastating losses in the event of LTCM's likely collapse. Preventing this crisis required the New York branch of the Federal Reserve to organize a banking consortium to bail out the firm. Until the end, the LTCM economists continued to believe that their investment strategies were fundamentally sound. They blamed their misfortune on other market actors who they believed had taken steps to sabotage LTCM's success (Lowenstein 2000; see also Coy and Woolley 1998 and Edwards 1999).

A second and far more consequential error resulted from the profession's failure to take advantage of the opportunity to learn from the LTCM debacle (*Economist*, August 31, 2000). At present (summer 2010), much of the world is grappling with the economic consequences of the failure of the United States and other governments to regulate financial markets sufficiently during a time of extraordinary financial innovation. Prominent economists since the 1980s argued forcefully against increased regulation on grounds that financial liberalization would induce greater economic efficiency and growth in the developed and developing world (see Chapters 9 and 10). Economists also claimed that financial market institutions could and would police themselves adequately to ensure against irresponsible and dangerous practices. Federal Reserve Chairman Alan Greenspan was among the most influential of the advocates of this view. Both before and after LTCM's collapse, Greenspan preached the benefits of financial liberalization. He opposed increased regulation of derivatives and other nontransparent financial instruments, though by the 1990s, they were expanding rapidly and were being used in part "to dodge the Fed's own margin rules" (Lowenstein 2000, 105). In response to these strategies, Greenspan called for eliminating the margin rules altogether. In his words:

> Removal of these financing constraints would promote the safety and soundness of broker-dealers by permitting more financing alternatives and hence more effective liquidity management . . . In the case of broker-dealers, the Federal Reserve Board sees no public policy purpose in it being involved in overseeing their securities credit (quoted in Lowenstein 2000, 106).

Suddenly this orthodoxy is in tatters. In a startling reversal, Greenspan pulled the thread that ensured the unraveling. On October 23, 2008, in the midst of global financial distress brought on by unsound financial practices, he admitted to the U.S. House Committee on Oversight and Government Reform that he made a fundamental error: "I made a mistake in presuming that the self-interest of organizations, specifically banks and others, was such that they were best capable of protecting their own shareholders." Speaking of a "once in a century credit tsunami," he continued, "[t]hose of us who have looked to the self-interest of lending institutions to protect shareholders' equity, myself especially, are in a state of shocked disbelief" (Andrews 2008). Coming from a disciple of Ayn Rand, this admission was stunning. In contrast, economists such as Robert Shiller of Yale University, Dean Baker of the *Center for Economic and Policy Research* in Washington, DC, and several others had warned for years of the dangers associated with the financial free-for-all that had emerged in connection with the housing bubble (see, e.g., Shiller 2005; Baker 2004). These warnings were dismissed in the halls of power in part because of Greenspan's constant opposition to increased public surveillance of financial markets when there was still a chance to head off the speculative activity that generated the crisis (Baker 2009b).[2]

A third error occurred in the context of the eagerness of leading economists to take on the role of social engineer without sufficient attention to the complexities attending that role. The case involves the design and implementation of the abrupt turn toward free-market (or, in the vernacular of political science, "neoliberal") economic policy regimes across the globe in places lacking the appropriate institutional supports, capacities, and inclinations. These reforms, undertaken as they were via what was called "shock therapy," have had traumatic effects on many developing economies in the South and in the formerly socialist countries such as Russia. Economists advocated abrupt economic transformation in both the developing and transition economies unencumbered by well-established, professional ethical principles that have emerged across other professions. These interventions created tremendous risk for communities that lacked the wherewithal to manage them. Moreover, economists neither sought nor received "prior informed consent" from those who would be most directly affected by the reforms they advocated.

In some cases, U.S. economists willingly advised governments that were clearly repressive. Funded by the Ford Foundation, economists from the University of California, Berkeley worked in advance of the overthrow of Indonesia's Leftist President Sukarno to prepare for economic reform that was in line with U.S. foreign policy. General Suharto installed himself as President in a coup in 1965 that left upward of a million people dead. The Berkeley economists trained the technocrats who would be appointed upon the overthrow of Sukarno and advised the Suharto government even after he had proven himself to be a violent dictator (Ransom 1975). A similar set of events soon played out in Chile. In this case, University of Chicago-trained economists (who would come to be known as the "Chicago Boys") designed and implemented the economic transformation plan for General Pinochet after the violent overthrow of President Allende in 1973, without objection to the authoritarian nature of the regime which ensured that Chileans would be deprived of any say in charting the country's economic course (Barber 1995). Indeed, the Chicago Boys rationalized the need for a dictatorial regime to dismantle the interest groups that in their view had up until then distorted public policy. The economists believed that by cooperating with the regime they could create the conditions necessary for true economic liberty (Silva 1991). Milton Friedman visited Chile upon the invitation of his Chicago colleague, Arnold Harberger, during the early stages of the economic transformation and insisted upon its full and immediate enactment. His involvement comprised a face-to-face meeting with Pinochet in which he assured the General that if he followed his advice, he would oversee an economic miracle; he emphasized to Pinochet that "gradualism is not feasible" (Friedman and Friedman 1999, 592; see Klein 2007). He also gave televised lectures and interviews on the need for shock therapy to cure the "sick country" of its inflation (Cárcamo-Huechante 2006).

For granting assistance to a brutal regime, Friedman was widely attacked. In response to his critics, Friedman had this to say about his own activities and those of the Chicago Boys:

> In spite of my profound disagreement with the authoritarian political system of Chile, I do not consider it as evil for an economist to render technical economic advice to the Chilean Government, any more than I would regard it as evil for a physician to give technical medical advice to the Chilean Government to help end a medical plague (*Newsweek*, June 14, 1976, cited in Letelier 1976, 1).

In defending the involvement of economists in countries where citizens would have no influence over economic affairs, Friedman anticipated what would become the predominant view among leading economists who later promoted radical reform across the developing world and transition economies. Indeed, in countries with formal democratic governance, the rhetoric and practice of shock therapy subverted meaningful prior consent of those who would be most adversely affected by neoliberal reform. As we will investigate in Chapter 9, economists believed that short-term pain associated with reform would engender a backlash from civil society that might block the needed economic transformation. Fearing backlash, leading economists such as Jeffrey Sachs and Anders Åslund advised policy makers in Russia and elsewhere to undertake the economic transformation all at once, before opposition could crystallize (Sachs 1991; Wedel 2001; Angner 2006). Their advice to officials in transition economies was, in the words of Sachs, to "figure out how much society can take, and then move three times quicker than that." To drive home the point, Sachs cited approvingly the words of a Polish economist: "You don't try to cross a chasm in two jumps" (Sachs 1991, 236). In Poland in 1989, he assured nervous legislators that "The crisis will be over in six months" (Wedel 2001, 21, 48).

Throughout the period of economic transition in Central and Eastern Europe, there was substantial consensus among the profession's most influential members about the desirability of rapid reform (see Murrell 1995). Given the absence of historical precedents for economic transformations of this scale, it is clear that the reformers subjected countries to economic experimentation without sufficient knowledge—let alone the permission—of those who would be most harmed by the interventions.[3] Economists enacted policies and designed institutions that they surely believed to be in the best interests of these communities. What they failed to do was to help these communities to design and implement policies that they might have reasonably preferred and that might have entailed less risk of harm.[4]

In some cases, the harm was severe. Indeed, a recent study reported in *The Lancet* finds that Russia, Kazakhstan, Latvia, Lithuania, and Estonia suffered a tripling of unemployment and a 41 percent increase in male death rates between 1991 and 1994, immediately following privatization (Stuckler, King, and McKee 2009). Factoring out other determinants, the researchers conclude that

> Mass privatisation programmes were associated with an increase in short-term adult male mortality rates of 12.8%. . . with similar results for the alternative privatisation indices from the European Bank for Reconstruction and Development . . . (2009, 1).

Between 1991 and 1994, life expectancy in Russia dropped by as much as 4.7 years overall and by 6.2 years for men (Angner 2006). While the economic advocates of shock therapy predicted "short-term" pain as a consequence of the reform, they certainly did not expect this kind of social trauma.

The Man of System

But they might have done so had they paid attention not just to Adam Smith's *The Wealth of Nations* and its passages that celebrate market organization, but also his *Theory of Moral Sentiments*. There, Smith derides the "man of system" who presumes to have in hand the blueprint of the ideal society and who believes himself to be authorized to implement it. Smith deserves to be quoted at length on this point. In his words, the man of system

> is apt to be very wise in his own conceit; and is often so enamoured with the supposed beauty of his own ideal plan of government, that he cannot suffer the smallest deviation from any part of it. He goes on to establish it

completely and in all its parts, without any regard either to the great interests, or to the strong prejudices which may oppose it. He seems to imagine
that he can arrange the different members of a great society with as much
ease as the hand arranges the different pieces upon a chess-board (Smith
1976, 233–34).

In Smith's view the man of system exhibits hubris that can only
do harm:

Some general, and even systematical, idea of the perfection of policy and
law, may no doubt be necessary. . .But to insist upon establishing, and upon
establishing all at once, and in spite of all opposition, every thing which that
idea may seem to require, must often be the highest degree of arrogance. It
is to erect his own judgment into the supreme standard of right and wrong.
It is to fancy himself the only wise and worthy man in the commonwealth,
and that his fellow-citizens should accommodate themselves to him and
not he to them (Smith 1976, 234).[5]

Smith was a reformer, to be sure. But for Smith, the responsible
reformer is not an ideologue or social engineer. Instead, he

will accommodate, as well as he can, his public arrangements to the confirmed habits and prejudices of the people; and will remedy as well as he
can, the "inconveniences" which may flow from the want of those regulations which the people are averse to submit to (Smith 1976, 233).[6]

It is striking the degree to which Smith's cautious, pragmatic, and
respectful attitude conflicts with the adventurism of leading economists
of our time. For instance, speaking of the "need for speed" in the transition
to the market economy in the former socialist countries, Sachs writes that
the reforms he proposes

will eventually produce great benefits, but they will be opposed by many
in the shrinking sectors. Populist politicians will try to hook up with coali-
tions of workers, managers, and bureaucrats in hard-hit sectors to slow or
reverse the adjustment. . .So it is crucial to establish the principles of free
trade, currency convertibility, and free entry to business early in the reform
process (Sachs 1991, 239).

Smith would shudder. Missing here is the humility that is central to
successful reform and any appreciation of the complexity, risks, and dangers attending abrupt institutional transition.

THE POLITICAL AGNOSTICISM OF PROFESSIONAL ETHICS

These three instances involve cases in which economists presumed the
virtues of and tried to profit from free markets (LTCM) and/or advocated
market liberalization in hopes of promoting prosperity for others. This
promarket bias is a consequence of the fact that the center of gravity in
economics since the 1980s has weighed heavily toward the substitution of
market mediation for government direction of economic affairs.

It is important to note, however, that liberal and left-leaning economists have been no more attentive to the ethical thickets that their work entails. In the post WWII period, Keynesianism was embraced with uncompromising vigor in the United States, and its advocates asserted without hesitation their unique competence and license to manage economic affairs (Bernstein 2001, 8). Keynesians quickly began to "fan out to the far corners of the US-controlled portions of the globe to preach their gospel to a variety of as yet unconverted natives" (Hirschman 1988, 6). Keynesianism embraced an approach to economic governance that emphasized and indeed depended upon economists' expertise and capacities. Keynesian macro-models comprised hundreds of simultaneous equations and were thought to capture the actual economy with such precision that they could provide the direction necessary to fine tune economic flows and outcomes. In the event the self-aggrandizement was unwarranted: during the 1970s, this form of Keynesianism proved itself unable to anticipate or respond to the combination of economic stagnation and inflation that had emerged, as critics such as Hayek argued consistently at the time. Most Keynesians today would not dispute his claim that "as a profession we have made a mess of things" (Hayek 1978, 23). McCloskey (1990, 122) is particularly scathing about the naïveté of economists of this era:

> As economists and other expert knights of Camelot realize now after much tragedy sprung from hubris, if an economist could see around the corner she would be rich. . . a fine tuner would see dozens of $500 bills lying around her neighborhood. The knowledge that would make fine tuning possible would make the economists who have it fabulously wealthy.

During the same period, left-leaning political economists did not flinch from asserting their influence across the developing world in order to enact their ideals. Leftist economists sometimes worked with nondemocratic governments to install government ownership over industry and resources and to implement strict management of economic flows and outcomes. Here, especially, we find efforts to engage in rather ambitious social engineering.

Neither the right nor the left within economics monopolizes hubris; nor does either refuse to violate well-established ethical principles in pursuit of what it takes to be the social good. As William Barber puts it:

> Economists operating within distinctly different analytic traditions have been willing to deploy their talents under conditions in which democratic processes were held in abeyance. . . The phenomenon on display here is thus not Chicago-specific, but (to borrow a Marshallian phrase) is a "specie of a larger genus." And the central characteristic of that genus is an attitudinal one: namely, an absolute conviction in the validity of one's doctrinal position and an unquestioning faith that its teachings will uplift the human condition (Barber 1995, 1947–48).

In light of this historical record it is vitally important to recognize that professional ethics is politically agnostic. It speaks to the practice of all economists, without implying one kind of policy regime as opposed to another. While my own inclinations are to the left of the mainstream of the economics profession, most economists who have raised concerns about the wisdom and ethics of economic social engineering are on the right. This is a consequence of the right's antipathy to expansive government, of course, but also of the historical fact that through much of the postwar period, liberal-left economists held the levers of economic management (Mankiw 2006). Only with the rightward political turn of the 1980s in the United States, the United Kingdom, and elsewhere and the crisis in Keynesianism did free-market economists find themselves in institutional positions where they could press their agenda forcefully. And when they did, they managed to overcome their historic antipathy to centralized authority in order to reengineer economic institutions across the globe.

By now, we have learned that economists of all political perspectives are willing to use their professional authority to secure economic transformations that they favor, without sufficient consideration of the ethical questions that professional economic practice raises. Not once over the past century has there been a serious conversation at the highest levels within the mainstream of the U.S. economics profession about its obligation to pursue professional ethics. Nor is there any tradition of inquiry into professional ethics among the various left- or right-leaning heterodox schools in economics. Though these schools differ among themselves on most other grounds, they are united in their historical disinterest in the ethical aspects of economic practice.[7]

On Economic Expertise

Throughout the postwar period, economists have presumed that they know best when it comes to economic affairs. Indeed, there is a widespread sentiment within the profession that political interference in sound economic policy making can and does cause severe harm. It follows that economists ought to be given wide berth in managing economic interventions. In this view, public understanding and evaluation of proposed economic interventions—let alone public participation in their formulation or prior consent to their enactment—are simply beside the point.

The issue that will concern us in this book is not that economists don't know best. Knowing best (or at least, better) is presumed whenever we are speaking of the professions (Hardwig 1994). According to sociologist Everett C. Hughes, professionals "profess to know better than others the nature of certain matters, and to know better than their clients what ails them or their affairs" (cited in Wueste 1994, 7). Professionalism entails the acquisition of knowledge and expertise that is not widely shared throughout society. Surely, medical practitioners often know best.

They generally have a much greater degree of expertise regarding their practice than do economists regarding their own. But in medical practice, the physician's expertise is hardly taken as a warrant to disregard the rights and autonomy of the patient. The physician anticipating the need for a medical intervention is required to inform the patient of her options, to discuss the possible benefits and dangers associated with each, and to secure the patient's permission in advance of any course of treatment. The physician is also directed to take into account the potential for harm associated with any intervention and to seek strategies that reduce that harm. This example illuminates the fact that expertise alone cannot possibly insulate economists against the demands associated with professional ethics. To the contrary, it is the asymmetry in knowledge between the professional and the client that stems from professional expertise that calls forth professional ethics (Hardwig 1994). Were there no particular economic expertise, the case for professional economic ethics would be substantially weaker, not stronger.

On Wrongdoing

Nor will we be concerned here with the matter of purposeful wrongdoing. I will not argue anywhere in this book that economists are disingenuous when they claim that they seek to advance the public good.[8] I will presume throughout (what I believe to be true), that the overwhelming majority of economists are dedicated to the advancement of the public good as they see it. Why, then, the need for professional ethics? I will argue that professional ethics should not be envisioned as principally focusing on purposeful wrongdoing (though it certainly addresses this case, too). It is oriented instead to the work of *virtuous* practitioners, people who try their best to manage the opportunities, challenges, and burdens that are associated with professionalism. This insight is often misunderstood even in those professions with mature bodies of professional ethics. Indeed, the two American doctors whose testimony was central to the Nuremberg Trial proceedings that established the Nuremberg Code to protect the rights of human subjects in medical experiments subsequently ignored those principles in their own work. They did not recognize that the Code applied to virtuous physicians like themselves (Shuster 1998). It must be emphasized, then, that the need for careful consideration of professional ethics arises from the complexities of professional practice, not from any purported character deficiencies of those who populate the profession.

The need for professional ethics derives from the fact that when economists teach, advocate, recommend, design policy or institutions, give testimony in civil litigation, publish editorials, or apply their expertise in other ways in the public or private sector, they are taking actions that affect others in consequential ways. In this work, they enjoy influence that is derived from their institutional affiliations and from their expertise over subject matter that is vital to social welfare. Their authority to affect the lives of others entails ethical challenges that are exceedingly difficult. They need the help of the best minds of their profession in sorting out how to act ethically. At present, they receive none. The refusal of the profession to recognize (let alone engage) these challenges is itself a gross ethical failure.

PROFESSIONAL ETHICS VERSUS CODES OF CONDUCT

What would professional economic ethics look like, were it to exist? What questions would it examine? What would it imply about how economists are trained and how they go about their work? I will take up these matters in later chapters, where I will explore what economists can learn from insights and pedagogical practices that have emerged in other professions.

For now, I must emphasize a distinction that is central to much of what follows and an appreciation of which must be kept in view throughout. *Professional ethics is distinct from and must not be conflated with a code of conduct.*[9] Professional ethics involves intellectual and pedagogical practices and traditions, not a list of rules that can be tacked to the cubicle wall. It exists only when there is careful and sustained attention within a profession to the full range of ethical matters that arise as a consequence of that profession's work. This is a purposely expansive view of professional ethics that ranges over the privileges, power, influence, responsibilities, challenges, institutional and epistemic milieu, and other features that mark the profession's place in the world. It draws attention first and foremost to the complexities that arise out of relationships—among the members of a profession, between professionals and their profession, and between these individuals (and their profession)—and those who populate the communities in which the profession operates and that are affected by the profession's work.

Defined as a field of inquiry, professional ethics engages all sorts of matters that arise in the context of professional practice. To that degree, professional ethics overlaps the kinds of issues that appear within codes of conduct—such as definitions of and warnings against conflict of interest, corruption, and so forth. But it extends far beyond these matters to engage issues that are more likely to be complex, ambiguous, and contested. For instance, what are the ethical implications of the intellectual barriers that prevent those whom economists serve from assessing economists' advice? How forthcoming should economists be about their confidence in their personal abilities or in their science when they engage in advising, forecasting, or other professional practice? When teaching students who will not go on to become economists but who as citizens will be affected by economists' practices, should economists emphasize the facility and capacities of their profession and, in so doing, cultivate trust in economic expertise and a sense of the power of economics? Or should economists temper their enthusiasm for their profession and encourage students to subject economists' pronouncements to careful scrutiny and also skepticism? To put it more directly, should they seek to cultivate true believers or skeptics?[10]

Unlike a code of conduct, professional ethics speaks to the obligations facing the *profession* as much as to those facing the *professional*. In part, this is because certain objectives cannot be achieved (entirely or at all) by the individual professional but only by an institution that speaks on behalf of the profession. For example, to what degree should economics commit itself to intellectual pluralism, and what would this commitment mean for the institutions that constitute the profession (university departments, academic journals, professional associations, funding agencies, and so forth) and for the individuals who belong to it?[11] What role should the profession play in cultivating ethical behavior in its members, not least by establishing mechanisms or guidelines for professional training? These kinds of obligations do not typically appear in codes of conduct since the latter typically are framed as guides for individual practitioners rather than for the profession as a whole.

Many professions, industries, trade groups, and others today have codes of conduct. Doctors, lawyers, engineers, and social workers, to be sure, but even cosmetologists and barbers have rules tailored to the particular character of their work. The ubiquity of such codes may help to account for skepticism in the public mind (and especially the minds of ever-skeptical economists) about the value of professional ethics. Most codes are widely disregarded or ignored. I have yet to meet a political scientist who has read or been aware of the existence of the code of conduct of the American Political Science Association.[12] And so I must emphasize that I am not going to propose in this book the adoption of a code of conduct for economists. Indeed, for a number of reasons, I will argue against the premature adoption of such a code. One is that I am far too imbued with the economics profession's fear of well-meaning regulation gone wrong to endorse such a thing. I worry that a code might come to serve as a weapon in the arsenal of those economists who seek intellectual imperialism and who are willing to argue that only their approach is "ethical." Another reason is that professional challenges require a willingness to confront and live with ethical ambiguity and aperture; they are not well met through the application of rules or commandments or what medical ethicist Howard Radest (1997) calls "moral geometry." That said, there may be good reasons for codes that apply to specific areas of economic work. Today, members of the National Association of Forensic Economists (NAFE) (who undertake economic analysis in juridical settings) subscribe to a code, and arguments have been advanced by some economists for ethical guidelines for econometricians (NAFE undated; Levy and Peart 2008). Moreover, two professional associations of applied economists in Sweden recently have adopted expansive codes (see Chapter 13). Whether a code is desirable in any area of economic practice should be sorted out carefully in the field of professional economic ethics. Professional ethics must come first; codes may or may not properly follow.

CONCLUSION

Outsiders to the profession might reasonably presume that those who occupy positions of authority in economic affairs are well versed in the ethical challenges that arise in their work. They might think that economics graduate students are encouraged during their training to adopt an ethically sophisticated approach to their work, and that in this work they are required to scrutinize the ethical consequences of their actions. They might presume the existence of economic ethics review boards populated by highly skilled economic ethicists who routinely advise researchers and other practitioners and who evaluate the economic interventions that economists craft, prior to their introduction, in order to ascertain their risk and appropriateness for the context in which they will be pursued; and to ensure that safeguards are in place to protect the most vulnerable in case things go wrong.

The truth of the matter, of course, is that we find none of this in economics. There is no professional economic ethics at all. Hence, there is no professional oath of the sort with which we began this discussion, no training of economists in any ethical matters that bear on their work, not a single journal or textbook that focuses on professional economic ethics, and certainly no economic ethics review boards. Economics appears to operate on the presumption that the answers to the ethical questions that arise in economic practice are so obvious that they require no sustained attention. As a consequence, the typical newly minted PhDs in economics, who may very well be mathematical savants and who may rise quickly to posts of tremendous influence over the lives of others, will arrive there without ever having had a moment's training in professional ethics. They may possess stunning technical facility. But they are unlikely to exhibit the least bit of ethical sophistication unless they have come by it on their own in their extracurricular hours. Unlike physicians, who typically treat patients one at a time, economists may very well make decisions that alter the life chances of millions of people all at once. Yet at no point in their professional instruction will they have been trained to confront the ethical dilemmas that this enormous responsibility entails.

This situation is intolerable. The economics profession faces an obligation to examine the ethical substance of its practice. A properly specified professional economic ethics would improve conduct not through legislation but through careful attention to the complex responsibilities that attend the economist's influence. At a minimum, it might raise awareness of the harms that Smith's "man of system" can cause, despite the best of intentions and the possession of extraordinary technical expertise. It just might prevent replication of the dangerous economic policy experiments that have been undertaken across the globe over the past several decades.

Equally important, professional economic ethics would also provide the public with a standard for evaluating the work of economists and for holding them accountable for the consequences of their actions. In short, professional economic ethics just might induce ethical economic practice, redounding to the benefit of the economics profession and of the communities that depend so vitally on its expertise.

Notes

1 Friedrich Hayek (1978), Albert O. Hirschman (1970), James Buchanan (1979), Deirdre McCloskey (1990) and other prominent economists identify and object to the aspiration of economists to the status of social engineer. In Hirschman's view, the profession exhibits an impulse to engage in "grand theorizing" and a related tendency to transform intellectual ideas into social design especially in the developing country context. He chastises "paradigm molders" for imposing simplistic models on complex societies and for suppressing the diversity of development strategies available to them. Buchanan emphasizes the mistaken focus of economics on the "problem" of maximization which calls forth unwarranted and obtrusive policy responses. In a similar vein, McCloskey identifies the inattention of the profession to the rhetoric it employs: "The social engineer promises to run the economy or the war or the culture with godlike expertise. But on the whole it is a wrong and naughty story, a wicked fairy tale" (1990, 3).

2 This is not to suggest that all prominent economists fought regulation; see Chapter 10.

3 Some knowledgeable observers at the time viewed matters just this way. See Wedel (2001, 172). For Latin America, see Hirschman (1970).

4 Among mainstream economists, Richard B. Freeman (1994) and Dani Rodrik (1998) represent important exceptions. Both raised concerns about the sufficiency of economic knowledge and the ability of the profession to orchestrate successful transitions. Rodrik argues that "Where knowledge is limited, the rule for policymakers should be, first, do no harm" (cited in Kirshner 2003, 271). This view is echoed by William Easterly (2006, 336): "The best rule of all for Western helpers is, first, do no harm." Unfortunately, economists rarely advance much beyond this component of the Hippocratic Oath in thinking through the ethics of their practice.

5 Hayek conveys a complementary sentiment: "To act on the belief that we possess the knowledge and the power which enable us to shape the processes of society entirely to our liking, knowledge which in fact we do not possess, is likely to make us do much harm" (Hayek 1978, 33). While Hayek is associated with the ideological right, of course, Burczak (2006) demonstrates that his chief epistemic insights are relevant to other economists, including those on the left.

6 I am indebted to Rob Garnett for suggesting the relevance of Smith's thinking in this area to the present project. For recent discussions of these passages in Smith, see Lock (2007), Wight (2007), and Hont (2005). One hopes that these passages will someday be as widely known and examined as Smith's arguments about the butcher, the brewer, and the baker.

7 I focus throughout on the U.S. economics profession because it has had such substantial influence over economics around the world for at least the past 50 years.

8 And so I will not explore the role of economists in various scandals of the late-twentieth century, such as the Savings and Loan crisis of the mid-1980s (see Black 2005) or the scandal that led to the closing of Harvard's Institute for International Development in 2000.

9 In the literature on the professions the terms "code of conduct" and "code of ethics" tend to be used interchangeably. Since it is central to my argument that professional ethics not be reduced to or conflated with a code, I will avoid the term "code of ethics" throughout this book.

10 Economists who deliver introductory courses in economics tend to recognize a civic duty to educate citizens about the world. In Mankiw's words, "Those of us who regularly teach undergraduates see our job as producing citizens who are well-informed about the principles of good policy" (Mankiw 2006, 43). I am asking whether it might also be their (ethical) duty to inform students about the capacities and especially the limitations of economics and economists.

11 The ethical imperative to nurture freedom of academic inquiry by sustaining pluralism can be taken to apply to individuals alone, to the profession as a whole and not at all to its individual members, or to both individuals and to the profession (though in different ways). We return to this matter in later chapters.

12 But see the symposium in the *International Studies Review* (10:4, 2008) on "responsible scholarship in international relations," which suggests that individual political scientists are concerned about professional ethics in their field.

Chapter 2

Economic Practice

What Do Economists Do?

Economics is what economists do . . .

Jacob Viner

. . . and economists are those who do economics.
Frank Knight (cited in Buchanan 1964, 213)

The economics profession comprises two categories of activity: academic economics, which involves research and teaching; and "applied economics," which involves a wide range of other professional activities. These include advising private and public sector clients; public service at the local, state, and national levels; expert witness services in civil litigation; employment in multilateral agencies such as the world's leading international financial institutions (IFIs)—the International Monetary Fund (IMF) and the World Bank and the major regional development banks—and in private sector firms (including investment banks, mutual and hedge funds, and other for-profit enterprises); service to industry trade groups (such as realtor associations); work for debt ratings firms; participation in think tanks that seek to affect public debate and policy deliberations; and involvement in the work of all sorts of nongovernmental organizations that engage economic matters in one way or another, such as the myriad institutions that focus on economic development. The world of applied economics also includes policy advocacy through public lectures, the publication of newspaper and magazine Op-Ed pieces and blogs, interviews, and participation as policy advocates in political campaigns.

In this chapter, I seek to accomplish just one objective: to present a rough sketch of the field of economics. How many academic and applied economists are at work in the United States today? Where do applied economists work, and in very general terms, what do they do? Answering these questions in detail would require a book-length treatment. The following discussion presents just a bird's eye view that will help us to begin to appreciate the ethical challenges facing professional economists.

MAPPING THE ECONOMICS PROFESSION

Counting economists is complicated by several factors. First, economic practice requires no licensing or certification; hence, there is no existent registry of economists (nor is there any requirement that those who work as economist have completed the PhD, MA, or the BA degree in economics). Second, many who provide professional economic services do not have the title of economist. Third, many who have earned the PhD or MA in economics and, in addition, some who hold the title of economist (regardless of their training) do not provide professional economic services.[1] Estimating the number of economists in each sector is therefore difficult: should we count by job title, credential, or the nature of the work that individuals actually perform? The first two are not ideal (while the last would require extensive work). For instance, the job titles that become attached to particular occupations often reflect factors other than the precise nature of the work performed, such as negotiation between the employee and employer, the incentive facing institutions to present their employees as experts for credibility or billing purposes, and so forth. Most agencies that hire large numbers of economists do not keep data on how many hold the PhD, MA, or BA degree in economics.

The numbers that follow are drawn from public sources and other published estimates, correspondence with various institutions, and interviews. They are, at best, approximations. Under these circumstances, the most prudent course is to present an array of data and estimates that together might best map the domain that concerns us.

Career Plans of Economics PhDs

One way to begin to map the profession is to consider the career plans of those earning the PhD in economics. Under contract with a coalition of government agencies, the National Opinion Research Center (NORC) at the University of Chicago prepares annual reports on the demographic and career profile of those earning the PhD degree in U.S. universities.[2] The data are derived from surveys of graduating PhDs which have been conducted by NORC regularly since 1958.

From 1980 until 2007, U.S. graduate economics programs produced an average of 908 PhDs per year, with an upward trend in recent years. From 2005 to 2007 an annual average of 1028 students earned the PhD in economics (NORC undated).[3] Of the 1980–2007 total PhD cohort, 60.1 percent had definite plans (including an accepted job offer) to begin their careers in the employ of universities, colleges, or other educational institutions (NORC undated). In the most recent period for which the data are available, 2005–2007, 59 percent started their careers in educational institutions. Among those with definite plans to pursue nonacademic careers during the period from 1980 to 2007, 13.9 percent entered industry and business (a cohort that grew dramatically over this period), 16.3 percent entered government (stable since the 1980s), and 3.7 percent (also stable) began their careers with nonprofit organizations. The remaining 6 percent were headed to other sectors. These data indicate that about 40 percent of all economics PhDs had definite plans to begin their careers outside of academia.

The NORC surveys also report the respondents' intended primary (and secondary) "activity" (as distinguished from the type of institution for which they intended to work). About half of new PhDs from 1980 to 2007 reported research and development as their primary activity, and this percentage grew considerably over the period, while about 30 percent reported teaching as their primary activity, although this percentage declined substantially over time (see Table 2.1). In contrast, fewer than 4 percent viewed administration, and about 9 percent listed professional services to individuals as their primary activity (this activity grew in importance over the period). The aggregate data indicate that 39 percent of the PhD cohort that began employment in the most recent period (2005–2007) did not intend to engage in teaching at all at the outset of their careers.

Since the 1960s, the percentage of non-U.S. citizens in economics graduate programs has grown steadily and considerably (Siegfried and Stock 2004; Siegfried undated). During the 1960s, over 73 percent of

Table 2.1 Primary and Secondary Activities, Economics PhDs with Definite Career Plans, 1980–2007

Activity		1980–84	1985–89	1990–94	1995–99	2000–04	2005–07
R&D	Primary	38.3	44.9	51.6	50.5	55.1	59.6
	Secondary	42.9	37.9	34.4	35.5	32.9	29.7
	Total	71.2	82.8	86.0	86.0	88.0	89.3
Teaching	Primary	49.7	44.8	35.9	31.0	26.6	27.0
	Secondary	16.9	23.9	28.4	27.0	32.2	33.9
	Total	66.6	78.7	64.3	58.0	58.8	60.9
Admin	Primary	3.8	3.3	3.9	3.9	3.8	4.5
& Mgmt	Secondary	5.9	6.2	6.4	10.2	10.2	10.7
	Total	9.7	9.5	10.3	14.1	14.0	15.2
Prof Servc.	Primary	4.1	4.2	5.2	10.1	11.0	7.0
to Indvs.	Secondary	3.5	4.0	5.4	9.3	7.1	5.1
	Total	7.6	8.2	10.6	19.4	18.1	12.1
Other	Primary	4.1	2.9	3.4	4.5	3.6	1.9
	Secondary	1.3	1.1	2.2	2.2	2.8	0.7
	Total	5.4	4.0	5.6	6.7	6.4	2.6
No Second. Employment		29.6	26.8	23.2	15.8	14.8	20.0

Source: NORC 2009. Private correspondence; available from author.

economics PhD recipients were U.S. citizens. That percentage declined in each successive decade and during the period 2000 to 2006 had fallen to just 34 percent (and in 2006 reached 28.2 percent—NORC 2006, Appendix Table A-3). In this regard, economics is an outlier with respect to other social sciences (excluding economics, 82 percent of social science PhD recipients in the United States in 2006 were U.S. citizens) and most other fields. It is much closer to computer sciences (where, in 2006, 33.3 percent of PhD recipients were U.S. citizens) and the physical sciences (44.4 percent). Of the non-U.S. economics PhDs in 2006 (including both permanent residents and temporary visa holders), 53 percent had definite plans to begin their professional careers in the United States, and an additional 6.3 percent planned to continue their studies in the country. The rest of these students with definite plans (about 40 percent) were headed for work or postdoctoral research positions outside the United States (NORC 2006, Table 33). In contrast, only 21 percent of all non-U.S. citizen PhDs across all fields had plans to work outside the United States (NORC 2006, Table 34).

Counting Economists

The statistics on the economics profession itself as opposed to economics PhD recipients are much less certain. There is no registry of economists or any professional organization to which economists must belong, and most professional organizations for economists do not survey their membership regarding the nature of their work. Moreover, while government agencies apply minimum educational standards when employing economists, most do not report on the educational credentials of their staff members.

What is an economist, and how many people work as economists in the United States today? According to the Bureau of Labor Statistics (BLS May 2008) estimate, there were 25,140 employed economists in the United States as of May 2008—although, as we'll see momentarily, this estimate is incomplete. This number includes those who perform functions associated with the profession, regardless of their credential or title. The profession is divided equally between academic and nonacademic careers. The BLS estimates that 12,540 economists are employed as faculty members by postsecondary educational institutions (Standard Occupational Classification, SOC 251063). According to the BLS, members of this group "Teach courses in economics. Include[s] both teachers primarily engaged in teaching and those who do a combination of both teaching and research." Colleges, universities, and professional schools employed 10,660 of these economists, while junior colleges employed the remainder.

The BLS reports that an additional 12,600 worked as economists outside the university (SOC 193011), and it is this category where undercounting occurs. This group comprises those who

> conduct research, prepare reports, or formulate plans to aid in solution of economic problems arising from production and distribution of goods and

services. May collect and process economic and statistical data using econometric and sampling techniques. Exclude[s] "Market Research Analysts" (http://www.bls.gov/soc/soc_e3b1.htm).

Undercounting results from the fact that the BLS does not attempt to include those economists working in the United States for the IFIs, which are among the largest institutional employers of economists in the country (see below). Nor does the BLS provide data on economists employed in the Legislative or Judicial branches of the Federal government. I provide estimates of some of the excluded categories below. In aggregate, they amount to several thousand additional economists. A better (though still conservative) estimate than that of the BLS for all nonacademic economists is perhaps 15,000.

The fact that the ratio of academic to applied economists differs from the career plans of new PhDs (i.e., a lower percentage of PhDs intend careers outside the university) reflects the fact that those working as economists within the university are much more likely than those in other sectors to have the PhD degree. The above data allow for a rough estimate of the number of applied economists with PhDs: if 60 percent of the 1980–2007 economics PhD cohort planned to work as teaching faculty, and their aggregate count in 2008 equals 12,540, then the number of applied (nonteaching) economists with PhDs is two-thirds of this number, or about 8360. This suggests further that there are approximately 6640 active, applied economists who do not hold the PhD degree.[4]

Where do applied economists work? By far, the largest concentration is found in government (see Table 2.2). The Federal government employs 4130 economists in the Executive branch, while state governments employ 2050, and local governments account for another 910 economists. All told, then, the BLS reports that the public sector accounts for 7090

Table 2.2 Employment of Nonacademic Economists, Largest Industry Employers

Industry	Employment
Federal Executive Branch (OES designation)	4,130
State Government (OES designation)	2,050
Scientific Research and Development Services	1,510
Management, Scientific, and Technical Consulting Services	1,510
Local Government (OES designation)	910
Religious, Grantmaking, Civic, Professional and Similar Orgs. (including Business, Labor, and Political Orgs.)	550
Mgmt. of Companies and Enterprises	420
Monetary Authorities—Central Banks	310

Sources: BLS. Occupational Employment and Wages, Estimates, May 2008 (19-3011 Economists). Available at http://www.bls.gov/oes/2008/may/oes193011.htm; BLS. Occupational Employment Statistics (OES), Estimates, May 2008. Available at http://data.bls.gov/oes/datatype.do.

economists. Assuming an additional 150 economists in the Legislative and Judicial branches (see below), a better estimate of the total number of economists in the public sector would be 7340. This likely represents just under half of all applied economists.

Table 2.3 provides a breakdown of Executive branch economists by agencies and departments in September 2008, including all those that employ 50 or more economists. The greatest numbers of economists are found in the Department of Labor (with 1262 economists, including its Bureau of Labor Statistics with 1208); Department of Agriculture (533, including its Economic Research Services, which employs over 200 economists); Department of the Treasury (473); and the Department of Commerce (462, including the 266 economists at the Bureau of Economic Analysis and the 35 economists at the Census Bureau).

Smaller numbers of economists are on staff at dozens of other agencies ranging from the Office of Management and Budget (with 48 economists), the Social Security Administration (35), the Department of Homeland Security (33), and the Securities and Exchange Commission (32) to many with fewer than 5 economists each (U.S. Office of Personnel Management, Sept. 2008). A small number of economists does not imply that the work is inconsequential or peripheral to the institution, however. For instance,

Table 2.3 Distribution of Federal Government Economists, Executive Branch, Sept. 2008 (Agencies with 50 or more economists)

Department or Agency	Number of Economists	Percent of Total Federal Exec. Branch Economists
Labor	1262	30.5
Agriculture	533	12.9
Treasury	473	11.5
Commerce	462	11.2
Defense	225	5.4
Energy	168	4.0
Environmental Protection Agency	163	3.9
Health and Human Services	137	3.3
Transportation	88	2.1
Interior	86	2.08
Fed. Trade Commission	74	1.8
Housing and Urban Dev.	62	1.5
Justice	61	1.5
FDIC	61	1.5
All others (below 50 economists)	275	6.6
Total	4130	100

Source: U.S. Office of Personnel Management, Employment-Sept. 2008. Available at http://www.fedscope.opm.gov/employment.asp.

the Council of Economic Advisors (CEA), which gives economic advice to the U.S. President, employs just seven economists.

In addition to these government agencies the Federal Reserve Board employs 225 economists who are spread out over several divisions. The majority performs economic research within three divisions: Research and Statistics (120), International Finance (56), and Monetary Affairs (38) (http://www.federalreserve.gov/research/mastaff.htm). An additional 85 economists work for the regional Federal Reserve Banks (together listed under "Monetary Authorities" in Table 2.2).

As noted a moment ago, the BLS does not provide data on economists in the Legislative or Judicial branch of the Federal government; nor does the Office of Personnel Management. Unfortunately, many of the agencies and offices in these branches do not keep data on their employment of economists. In response to queries, the Congressional Budget Office reported that it includes 93 economists on its staff of 248, 78 of which have the PhD degree, and a further 5 have the MA degree in economics. In contrast, the Joint Economic Committee reported just 14 economists among its staff.

It is unfortunate but perhaps inevitable that the BLS statistics combine in the same data set employment by type of institution with employment by task. Those who work for the government and for certain other industries are listed as such, regardless of what specific economic services they provide. For instance, the BLS reports that 550 economists work for "Religious, Grantmaking, Civic, Professional and Similar Organizations." For this category, the BLS does not report on job functions. In contrast, other economists are listed by function with no reference to industry. Two categories are particularly important in this regard: "Management, Scientific and Technical Consulting Services" and "Scientific Research and Development Services." Each of these categories includes 1510 economists. These economists populate industries not identified separately in the BLS statistics. The former category includes those who provide management, human resource, marketing, environmental, and other consulting services, while the latter category comprises those who perform research and development in sectors ranging from the physical, engineering, and life sciences to the social sciences and humanities (BLS Occupational Employment Statistics, May 2008; available at: http://www.bls.gov/oes/2008/may/oes193011.htm). The BLS also reports that in 2008, 1200 economists (representing about 8 percent of all applied economists) were self-employed. The BLS does not provide any information on the work of these economists (ftp://ftp.bls.gov/pub/special.requests/ep/ind-occ.matrix/occ_pdf/occ_19-3011.pdf).

Multilateral Institutions

The IMF reports that of its approximately 2660 employees, 1105 were economists in 2008, accounting for 46 percent of its total workforce (http://www.

imf.org/external/np/adm/rec/workenv/aboutst.htm#StaffStatistics).
The vast majority of these economists work in the IMF headquarters in
Washington, DC, and most hold the PhD degree. In contrast, the World
Bank does not report on and would not provide the occupational break-
down of its employees. Although the Bank is a much larger employer
than is the IMF, a smaller percentage of its employees are economists,
and a smaller percentage of its employees are stationed in the United
States. Of its 10,000 employees worldwide, about two-thirds work in
Washington, DC. Moreover, the BLS does not report on the numbers of
economists who work for the IFIs, as noted above.[5] It is certainly reasonable to assume that the Bank employs well over a thousand economists in
Washington and possibly many more.

The United Nations (UN) system also employs economists in various departments. For instance, the Department of Economic and Social
Analysis, based at the UN headquarters, employs approximately 30 economists on its staff of about 200 employees. Economists are also found on
the staffs of the various UN agencies (such as the ILO and WHO) and
Programmes and Funds (such as UNICEF, UNCTAD, and the UNDP),
although most of these are based outside the United States. For example,
UNCTAD employs 190 economists (at its Geneva headquarters) while
the WTO employs 30 staff economists (private correspondence with
UNCTAD and the WTO, respectively, 12/2008).

THE WORK OF ECONOMISTS

This provisional mapping of the economics profession tells us little about
just what economists do and less, still, about the challenges they face as
they seek to perform their work with integrity. Here we will examine the
kinds of work that applied economists perform.

Federal Government Economists

One way to begin to approach this matter is to distinguish among the
federal agencies, departments, and bureaus that employ the largest numbers of economists by reference to their mandates and what these imply
about the kinds of work performed by the economists in their service. The
problem with this approach, however, is that economists within many
agencies undertake a wide range of distinct professional activities.[6] The
work of one economist at the U.S. Department of Agriculture (USDA)
may have very little in common with that of another at the same agency.
Complicating matters, the mandates of many agencies overlap. Hence,
an economist working for the Bureau of Economic Analysis (BEA) may
have much in common with another working at the Energy Information
Agency (EIA) since both are generating official statistics. But occasion-
ally, so might economists working for a regulatory agency who come to

find that they require certain kinds of data that are not available. This may require the design and implementation of a new survey to gather the needed data. Now they, too, are doing statistical work and face many of the challenges that would be familiar to their peers at the BEA and EIA.

Several of the largest federal employers of economists are statistical agencies. This category includes most importantly the Bureau of Labor Statistics under the Department of Labor and the Bureau of Economic Analysis and the Census Bureau under the Department of Commerce. Economists at these agencies gather, synthesize and analyze data, produce a broad array of official government statistics, and generate official government estimates (such as "now-casts") that are relied upon by other government agencies, academic economists, and private sector institutions. They also undertake research on how to improve data collection and the interpretation of these data. Important statistical operations also exist within many other federal institutions such as the USDA—especially within its Economic Research Service—the Department of the Treasury, and the Federal Reserve.

A second broad category comprises those agencies that are engaged in regulation. This group includes the Environmental Protection Agency, the USDA, the Department of the Interior, the Federal Trade Commission, the Department of Energy, the Consumer Protection Safety Commission, the Occupational Safety and Health Administration, and the Federal Reserve, to name just some of the federal institutions that generate and police government regulations of all sorts. Much of this work involves applied microeconomics. The economists in this field participate in two broad practices: generating and revising regulations, pursuant to legislative or executive mandate; and conducting economic analysis that contributes to investigations of whether existing regulations are effective and/ or whether they have been violated. Regulatory economists undertake benefit-cost and cost-effectiveness analysis and seek to direct the work of their agencies toward efficient strategies that are derived from the application of basic economic reasoning. For instance, new legislation that calls for regulation must be translated into particular rules that will implement and enforce the regulation. In this context, economists may seek to present and advocate for rules that realize the legislation's objectives in ways that minimize social costs.

A third category covers those government institutions that provide support and impose penalties of one kind or another or that otherwise redistribute income. This category includes income support programs and subsidies and tax credits on the one hand, and fines, fees, and taxes on the other. Notable here are the Social Security Administration, the Internal Revenue Service, the Department of Health and Human Services, the Department of Housing and Urban Development, the Department of Labor, and the Department of Veterans' Affairs, as well as the Office of the U.S. Trade Representative, the State Department, the International

Trade Commission, the Agency for International Development, the International Commerce Commission, the Overseas Private Investment Corporation, and several agencies within USDA. Economists at these institutions do much more than participate in decisions concerning support and penalties. For example, the International Trade Commission provides technical assistance and political support to U.S. exporters, helping them overcome political barriers to imports abroad.

There are many other ways to classify the work of Federal government agencies and economists. One is to distinguish between those whose work focuses on the household sector (including involvement in household-level studies and service programs) and those whose work focuses instead on the industrial sector (although some institutions, such as the Federal Reserve and the USDA, focus on both).[7] The former would include those performing studies of rural households, public health, employment (and income), immigration, minorities, and so forth. The latter would include those who are engaged in studies and programs that relate to the financial sector (from banking to securities), manufacturing, services, international economic activities, science policy, and defense (among others). Taking this approach helps to illuminate the intra-agency diversity in work assignments among economists. To illustrate, one economist at the USDA might focus on food industry regulation, another on food security, another on farm operator household incomes, and another on the food stamp program.

Many industrial or sectoral groupings involve several departments and agencies and a wide range of economic activities. In the area of defense, economists work for the Central Intelligence Agency, the Department of Defense, the Department of Homeland Security, and the various branches of the U.S. military. These economists serve as country or regional economic experts that track economic developments and generate forecasts, study critical economic sectors, and examine economic drivers of political instability. In the context of the current global economic crisis, the CIA has stepped up its economic surveillance and forecasting and now reports daily on global economic affairs to the U.S. President. Along with accountants and other financial experts, economists also develop and implement economic tools for detecting illicit financial flows such as those that sustain terrorist operations. Economists also provide technical analysis of logistical matters for the armed services, such as the efficient allocation of resources across its bases and departments, often with the assistance of outside economic consulting firms.

A final distinction merits attention. Federal government economists can be distinguished according to their audiences. Some produce analyses that are intended for internal consumption by other government staff members or officials, others produce work that will be used by those outside of government, while others produce scholarly work that targets other economists and other specialists. This distinction bears on the matter of the degree to which economists can speak freely and honestly about the matters on which they work.

In all of these agencies, economists are likely to face a constant barrage of requests for information, analysis, and economic advice while they attend to their other regular duties. A study of the Economic Research Service of the USDA found that responses to requests for questions from the Office of the Secretary of Agriculture, the Office of the Chief Economist, other USDA divisions, Congress, the Council of Economic Advisers, and other government units absorbed about 20 percent of its staff's time in 1997. In that year, the staff responded to "about 350 such requests" (Commission on Behavioral and Social Sciences and Education 1999).

State and Local Government Economists

Among the activities of economists who work for state government, the most common include the generation of frequent state-level fiscal, industrial, and other forecasts (including state university enrollments and tuition revenues, prison populations, park user fees, revenues from licenses, etc.); the assessment of the fiscal impact of proposed bills as they make their way through the legislative process; and the generation of research and analysis on matters related to state governance. At the same time, and just like their counterparts in Federal government, these economists field requests for data, analysis, and advice from elected officials in the legislative and budgeting process. During the legislative session, those state economists involved in budgeting face particularly intensive demands for their services. Most pressing is the task of assessing the fiscal impact of every bill that comes before any legislative committee and revising these estimates as the bill undergoes substantial amendment. These economists also field myriad requests from state legislators for technical assistance on proposed and pending bills. State government economists undertake benefit-cost and economic impact analysis, such as in cases involving private sector investment incentives. In this context, elected officials need to have a basis for weighing the merits of subsidies. Economists doing this work are called upon to provide testimony and answer questions about their economic analysis before legislative committees and to respond to inquiries from the press and other interests.

With the exception of the largest cities, municipal governments typically employ few economists. These economists often work for agencies that are involved in providing technical support to municipal economic development strategies. Cities often depend on outside economic consultants for more intensive economic analysis—such as the evaluation of the economic impact of proposed private and public sector initiatives (see below).

The International Financial Institutions

The IFIs face broad mandates; as a consequence, their economists perform a wide range of activities. The following discussion of the IMF and World

Bank presents just a glimpse of these institutions and the work of their economists.

IMF staff economists are divided into two kinds of departments: "area" departments that concentrate on the economic affairs of countries in a particular geographic region (such as Sub-Saharan Africa) and "functional" departments that focus on research and policy matters of a specialized nature (such as the Fiscal Affairs and the Monetary and Capital Markets Departments). On its Web site, the IMF describes the range of functions of its economists as encompassing "economic analysis," "policy and program design," and "technical assistance" to member countries. These responsibilities entail surveillance of economic developments in member countries; analysis and design of "an appropriate mix of fiscal, monetary, and exchange rate policies to promote and maintain macroeconomic stability"; examination of "issues of good governance" and "issues of fiscal and external debt sustainability"; and the development of initiatives that promote "regional and broader trade liberalization." The work also requires maintenance of comprehensive databases, forecasting, and the development of various aspects of IMF lending programs. The work of the functional departments encompasses the full range of fiscal and financial affairs—from tax and customs policy and administration to financial market development, currency convertibility, bank supervision and restructuring, and the implementation of international standards. All of these activities require extensive statistical research.

The World Bank is an even more complex organization owing to the breadth of its mandate. Its work includes projects in poverty reduction, human development, physical and financial infrastructure development, private sector and global capital market enhancement, financial crisis management, the promotion of sustainable development strategies, and many other activities. Each of these areas encompasses diverse and complex sub-fields of engagement. For instance, human development involves the enhancement of education, health and nutrition, social protection and labor policy, the provision of children and youth services, and other activities.

Owing to the interdisciplinary nature of World Bank projects, its economists work closely with professionals from the fields of law, medicine, ecology, accounting, agronomy, education, and beyond. Many of its economists provide research and forecasting in support of the Bank's programs and projects (such as in the Bank's DEC Research Group and its Development Data Group), and in this work, they are much more likely than academic economists to engage in survey design and implementation and in field work to gather the appropriate data. Bank economists have been in the forefront of the adoption of randomized controlled trials (or RCTs) in economics, where researchers undertake experiments in the communities that are to be targeted by an intervention.[8] The DEC Research Group also produces many publications of the Bank that summarize its research findings and lay out its philosophy, including not least, the annual *World Development Report* and *World Development Indicators*, the Bank's development journals and working papers. This unit is also responsible for global monitoring of trends (such as capital flows and the development and effects of regional trade agreements) and global projections (such as countries' performance in meeting the Millennium Development Goals).

In many of the Bank's operations, research and reporting is combined with planning, advising, technical assistance, impact evaluation, and funding of development projects. The Bank plays a central role in the coordination of donor aid (from governments, humanitarian organizations, and development banks). Owing to the breadth of its activities and the resources that it can marshal, the Bank is also a central actor in influencing development strategies among the world's low-income countries. All of these activities involve the Bank's economists (to varying degrees) in assignments ranging from research (and publication of findings) in policy, strategy, and impact analysis to government advising and participation in funding decisions and the implementation of Bank-funded projects.

The Federal Reserve Bank

As we have seen, the largest numbers of Federal Reserve Bank (the Fed) economists work in three research divisions: Research and Statistics (the largest of the units), International Finance, and Monetary Affairs. Smaller units exist in the areas of Banking Supervision and Regulation, Reserve Bank Operations and Payment Systems, and Consumer and Community Affairs. The Fed is considered by many economists (including its own) to be the most rigorous producer of independent economic knowledge in Washington, DC.

Economists at the Fed engage in diverse research ranging over financial economics, industrial organization, international economics, and public finance. Fed economists monitor "the money stock, commercial banking, the flow of funds accounts, and industrial production and capacity utilization" (http://www.federalreserve.gov/careers/economist.htm). The economists generate regular studies, reports, and forecasts for and advise the Federal Open Market Committee (FOMC), the Board of Governors, and the Federal Reserve Banks. They also assist Federal Reserve officials in preparing Congressional testimony and speeches.

In general terms, Fed economists are primarily involved in two vital functions: macroeconomic analysis and forecasting (along with the statistics generation that those functions entail), and bank supervision and regulation. Research and forecasting requires substantial econometric work and modeling, of course, but the Fed also values and draws extensively on other sources of information and on the subjective judgments of its economists in discerning appropriate monetary policy. Forecasting at the Fed often entails expert analysis and intuition, informal data collection (through surveys, interviews and informal conversations with others), monitoring various factors that contribute to GDP and inflation trends, and so forth. This implies that Fed economists must demonstrate reliable judgment as well as technical proficiency. Staff reporting to the FOMC and the Board of Governors also sometimes requires negotiation and reconciliation among staff members when they have competing views about the matters before them. Questions arise routinely about whether and to what degree institutional innovations (such as new banking activities or financial assets) complicate in some way or other the basic macroeconomic relationships upon which FOMC decisions are based. At such times, judgments must be made about which indicators are most reliable, how to interpret the new data, and/or about whether the historical data are of much value for interpreting present developments. The stakes are high in these deliberations, of course, since the outcome will bear on the advice that is given to the Fed's critical decision makers. In these cases, staff economists must balance the imperative to collaborate and compromise with their peers against the obligation to advance views that they take to be most tenable in the face of the evidence before them.

Private Sector Economists

As we have seen, the two largest categories of nongovernment functions reported by the Bureau of Labor Statistics (and given above, see Table 2.1), "Scientific Research and Development Services" and "Management, Scientific, and Technical Consulting Services" together comprise one-quarter of all nonacademic economists and 58 percent of those working outside of government. The largest number of economists in this group are found in private sector consulting firms and research entities (such as independent think tanks). It is likely that most of the 1200 self-employed economists also provide consulting services while many also provide forensic services to the legal profession. This is because while just 30 economists were employed directly by the legal industry in 2008, the National Association of Forensic Economists reported 631 members as of July 2009. Much of the difference is accounted for by consultants that provide expertise in civil litigation.

Economic consultants provide a range of functions for a diverse array of clients. Some of the most common functions include "economic impact assessments" of recurring or discrete events, such as infrastructure projects; benefit-cost analyses; demographic, economic, or financial forecasting for a particular industry or for a local economy; market studies; industry location studies; expert witness testimony; and so forth. Government at all levels is a major client in this market, and some firms focus exclusively on government advising. Other important clients include organizations engaged in the promotion of economic development (both private sector consortia like the Chambers of Commerce and public-private development organizations), industry trade groups, real estate developers, and a wide array of nonprofit organizations that need economic analysis to assist them in their decision making and the achievement of their respective missions.

A smaller but influential group of economists populate the policy think tanks, most of which are based in Washington, DC or in the leading universities across the country. The most prominent of these are well known owing to the important roles they play in national policy debate. These include the Brookings Institution, the American Enterprise Institute, the Economic Policy Institute, the Heritage Foundation, the Peterson Institute for International Economics, the Center for Economic and Policy Research, and the Political Economy Research Institute to name just a few with a presence in the field of economics. These think tanks range from right- to left-of-center, with the most influential clustered around the middle of the ideological spectrum. Economists at these institutions attempt to affect the policy debate through the generation of empirical research, public policy analysis, and public education. The reports generated by these institutions supply candidates, elected officials, and government staff members with arguments, evidence, and the cover of expertise in support of their policy positions.

CONCLUSION

The foregoing discussion indicates that economists engage in a wide range of activities and that they perform important and consequential functions in the public and private sectors. It suggests that in their professional work, economists exert substantial influence across the economy and thereby affect the lives of others. Economic work bears directly on decision making in government and myriad private sector institutions. But this description of the profession does little to illuminate the ethical quandaries economists face as they attempt to do good work. Achieving that goal requires a different kind of analysis—one that draws directly on the experiences and insights of economists. This is the goal of the next chapter.

Notes

1 These points might be taken as reasons why economics is not a profession in the traditional sense, which implies, in turn, that there can be no professional economic ethics. We will return to this matter in Chapters 5 and 6.

2 The annual reports are available at http://www.norc.org/projects/Survey+of+Earned+Doctorates.htm.

3 At the time of this writing, NORC had not yet released the full report on the 2007 PhD cohort, but its preliminary report indicates that 993 economics students completed the PhD degree in that year.

4 This estimate assumes that 100 percent of academic economists hold the PhD degree, that the occupational migration between the academic and nonacademic sector among PhDs over time is on balance zero, and that all economists

with the PhD working in the United States earned their degrees within the country. The first assumption is most certainly incorrect, and a more accurate estimate would yield a greater number of PhD degree-holding applied economists. The second assumption may also be incorrect since it is likely given the hiring practices in academic and applied economics that on balance, there is a net migration from academia to applied professional pursuits. This, too, would increase the relative presence of PhD economists in applied fields. The third assumption is incorrect but likely insignificant in the aggregate, except perhaps in regards to estimating the number of economists at the IFIs.

5 These economists are classified under NAICS 928120 "International Affairs," but the OES does not provide an estimate for this category.

6 I am indebted to Steve Payson and Martha Starr for clarifying the complexity of the work of federal government economists. I draw on their insights in this section, though any errors are of course my own.

7 Another would be to distinguish among Federal government economists by the nature of their appointments (see Henderson 1977).

8 We will return to RCTs in Chapter 11 where we explore the content of professional economic ethics. For now, it should be said that difficult ethical issues arise in the context of RCTs.

Chapter 3

Ethical Challenges Confronting the Applied Economist

Fortunately, or unfortunately, depending on one's point of view, the law does not allow malpractice suits against economists. If the world looks a certain way, if we are mistaken in our understanding of this, and if this misunderstanding gets translated into misinformed policies, it is not mainly economists who bear the brunt of the ensuing pain and misery. Even if we are not mistaken, implementation of any particular policy will have costs to someone.

Samuel C. Weston (1998, 38)

The preceding chapter provided a rudimentary mapping of the economics profession. The next step in the case for professional economic ethics requires an investigation into the particular challenges that economists face as they attempt to render their professional services with integrity. Gaining this insight requires a more fine-grained investigation that draws upon what economists have to say about their work. A small number of academic economists have begun to explore ethical questions that arise in certain branches of economic research, and we will examine these matters in Chapter 11 where we consider the content of professional economic ethics. Unfortunately, applied economists have written little about the nature of their work or about the challenges they face.[1] And so the available material must be supplemented by interviews with applied economists. The following discussion draws on both kinds of evidence, including over 35 interviews with applied economists that I conducted in 2008 and 2009. The goal is to shed light upon some of the incentives, constraints, and pressures that applied economists face as a consequence of the nature of the institutions they serve and the relationships within which they are embedded, and to tease out some of the ethical dilemmas that these forces induce. This discussion will not explore cases of explicit misconduct by economists or the institutions they serve. Instead, the focus will be on the everyday difficulties that well-meaning economists grapple with as they attempt to do good work. If we discover that these difficulties are common, complex, and consequential, then we will have taken one step toward making the case for the need for professional economic ethics to help economists prepare for and manage the tensions that bear on and can undermine the quality of their professional services.

THE ECONOMIST AS PARTISAN

A frequent theme in the literature on nonacademic economic practice is the need to correct the misconception that applied economics involves nothing more than objective, technical work (e.g., Nelson 1987; Allen 1977). Economists who have reflected on their work in government and other institutions emphasize that effectiveness requires economists to abandon the role of neutral technocrat and arm themselves with an arsenal of rhetorical, political, and other strategies. Economists in dense bureaucracies of competing interests and values must cultivate the ability to translate economic ideas into everyday language, build alliances, win votes, and marginalize opponents. Those who instead rely exclusively on their technical expertise often lack influence when the most important decisions are being made.

The partisanship required of applied economists raises difficult questions. To what degree is an economist warranted in making whatever plausible arguments are necessary to prevail in a departmental dispute when he knows that, owing to the relative ignorance of his colleagues or superiors, the arguments that are apt to persuade are in fact specious or otherwise deficient? When and to what degree should he conform to a prevailing institutional practice in order to be effective, when doing so entails conflicts with his best judgments? What is he licensed to do when he loses an important argument about a particularly important matter? Does professional responsibility require him (always) to submit to the decisions of the relevant authority, or should he (at least sometimes) dissent and disrupt implementation of the decision taken (see Applbaum 1999, Chapter 9). Under what conditions (if any) should he avail himself of back-channel opportunities to reverse decisions that he believes to be harmful?

These questions do not arise if we hold to the view of the economist as neutral technocrat. Such an economist would have little reason to worry about whether his work is decisive or, indeed, if it has any effect at all. He would simply submit his research findings, satisfied that he had fulfilled his professional responsibilities. But the economist who recognizes an obligation to be effective in advocating for the insights that his work generates cannot ignore questions about how to comport himself in a professionally ethical way. To be efficacious, he must decide which battles to fight and when to compromise—not least so that he doesn't acquire a reputation as an irritating pariah. He may find that a given issue is not worth the risk to the relationships with colleagues and superiors that are vital to his effectiveness. He may perceive that there is nothing he can do in a given case to alter the outcome, and so he may seek ways to absent himself from participation in a process that is going to yield a result that he does not support. The economist facing all these questions also must interrogate his motives to discern when he is being wise, prudent and strategic, and when, instead, he is being cowardly, indifferent, or opportunistic.

An economist who feels an ethical responsibility to be effective—to be what Robert Nelson calls "a proselytizer for efficiency and other economic values; for economic progress"—therefore faces decisions that he would be spared were he a technical automaton, some of which entail ethical substance that is difficult and important. Reflecting on his long career in government service, Nelson argues that many applied economists have come to realize that the self-conception of economist as technocrat is misleading. In his view, however, self-aware economists do not know what conception of professional practice should take its place.[2] They find that their profession does not provide the resources necessary to think through what it means to be an ethical yet partisan economist. For his part, William Allen (1977) wonders how much courage it takes to be a government economist—and he is right to do so. Once we understand the complexity that attends partisanship, we come to see that it takes not just good judgment and self-awareness but also fortitude to act in ways that are professionally ethical.

TIME AND RESOURCE CONSTRAINTS

Above all other concerns, applied economists emphasize time constraints as the biggest obstacle to doing good work (Allen 1977). In comparison with academic economists who typically enjoy flexibility in their deadlines and a substantial measure of control over the pace of their work, applied economists face an unrelenting clock. Work flow through bureaucracies is not generally under economists' control. Instead, applied economists receive assignments from others, and the deadlines imposed are often unrealistic relative to the amount of time required to do first- or even second-rate work. Economists speak of being expected to produce data, reports, or recommendations by the close of business the following day and sometimes later in the same day that the request is received. Economists in this position realize that what they can produce in the time available will be inadequate and misleading in critical respects. Often the economist knows that the most readily available data are inappropriate for the purposes to which they will be put, and yet there is often no time to generate or find more reliable data. Applied economists must rely frequently on the work of others without checking its reliability; they must grab and go with what they can find laying ready to hand. In an interview, one highly regarded economist put it this way: "The correct answer a day late is useless. You have to provide an answer in the time you have, with the resources you have."[3]

Applied economists appear to have few opportunities available to them to address the problem of time and resource constraints. Several economists reported to me that their supervisors judge their work by quantity of output and deadlines met rather than by quality. None of the economists who identified time constraints as a major problem could cite effective strategies for managing it. It appears that individual economists are left to make the compromises that they can justify to themselves, with no assistance from their profession.

Why can't economists simply refuse those assignments that are untenable with the resources available and in the time given? In conversation with economists, it became clear that they must be judicious in deciding when to yield to and when to resist unrealistic requests so as not to earn a reputation for being undependable. The default is to try to comply with work requests—to produce *something* in the time given—rather than to refuse assignments. And as a consequence, applied economists must be prepared to compromise quality for punctuality as dictated by the circumstances of their positions and their professional conscience. Those who find themselves in situations that are unbearable in this regard sometimes look to move to other work environments that appear to be more conducive to doing good work.

Time constraints bear unevenly on economists across institutions, though not in the ways that one might expect. For instance, it is not at all clear that the work flow in private-sector institutions facing competitive pressures is more demanding than in the public sector. Indeed, economists closest to the legislative process at the state and federal levels spoke of work flows that were more demanding than those described to me by any other economists. Factors that bear on time constraints were more subtle. In those institutions that are headed by economists and reflect an economists' culture, supervisors tend to appreciate the time and resource requirements of particular projects. Economists in these institutions often are in a better position to raise concerns about the pace of work. In contrast, where economists are in a minority and where they report to noneconomists, there is less understanding of the demands of economic analysis.

Time and resource constraints also bear unevenly on economists at different stages of their careers. Those economists with long tenure and established reputations spoke more confidently about when and how to resist unreasonable pressures. In contrast, younger economists face greater pressures to generate work asked of them in the time frame given, despite a lack of resources or expertise. Lacking experience, it is more difficult for them to ascertain when it is appropriate or acceptable to refuse unreasonable requests. New economists also face pressure to prove themselves, which may induce them to meet all requests that come their way. It is potentially damaging to one's reputation to refuse any particular request, especially when one is not yet in a position to know which requests really matter and which are of little consequence.

Referring to this pressure and lack of experience, one senior economist said, "You should never trust the forecast of an economist who has less than three years experience."

INSTITUTIONAL PRESSURES TO GENERATE BIASED WORK

A frequent complaint among applied economists across sectors is the pressure to generate data or draw inferences from the data that sustain the mission of their institution or serve the interests of their managers. Outside observers of the profession register the same complaint (e.g., Silk 1972). All too often, economic research follows rather than precedes decision making; in this case, economists are expected to produce evidence after the fact that justifies the decisions taken. William Allen (1977) cites a notable (but not uncommon) example: a new member of the Council of Economic Advisors was instructed to produce (*in six hours*) an estimate of "the balance of payments impact of a West Coast dock strike" for government attorneys who would "seek a Taft-Hartley injunction in court the next morning." He continues:

> The legally specified basis for the injunction was demonstration of existence of a national emergency. So, first the Administration made the decision to claim a national emergency, in order to obtain the injunction, and then economists were to provide supportive data and analysis (Allen 1977, 52).

The expectation to supply research to sustain decisions already taken was raised in interviews by economists working on judicial cases and in explicitly political contexts, as we might expect. For instance, economists working for an organization that works on climate change understood that their role was to produce evidence that supported the position taken by the institution, full stop, despite what the economists understood to be severe methodological and data problems with the very long-term forecasts that the organization was generating. They were expected to produce reports that presented the case on climate change much more forcefully and with more certainty than was warranted by the evidence. In other contexts, economists report being told which specific policy interventions to justify in their work. But interviews revealed that the problem also arises frequently in contexts that appear on their face to allow for disinterested, objective work. Even in depoliticized contexts, economists face pressures to generate work that establishes a position or reaches a conclusion that is decided in advance by those who direct their work. This problem was reported to me both by economists working in the public and private sectors, in institutions whose focus was explicitly economic and those whose principal mission was noneconomic, and in institutions that were run by economists and those run by noneconomists. In the public sector, several spoke of the imperative to justify their respective agencies' regulations on economic grounds, regardless of their economic merit.

In the private sector, clients of economic services often place pressure on economists to generate biased work (see below).

The pressure to produce certain results can be explicit or implicit. In some institutions, managers return work to economists with instructions to change not just the inferences drawn from the empirical findings but also the data that support these inferences. In other contexts, economists are given a target for an economic estimate prior to commencing their work, and they are instructed to do what is necessary to generate that target. The economists are then expected to choose data sources, models, techniques, and judgments that together produce the specified estimate.

Do economists often find themselves in this position, and do they often comply with instructions to alter their work in ways that serve the interests of their managers or institutions? The sense one gets in conversation with economists is that such requests are extraordinarily rare and perhaps nonexistent in many institutional settings but common in others. In the former, requests to alter findings would be viewed by all concerned as extremely inappropriate. In the latter, where instructions to revise work are normalized, economists report that they are apt to comply if they can justify to themselves the changes being asked of them or if they can see no practical way around making the adjustment. One economist explained to me that economists working under such arrangements try to draw a line between misdemeanors and felonies: while they are apt to comply with requests for minor distortions in their work without complaint, they do what they can to resist major distortions that substantially alter the primary conclusions of their work. Some economists emphasized that research which conflicts with the vision of their supervisors or the mission of their institution may very well be suppressed altogether. If they want to have an impact, then they must make compromises that they can live with. Some also cited instances where instructions to revise work led them to consider resignation.

Economists are expected to contribute to predetermined outcomes in ways other than through biased research. In the legislative arena, for example, economists influence the outcome of committee hearings through their involvement in the selection of those outside economic experts who will provide testimony. By selecting one expert as opposed to another, one can ensure that the testimony will be supportive of one's agenda. Economists also influence proceedings by preparing legislators for hearings—by drafting questions that they should put to the experts who will give testimony. Next, government agencies at all levels rely on economic experts (from academia and consulting firms) to gather and analyze data and undertake all sorts of economic research (see below). But, of course, economic experts have track records that reveal much not just about their competence but also about their political commitments, policy biases, and methodological predilections. When it falls to a government economist to vet outside economic experts, the economist can influence the content of the research that the government agency ultimately receives. In these ways, the economist can take steps to ensure that an agency's (or a legislator's) bias is confirmed through nominally independent outside economic expertise, or the economist can instead subtly lean against this bias to ensure that opposing views are heard.

MARKET PRESSURES: "SELLING EXPERTISE" VERSUS "SELLING OPINIONS"

Many economists with whom I spoke identified the economic consulting industry as among the most ethically fraught of all the places in which economists work. Former consultants, in particular, expressed the strongest concerns about the pressures that bear on the quality and integrity of the work that is produced in this sector. One prominent economist argued that ethical economists could not survive in the business since there would be no call for their work. These concerns were echoed—with less intensity, to be sure—by some active consultants.

Several economists identified the market pressures that operate on the economic consultant—pressures that sometimes push the economist in the direction of providing the client with the result that best serves its interest rather than that which is best supported by the evidence. There appears to be substantial opportunity for gain in some sectors of this industry from selling "opinions" rather than "expertise," as one economist put it, especially when large financial interests are at stake. A developer may need to brandish a favorable economic impact analysis before an urban planning agency—one that confirms that a new building project will on balance augment rather than diminish municipal resources or will generate benefits that more than make up for the environmental costs that it will impose on the community. The stakes in such cases can be very large; this implies that an economist who can produce a persuasive report that supports the developer's position stands to earn substantial fees. Pressure to sustain the position of the client can be particularly intensive in civil litigation where the parties often contest vast sums. Speaking of this situation, Michael Weinstein expressed deep worry about

> economists writing one-sided accounts, purposely side-stepping counter claims and arguments . . . [F]or academics to twist the facts, no matter how brilliantly, to fit the preconceived interests of their clients is disturbing (Weinstein 1992, 75).

It is unsurprising, then, that the National Association for Forensic Economics is the only U.S.-based economics association to have adopted a code of conduct for its members (see Chapter 13). But the incentives for bias that arise in the judicial arena also infuse the economic consulting industry more generally.

The market for economic consulting services is segmented.[4] Many clients need reliable, unbiased information about the economic landscape.

This is true of both public-sector and private-sector clients. A regional transit authority may need good projections on demographic trends, the locational match or mismatch between new housing developments and new employment centers, and income and employment projections as it attempts to ascertain how best to utilize its resources to provide transportation services. A grocery store chain may need reliable information on population density, market penetration by other grocers, neighborhood household income data (and projections), and the like as it attempts to ascertain where to site a new outlet. These clients require high-quality analysis of the sort that competent economists with a comprehensive knowledge of the local area can provide. In such cases, there is generally no conflict between the goals of the client and the professional imperatives driving the economist.

In contrast, situations frequently arise in which clients operate in a contested environment and where they seek economic validation for their projects. A corporate client may face opposition from another firm, such as in litigation, or from politically organized interests, such as in economic development disputes where the client is seeking zoning variances or tax subsidies. In contested markets, the economic consultant may confront clients who want to buy validation and legitimacy, not economic expertise. As one economist put it, there is no demand in this context for "'on the other hand' analysis: the client wants unambiguous and unwavering support." And in this case, a wide chasm may indeed exist between the interests of the client and the professional obligations of the economist.

Economic consultants hold a range of views about the relative size and significance of the market for expertise and the market for opinions, the degree to which economic consultants face pressure to compromise their work to win and satisfy clients, and perhaps most importantly, the mechanisms that either imperil or protect good, honest work. Some argue that the rewards for selling opinions are so substantial as to seduce well-meaning economists into finding ways to meet client needs. The skeptics argue that though economists find ways to justify their behavior, they ultimately produce compromised work. Those who are most pessimistic about the consulting industry express a view that reminds the economist of Gresham's Law, with bad consulting practice driving out the good. Especially when the stakes are high, a client will shop for the consulting firm that promises to deliver just the opinion that the client needs. Since these are the cases where potential fees may also be highest, there is a powerful incentive for consulting firms to find a way to provide the opinion that the client seeks.[5]

The majority of those with whom I spoke took a far more sanguine view, arguing that good consultants predominate in the industry. One factor that weighs in this direction is a strong moral aversion in the industry to doing work that lacks integrity. No other group of economists with whom I spoke conveyed this sentiment with equal passion. All emphasized that they would not take on clients who dictated findings prior to the commencement of economic analysis. This may be a consequence of the fact that they operate in an environment where the risks of professional ethical erosion are severe, owing to the rewards that can follow from doing biased work. Confrontation with explicit ethical challenge may yield a heightened self-awareness that other economists are not forced to cultivate.

Two mechanisms seem to fortify the ethical bearing of consultants and, at the same time, offset the pressure for biased work. First, in cases where substantial financial or other interests are at stake, the work of the economic consultant is exposed to intensive scrutiny by those opposing the client's mission. The greater the stakes, the more intensive is this scrutiny. This is true whether the case involves litigation among private parties or a controversy involving public policy or decision making. There is no peer review such as occurs in academia in these arenas but the economist's work undergoes a more rigorous test than it would under the review process of a prestigious journal. The adversarial process ensures that tainted or otherwise inadequate work will fail to advance the client's interests; hence, clients will rationally come to demand expertise rather than opinion.

Second, except in perhaps the very largest cities, the number of economic consultants in any particular locality is rather small. Economic consultants tend to know a good bit about each other's work. Moreover, it is relatively easy for potential clients to ascertain which consultants do good work in the sense of producing credible analysis. Reputational effects are therefore substantial in this industry. If a particular consultant is willing to contort the data to support the client's interests, such behavior is not sustainable given the tarnish that will attach as a consequence to the consultant, his work, and his firm.[6]

Economic consultants employ several strategies to protect the integrity of their work. First, consultants are explicit about their professional principles; they signal to potential clients the market in which they will and won't participate. One emphasized to me that he won't do "MAI" work, or "made as instructed." In this way, consultants hope to dissuade those clients seeking opinions from knocking on their doors. Second, some firms subject their own work to intensive scrutiny before releasing it to the client. In-house review is designed to simulate the criticisms that the work will attract when it sees the light of day; the work is released only when the firm's economists are satisfied that it will stand up to all legitimate criticisms.

A third strategy divides optimists from skeptics. Those with an optimistic sense of the industry tend to be willing to work for just one class of client (such as one industry) and do not see this practice as in any way compromising the integrity of the work. Among this group are those who speak of the need for a "philosophical affinity" between the consultant and the client. Consultants in this camp take on as clients only those whose aspirations they admire (or, minimally, can tolerate). That said, they emphasize that though they serve a limited range of clients, their work is fully objective. One consultant explains that he and his colleagues pass potential clients through two filters: an ideological filter to ensure that clients seek an appropriate agenda and a bias filter to ensure that the clients seek expertise rather than opinions.

Consultants who impose an ideological filter face a difficult balancing act. On the one hand, they express an explicit desire to assist the client to achieve its objectives. On the other, they try to avoid compromising their professional integrity. One economist put it this way (and I paraphrase):

> While an academic economist places all the evidence he can find on both sides of the scale and sees how things balance out, the economic consultant's job is to load up as much evidence as he can find on just one side of the scale—that side that advances the client's interests. But all this evidence must nevertheless be legitimate and honest.[7]

Do the ethical obligations facing the economist change in this way as one migrates between academic and applied work, as this economist claims? Michael Weinstein worries about the corrosive effect of this presumption on the work of the large number of economists who work in both sectors. In his view,

> A scholar's foremost responsibility is to expose all relevant evidence, even if disconfirming. Gnawing at our collective insides should be the question of whether academics who serve as hired guns will subsequently serve their students, colleagues and the general public equally well (Weinstein 1992, 75).

Those with a more skeptical view of the industry share Weinstein's concerns. They argue that an ethical consultant must "work both sides of the street," accepting contracts from any potential client who seeks legitimate work. Providing services to clients of divergent interests is consistent with the conception of the work as objective and unbiased. At the same time, as several consultants explained to me, it enhances the consultant's professional reputation. Some of these economists express concern about the work of consultants who serve only particular classes of clients. The skeptics are also more likely to refuse work which they view as particularly prone to bias. In conversation, various economists identified real estate and development work and forensic cases involving the assessment of damages as among those tasks that they refuse to perform.

Economic consultants face other challenges as they seek to undertake their work with integrity. It is not unusual for a consultant to provide expertise to a particular client over an extended period of time. Some consultants argue that a close working relationship with clients can improve the quality of their work by helping the economist to gain a deep understanding of the matters at hand. In contrast, other economists emphasize that they always keep their clients at arm's length so as to prevent them from influencing their work. They worry that an enduring relationship can encourage them to adopt the vantage point of the client to such an extent that it blurs their professional obligations and judgment. The relationship between economist and client can become particularly fraught when the client offers to provide some or all of the consultant's compensation in equity or a share of profits rather than in a fixed fee; and when the consultant provides not just up-front economic analysis of an intended project but also, for instance, engages in project management or other support activities once a project is undertaken. In the latter case, as one consultant explained to me, one has to work hard to ensure that the prospect of securing subsequent contracts in project management does not influence one's prior economic analysis.

The pressure to adopt and shade one's findings toward the viewpoint of the client is particularly acute in forensic economics (Johnson 1991, 1995; Sattler 1991; Fox 1991; Mandel 1999). In the words of one economist with whom I spoke,

> The forensic economist's chief obligation is to serve the mission of fact-finding and the illumination of the truth. But once you've been hired by one side or the other, it is very difficult to insulate yourself from the lawyer's adversarial ethic. You can come to think of yourself as serving the client rather than the court (see also Mandel 1999).

The further a case progresses, and the more the economist has already been paid for her services, the more difficult it is to resist the pressures to find ways to support the client's case. Managing these pressures may require delicate negotiations between the economist and the attorney over what claims the economist can and cannot legitimately sustain in court. In the extreme, the economist may have to separate herself from a case in order to protect her reputation and the integrity of her work, though forensic economists tend to view this as a last resort.

An additional problem concerns the ways in which the consultant's work is used by the client. While the work products of the economic consultant are "client confidential," the client can (and often does) publicize the research for some purpose or another. In contested contexts, the client generally wants to publicize the results of the research to convince others of the virtues of its position, and it may hire media consultants to package and disseminate its message. In the process, the client may choose selectively from the consultant's report—emphasizing only those findings that are most favorable to its case—while referring to the consultant by name to establish the credibility of the research upon which it relies. This can place the consultant in a difficult position of having to decide how much public misrepresentation of her work she can tolerate since the client is not apt to be pleased if the consultant demands public retractions or corrects the record herself in ways that contradict the client's claims.

The consultant also can face ambiguity concerning to whom she is obligated when the client is an institution rather than an individual. In such cases, a member of the client firm typically serves as the agent of the firm for the purposes of contracting and working with the consultant.

Who, then, is the consultant serving in this context—the principal or the assigned agent? And who is the principal in this case—the firm's CEO, board of directors, or shareholders? The question arose with particular urgency for one consultant with whom I spoke. The consultant was engaged by a firm to evaluate the effectiveness of various programs undertaken by one of its departments. His contact for the project was the director of the department under evaluation. As an interested party, the director was eager to receive evidence that his initiatives had been successful. The consultant discovered that this was not at all the case: the millions spent on these programs had failed to have any effect at all on the firm's efficiency or profits. When this news was delivered to the director, the consultant's contract was terminated, and his report was suppressed. The consultant expressed discomfort about this. Had he fulfilled his professional obligations when he reported his findings to the firm's agent, or did he have a professional responsibility to provide the report to the CEO who would otherwise never receive the benefit of the consultant's research services?

Finally, the consultant may confront a client that is unwilling to pay for the collection of data that are necessary to examine the case at hand. The economist must then decide where to draw the line between working with inadequate data that are readily available and declining the contract altogether. And if the economist does undertake the project despite the data problem, she must then decide whether and to what degree to emphasize this inadequacy in her report and whether and to what degree to restrict the inferences she is willing to draw from these data. Both of these strategies may be vital to protect the integrity of the economic analysis, but they may displease the client that needs an unequivocal report that draws clear inferences.

There is another book to be written on the ethical challenges facing the economic consultant; this discussion barely scratches the surface. For now, it should be said that many in this field are highly attentive to these challenges and have adopted strategies to manage the pressures they confront as they do their work. At present, they must do so on their own, without any assistance at all from their profession.

BUREAUCRATIC INERTIA

Several economists cited the inertia in their institutions that impede good work. One spoke of her department as a "crank and turn" operation that tolerates no innovation whatsoever. Like time constraints, this obstacle bore in particular on newer economists. New economists often appear in the workplace armed with expertise in the newest econometric techniques and theoretical insights. Existing staff often lack this expertise. Given the speed with which economic techniques have advanced in recent years, one need not be a long-term veteran in order to be methodologically dated. Incumbents tend to be committed to the perpetuation of the techniques already in use—over which they have expertise and the virtues and limitations of which they understand.

This unevenness in skill sets can generate conflict. The new economist must make difficult decisions about whether and how hard to press the case for methodological reform. When the department manager, too, exhibits little interest in or resistance to change, the dilemma for the new economist is more acute. A common theme in interviews with newer economists is the challenge of balancing the desire for career advancement with the desire to produce quality work. Sometimes the former impulse wins out, and the new economist conforms to procedures and techniques that she believes (and may know) produce inaccurate results.

GURU WORSHIP AND GROUP THINK

Pressures to conform can take other forms besides institutional self-interest and bureaucratic inertia. In interviews, several economists in the public, private, and multilateral sectors cited the problem of "group think" that often emerges within the economics profession generally and/or within the institutions where they work. This refers to the tendency of members of a community to identify problems and strategies for addressing them in ways that reflect the conventional wisdom that often emerges within a professional community, and to dismiss alternatives out of hand. In the economic policy world, economists also speak of the tendency of their institutions to chase the latest theoretical fad, hopping from approach to approach as the theoretical winds within the academy shift.

The tendency of groups to converge in their judgments is now the subject of extensive research, including that of economists. Work in behavioral economics reveals the degree to which nominally independent actors come to mirror each other's worldviews and behaviors. In the financial sector, behavioral convergence can have dramatic consequences for asset price movements (Shiller 2005; Thaler and Sunstein 2008). And so it is no surprise that economists, too, can converge on how to think about the matters that arise within their areas of expertise.

In the case of economics, the problem of group think is exacerbated by a professional hierarchy that accords the highest status to academic as opposed to applied economists. Often, applied economists cannot pass judgment on the technical work of academic economists since the pressures of their work leave them with little time to keep abreast of the newest research. As a consequence, they feel pressure to defer to the judgment of academic economists. This is not the case in most other professions (such as architecture) where nonacademic practitioners can and often do achieve a level of respect and influence unmatched by their academic peers. Several economists with whom I spoke cited the "guru worship" that results. As a consequence, applied economists sometimes feel the need to seek out a prominent academic champion in order to enhance their influence.[8] And as an academic economist's star rises, reflected perhaps in prestigious appointments and awards, it becomes far less likely that applied economists will come to challenge her insights or policy prescriptions even if they have a better understanding of the policy terrain in their own field. The result of this peculiar status alignment in economics can be group think masked by an ideology of best practice.

SPEAKING ONE'S MIND VERSUS SPEAKING FOR ONE'S INSTITUTION

Most applied economists have just a sliver of the freedom that academic economists take for granted. An academic economist can give an interview or write an Op-Ed piece on virtually any topic without the least thought to the ramifications of her statements. Generally, she can take positions that conflict directly with the mission of her employer or cause embarrassment to colleagues. In contrast, the applied economist must take care to avoid harming the institution that she serves. Often, she must secure permission to speak publicly, and she must calibrate her comments to ensure that they square in important respects with the mission of her employer.

Speaking as an economist can raise difficult ethical issues when it requires the economist to say things that she believes not to be true. In this case, we find a conflict between two duties: the duty to serve the mission and interests of one's institution and the duty to oneself and one's profession to be truthful (see Chapter 8). Several economists from the private and public sectors spoke of strategies to avoid lying while being faithful to one's institution. The simplest involves refusing to comment at all when one is not free to tell the truth, though this strategy is not always available since it might be interpreted by others (correctly) to imply a criticism of or disagreement with one's institution. Other strategies involve telling half-truths that omit or gloss over those aspects of the case that are problematic, exaggerating the strength of one's beliefs so as to enhance the plausibility of the institution's position, and so forth. As one economist put it, "outside of academia it's your job to sell something. You want to build confidence in what it is you're doing." Similarly, Charles P. Kindleberger reported in an interview with William Allen that in the context of advocating for the Marshall Plan,

> we all understood the political process . . . you oversell these things terribly. You really don't quite dare, in the face of a lot of opposition, say that we really don't know about how this will work (Allen 1977, 67).

Sometimes applied economists are in a position to influence events simply through their public statements, and these effects can be helpful or harmful to himself or others. In these cases, the economist faces several problems. One is an appearance of or actual conflict of interest—the economist might be able to secure advantage for himself and/or his institution simply by shading his reporting in one way or another. Since the pathways of causation by which a public statement generates effects are complex, it is not always easy to ascertain in advance what kind of statement will in fact have a troublesome, consequential effect. In this case, it is not enough to be in the right legally; it is also necessary to exercise good judgment and prudence (not least since apparent conflict can be just as damaging to an institution as actual wrongdoing). Both private-sector and public-sector economists spoke of instances where they or their colleagues had erred in this respect with deleterious consequences for their institutions and themselves.

Strategic speaking arises in many sectors where economists work. Politically aligned think tanks may expect their economists to exaggerate the potential gains or harms associated with a policy or regulation in order to garner the attention of the media and to satisfy donors who look to the think tank to give voice to their concerns. Moderation may not serve such institutions very well on any count. Instead, the incentive structure and the competition to command center stage on an issue might push them "to be louder than they would otherwise be" on an issue, as one economist put it—to stake out more extreme positions than they otherwise have reason to adopt. On the other hand those think tanks that present themselves as centrist may find it necessary to equivocate with respect to the inferences they draw so as to appear responsible, credible members of the DC-based policy establishment. In either event, the concern is the same—the needs of the institution may trump the economic findings and require economists to take public stands that they privately believe to be incorrect.

In the public sector, speaking strategically can serve as an effective means to influence political events through backdoor channels. A government economist can influence the legislative process by leaking data or reports or by giving anonymous statements to the press that can force the hand of elected or appointed officials. Or the economist can contact legislative staffers and coach them to request a particular kind of study that the economist knows will yield a particular result. High-placed economists in particular face many opportunities to exert such influence, and it can be difficult to resist the temptation to overstep one's authority when one believes that the political process needs to be redirected in some way or other. The most self-aware of economists think carefully about if, when and how to intervene in these way. Several explained to me that they think that it is appropriate to exploit such strategies to ensure that economic rationality informs the policy-making enterprise. Others disagree. As one economist put it, "you are paid to be anonymous, and you have to be careful not to forget that you don't have the election certificate on your wall. You can't say things that will make trouble for those you serve."

THE REVOLVING DOOR AND THE PRESSURE TO CURRY FAVOR

It may be discomfiting for academic economists who prize liberalized labor markets (while ourselves enjoying tenure) to hear that job insecurity can present a severe challenge to professional integrity. Many applied economists face constant pressure to attend to their job prospects. This is particularly true in certain branches and at certain levels of government (among those lacking civil service protection), but it is also true of the many economists who serve organizations (such as multilateral agencies) as long-term but contingent consultants. It behooves economists in these kinds of positions to look at least passively for the next job opportunity. And this may generate pressures that bear on one's work.

Many economists in and outside of government regularly interact with and are in a position to either befriend or antagonize outside interests that are potential providers of future employment. The economist with uncertain job prospects might be tempted to calculate how to modulate his behavior so as to do good work, while at the same time not foreclosing on professional avenues which he might want to pursue. An economist involved in the promulgation of government regulations in a particular industry might have the kind of expertise that is valuable to firms in that industry; an economist who is engaged in the nitty-gritty of legislation may rub elbows constantly with interests that could provide more lucrative employment. Managing these pressures ethically is difficult—in principle and in practice—not least since being effective might require the economist to maintain good working relationships with others from whom he both needs cooperation and stands to benefit in the future.

Economists in this situation and who place a high priority on doing good work face risks and temptations, some of which are quite subtle. When an economist anticipates that a particular research project could risk important relationships upon which she might want to draw in the future, she can always justify to herself turning her attention to another project instead—one that might also be valuable but that does not risk offense. As one economist put it to me, "The danger is that you can always find something to write about that's safe—so why not do just that?" The responsible economist must make such decisions—she certainly cannot dress for battle every day of her working life and maintain her sanity or effectiveness. But this is an area of judgment where self-interested rationalization can easily trump disinterested professional judgment. Over time, the economist can come to avoid projects that are professionally risky as a matter of course. The largely invisible but potentially large social cost that results is the important but tendentious economic research that never gets done.

ECONOMIC SOCIAL ENGINEERING

Above, we considered economic consulting in the purest sense. A client contracts with a consultant to undertake some sort of economic analysis, and the client then uses that analysis as its sees fit in its decision making, lobbying, or other work. In this case, the consultant exerts influence only by virtue of the strength of her analysis and by the suitability of her work to the needs of the client. Here, the client is in charge of the relationship and the uses to which the consultant's work will be put.

A second arena of economic consulting involves an inversion of this relationship. The consulting undertaken by IFI economists often involves a situation in which the client state faces economic difficulty or even desperation and in which the IFIs provide not just advice but also the material resources that the client state requires to meet basic needs, retain or restore credit, and achieve other vital objectives. Here, the economic consultant wields influence not just by virtue of the quality of the advice that she has to offer but also by virtue of the institutionalized power she enjoys. In these cases, economists may transcend the role of subordinate consultant or advisor and operate instead on the level of social engineer.

There may be no other terrain on which economists operate that is as ethically fraught as that of social engineer. We will explore this matter in greater detail later on (Chapter 9). For now, it is important to describe some of the ethical challenges facing the social engineer.

Economic social engineering entails deciding for others while shaping the institutions and processes that are central to the meaning and quality of people's lives. Presumably, the economist as social engineer should try to make the decisions that these others would make, were they to be in a position to do so for themselves and were they to have a comprehensive understanding of the situation they face. In this sense, the economist may think of herself as in a situation that is akin to an emergency room doctor who must act on the patient's behalf without the benefit of detailed conversation with the patient about how he wants to be treated. Especially in crisis situations, the economist must act fast to restore order—and in such circumstances, building a consensus behind the necessary policy interventions is out of the question (Sachs 1993). This conception would license the economist to substitute her own professional judgment for those she serves. And in this case, perhaps it is not ethically troublesome that those who are affected by the economist's actions do not have the opportunity to govern themselves.

This line of argument invites dissent, however. On what ethical or professional grounds is the economist ever justified in engaging in social engineering? By what warrant is the economist to view herself as a legitimate decision maker for others? Surely she cannot be certain that she has sufficient information about the community she now governs—including their deepest aspirations—to make the choices they would make if in a position to do so. Moreover, even if she could presume this knowledge, she must confront the fact that choosing for others might violate their right to self-governance. Perhaps instead of embracing her role as social engineer, she should refuse on professional ethical grounds to exploit the opportunity provided to her to govern and look, instead, for ethically appropriate ways to assist the community to govern itself.

If the economist somehow manages to convince herself that she is indeed warranted in occupying the role of social engineer—perhaps because she judges the alternative to be too dangerous for the target community—she confronts myriad difficult challenges. First, what values should guide her work: what outcomes should she target in her interventions? Should she advance the cause of efficiency and growth, or equality, or community stability, or something else? The textbook version of this choice presents things far too simply—often as a trade-off between "equity" and "efficiency," as if each of these terms is self-evident. But economists know that this is never the case: any particular target is itself internally complex and so involves trade-offs and value judgments. For instance, the target of improving health outcomes can be achieved in myriad ways, and these diverse ways imply that different people's lives will be saved and lost. Should resources flow to illness prevention, or to treatment of those already infected? Should programs target the young or the elderly? Should emphasis be placed on extending life, regardless of the quality of the life achieved, or on enhancing the quality of life even if that means that fewer are saved? When the economist is placed in the position of social engineer, these decisions necessarily fall on her shoulders. The ethical challenges confronting this economist could hardly be more daunting—and the outcome of her decisions hardly more grave.

A second difficulty derives from the complexities of the world that economists confront. Each instance of social engineering is *sui generis*: the particulars of the context are unique and so are the outcomes of any particular economic intervention. While the economist may be able to exert substantial influence over events, she certainly does not enjoy the power to control them. The economist as social engineer, therefore, faces the risk of doing substantial unanticipated harm, and this situation raises particularly daunting ethical questions. Is it sufficient for the economist to try to engineer that outcome which promises greatest net benefit, irrespective of the distribution (and form) of benefits and costs? Does she instead face an obligation to minimize harm, especially to those groups that are most vulnerable and least able to absorb an economic shock? Or is there some other decision rule that should guide her decision making? We will return to this matter frequently in later chapters since it relates so directly to the case for and the content of professional economic ethics.

A third difficulty that arises, particularly in the context of social engineering but also in other cases, concerns the legitimacy of "inappropriate" means. The difficulty arises when an intervention that is vital to the achievement of some important social objective requires the economist to violate some nontrivial moral imperative or involves some other kind

of ethical or professional compromise. For instance, development economists often operate in contexts where governance is marred by autocratic
structures and corruption. In these contexts, economists confront dilemmas about the extent to which they should "dirty their hands"—perhaps
by exploiting the government's coercive apparatus—in order to achieve
policy agendas that will ameliorate suffering among vulnerable communities (see Chapter 8). Alternatively, development economists might confront situations in which they know that the projects that they administer
help to sustain oppressive governance structures. What are they to do in a
case such as one described to me by an experienced economist: where an
aid project reduces pressure on governing elites to respond to the claims
of the dispossessed and so serves primarily as a subsidy for the wealthy
that retards meaningful political and economic reform? In cases like this,
the self-aware economist faces the daunting problem, as the economist
put it to me, of distinguishing good argument from rationalization in a
context where one is expected to get things done despite insuperable
obstacles.

CONCLUSION

The foregoing discussion is by no means comprehensive. It seeks merely to
identify some of the ethical difficulties that applied economists encounter
as they attempt to do good work. A fuller mapping would require a textbook of cases that explore the field. But I hope the discussion suffices to
indicate just how interesting, ubiquitous, difficult, and consequential are
the ethical questions that arise within professional economic practice.

Academic economists are spared many of the ethical quandaries that
we've encountered here and may not be aware of their existence. This
might help to explain why the profession, led as it is by academic economists, has resisted calls for the advancement of professional economic
ethics. To that resistance we now turn. The next chapter explores the
history of the American economics profession and demonstrates its historical aversion to professional ethics. The subsequent chapter attempts
to explain this aversion in terms of the way that economists view their
profession and the world.

Notes

1 Recent exceptions include Stiglitz (2002), Griffiths (2003), and Meyer
(2004).

2 Interview with Robert Nelson, May 26, 2009.

3 Not all economists with whom I spoke raised this concern. Several pointed
to the culture of their respective institutions as a guarantor of good work. Some
institutions (or departments) emphasize quality of work above speed or quantity
of output; others do not.

4 Hardwig (1994) discusses this problem in the context of professional services more generally.

5 In contrast, one economist cited uninformed buyers as the chief driver of bad economic consulting. Though such clients often seek expertise rather than opinions, they are not sufficiently sophisticated to discern good from bad consulting work. Consumer ignorance allows those firms with brand recognition and substantial marketing budgets to secure the lion's share of certain sectors of the business, even if the quality of their work is substandard.

6 One might think that the same sort of reputational incentive ensures high quality work by economists at the leading policy think tanks. But in an interview, an insider reports that this is not true—that at the largest of these institutions funding is so secure that neither the institutions nor their economists face sanctions for generating biased or unreliable work. We will consider means for improving on this situation in Chapter 11.

7 This way of thinking also characterizes the work of economists at politically aligned policy think tanks. Some of these organizations are implicitly partisan, and yet they present their work as objective economic analysis. They, too, can defend their work as loading up one side of the scale with supporting evidence and argument.

8 In this context, it is not surprising that applied economists can come to devalue their own comparative advantage which involves a wealth of knowledge about economic affairs and institutions and sophistication with respect to economic data that most academic economists cannot begin to match.

Chapter 4

Historical Perspective

"Don't Predict the Interest Rate!"

November 15, 1929

My dear professor Deibler:

The Monday Council of the Sunday Evening Club . . . is engaged in a study of Business Codes of Ethics as adopted by various organizations. Has your organization adopted such a code or do you have any formal statement of what may be regarded as the proper standards of practice in the line of business which you represent? . . .

Very truly yours,
Rudolph A. Clemen,
President, Monday Council

November 19, 1929

Dear Mr. Clemen:

You should know that our middle name is "Ethics", but we have no particular code, consequently, I cannot comply with your request.
Very truly yours,
F.S. Deibler
Secretary, American Economic Association[1]

PROFESSIONALIZATION IN HISTORICAL CONTEXT

Occupations that come to view themselves as professions tend to adopt codes of conduct early in the course of their evolution. Some professions take the far more important step of launching the study of professional ethics in their respective fields. Advancing a set of ethical ideals reflects an occupation's maturing identity as a profession. By doing so, an emerging profession signals to its own members and society that its work is vital to the public good, and that it therefore holds itself to standards that transcend the pursuit of its own interests.

The drive toward professionalism in the United States gained substantial momentum in the decades surrounding the turn of the twentieth century, during the Progressive Era. This period witnessed a series of dramatic social and economic discontinuities that were associated with industrialization in rapidly expanding urban centers. For many analysts, this era marked the displacement of competitive capitalism, characterized by small, locally owned firms which competed on level playing fields, by corporate capitalism that featured large oligopolies which managed to assert control over vital input and output markets through the exercise of formidable economic and political power (Weinstein 1968; Larson 1977; Ross 1991; Crunden 1982).

The economic transformation of the late-nineteenth century produced unprecedented effects across U.S. society. At one pole, industrialists and the enormous firms they piloted became extraordinarily wealthy and influential. At the other, impoverished migrant laborers from the countryside and from abroad found themselves inhabiting an urban landscape that lacked the social and institutional infrastructure necessary to mediate the dislocations associated with rapid industrialization. At the same time, farmers faced stresses stemming from recurring economic crises coupled with national policies that favored industry. In this context, agrarian protest against industrial and financial capital waxed and waned while cooperative, socialist, and anarchist agitation spread widely and came to achieve influence and support among a restive industrial working class. Worker unrest gradually became more organized, such as through the rapid growth of the Knights of Labor during the mid-1880s. More radical elements soon eclipsed this worker cooperative movement. Incidents such as the Haymarket Riot in Chicago (1886) and

> [t]he depression of 1893–7, a series of major strikes, notably Homestead in 1892 and Pullman in 1894, the march across the nation of Coxey's army of unemployed in 1894, the rise of the Populists, and the presidential campaign of 1896, all brought conflict, anxiety, and reaction to fever pitch (Ross 1991, 101).

These developments raised the specter of socialism in America and induced political and intellectual repression as industrial and political leaders came to fear the growing confidence and power of an emerging working class.

From the perspective of an increasingly well-educated middle class, these trends signaled a new and pressing need for the careful application of professional expertise to resolve the deepening tensions and fissures that afflicted society. In Ross's view,

> The new concentrations of economic power, the teeming, polyglot cities, and the expansion of urban, state, and federal governance created new worlds that required detailed knowledge (Ross 1991, 156).

Progressive reformers identified the need to apply the principles of the new social sciences and scientific management to the confounding problems facing society. Progressives believed that professional expertise could ameliorate the most deep-seated social problems. The goal was to rescue the liberal economic and political order from social unrest by ensuring that the prosperity associated with industrial progress would benefit the dispossessed as well as the privileged. In the new order, professional management of public affairs through rational public policy would play the pivotal role in securing efficiency, fairness, social stability, and progress (Larson 1977; Sullivan 2005).

The Progressive Era was marked, then, by heightened self-awareness and purpose among professions that recognized a historic mission that they were to fulfill. Neither the captains of industry nor a radicalized working class could manage the tensions and meet the challenges of the new industrial order. Neither had a sufficient grasp of the whole; neither could see beyond its own interests. Only the emergent professional class armed with the requisite scientific methods of inquiry, a broad cosmopolitan conception of what was best for society as a whole, and a heightened and refined ethical sensibility that directed them to serve the public interest could tend the rudder of social affairs and ensure safe passage to a rational social order. In short, this was "the age of the expert": "At its most expansive, the new notion of expertise meant the capacity to solve problems, the kind of skill that expanding industrial America greatly needed and very much admired" (Sullivan 2005, 84). For the Progressives, "Government 'by science, not by people' was a creed, not a contradiction" (Bernstein 2001, 12).

The emerging professions formed new professional associations and took care to craft bodies of professional standards to guide the privileged members of their communities as they sought to achieve their purposes. The motivations behind professionalization were diverse, of course, ranging from a genuine commitment to serve society, on the one hand, to the more mundane aspiration to elevate the status and (no doubt) remuneration of professionals, on the other. At the time, these aspirations were viewed as complementary: only by achieving recognition among the social elites and the broader public could the emerging professions acquire the influence they needed to work efficaciously. Hence, Edgar Heermance could write in the 1920s, introducing his compilation of professional and industrial codes of conduct:

> Unethical practices are not only a menace to society. They jeopardize the standing of the [professional] group as a whole, and tend to depreciate the value of its service. The enforcement of the standard becomes a matter of self-preservation (1924, 1).

Heermance's book gives ample evidence of just how far the movement to install professional standards had progressed in early-twentieth-America. The book reproduces the codes of 130 occupations, industry associations, and professions—ranging from accountants, architects, and doctors to ice cream makers, peanut butter manufacturers, shoe wholesalers, and most everything in between. The list reveals the extent to which even those occupations with little association with professionalism per se thought it right, necessary, or merely expedient to embrace the contemporary emphasis on public service rather than mere self-interest.

Absent from Heermance's list is the economics profession. The profession did not adopt a code of any sort, despite the fact (as we shall see momentarily) that leading economists from the late-nineteenth century onward were determined to establish economics as a profession on par with its most prominent peers. This refusal was striking given how central was the recognition of professional responsibility to the Progressive vision of a "meritocratic order" (Bernstein 2001, 12). From the Progressive Era onward, the profession simply dismissed as unworthy of its attention the idea of a code of conduct and, more importantly, the need to investigate its professional responsibilities. No other important profession has been so cavalier in its treatment of the matter. The roots of this attitude lie in the early and enduring conception by economists of the nature of their field.

THE PROFESSIONALIZATION OF ECONOMICS: THE ORIGINS AND FORMATIVE YEARS OF THE AMERICAN ECONOMIC ASSOCIATION

The most prominent professional association of economists in the world is today, and has been for well over half a century, the American Economic Association, or AEA. Founded in 1885, the AEA sought to promote the profession at a time when economics comprised as many amateurs as professionals, was widely regarded as having weak theoretical foundations, and enjoyed little influence over public affairs. In the early decades, the organization was preoccupied with the need to enhance the legitimacy and influence of the economics profession (Bernstein 2001). But there was no consensus within the profession about how it would come to define its mission and achieve these purposes. And the primary controversy of the time bears directly on the matter before us.

The pivotal figure in the formation of the AEA was Richard T. Ely, a dynamic economist and a leading member of the 1880s social gospel movement (Nelson 2003). For Ely, economics was by its nature historical, inductive, and deeply normative. In particular, and very much in the spirit of Progressivism more generally (Sullivan 2005), Ely emphasized the necessary commitment of the profession to the principles of social engagement and reform. Ely and other reformers based this commitment squarely on Christian theology—indeed, "20 of the 50 founding members of the AEA were former or practicing ministers" (Nelson 2003, 1). He believed that economics departments should be located in theology schools; he hoped to bring about a "kingdom of righteousness" on earth. For Ely, ". . .the teachings of economics should provide the knowledge base for 'a never-ceasing attack on every wrong institution, until the earth becomes a new earth, and all its cities, cities of God'" (Nelson 2003, 2).

The AEA's initial *Statement of Principles* reflected these commitments. In it, Ely emphasized "the positive role of the church, the state and science in the solution of social problems . . ." (Coats 1960, 557–58; Furner 1975, 71). Ely wrote of a "movement 'which will help in the diffusion of a sound, Christian political economy'" (cited in Crunden 1982, 13). Reflecting Ely's socialist commitments, the document "named the 'conflict of labor and capital' the central problem of modern economics" (Ross 1991, 110). In establishing the AEA, Ely sought explicitly to rescue the field of economics from two related vices. First, Ely hoped to displace deductive formalism, which he viewed as a barren method. He sought to pattern American economics on the German historical school which he took to be better suited to the generation of a realistic and socially useful science. Second, Ely detested the *laissez-faire* orthodoxy which was embraced by many economists at the leading universities. The *Statement of Principles* goes so far as to disparage *laissez-faire* as "unsafe in politics and unsound in morals" (Crunden 1982, 13). Ely recognized a moral imperative to examine the sources and nature of economic oppression and to press for state interventions that would liberate those who suffered its effects. "It rests with us," he argued, "so to direct inevitable changes that we may be brought nearer that kingdom of righteousness for which all good Christians long and pray" (Ross 1991, 107).

The "traditionalist" camp which Ely attacked drew on an equally important though conflicting tenant of Progressive thought—an uncompromising commitment to objective scientific practice. The traditionalists viewed Ely's moralism as a retreat from science. These economists "had been trying to free themselves from the domination of the clerical colleges and moral philosophy"; for them, "the direct identification with ethics summoned up a moralistic and impractical clerical connection they wished to avoid" (Ross 1991, 115). Simon Newcomb, one of the most vociferous critics of Ely's AEA (and a staunch defender of *laissez-faire*), dismissed the organization as a "sort of church, requiring for admission to its full communion a renunciation of ancient errors, and an adhesion to the supposed new creed" (Furner 1975, 73). J. Laurence Laughlin, another prominent traditionalist, refused to accept an appointment to the advisory council of what he took to be a "class of disciples"; he announced derisively that he would not join any organization that ". . .has any constitution save love of truth" (Furner 1975, 78).

In Ely's view, the criticisms betrayed all that was wrong with economics—not simply because it ran contrary to his convictions about the field and its ethical obligations, but also because he viewed it as obstructing the critical work of building the AEA as a professional association. In his words, ". . .it is not easy to arouse interest in an association that professes nothing" (Coats 1960, 558).

The controversy over the appropriate methods, purposes, and ethical content of economics reached the public through the attention of the press and other publications. *Science* published a debate in 1886 in which the principal combatants dismissed the value of the economics pursued by their opponents (Ross 1991, 110). But for the common aspiration among the two camps to enhance the standing of the economics profession, it is not clear that the organization would have survived at all. In the event, leaders of both factions shared the goal of emphasizing whatever common ground they could find in order to achieve respectability for economics (Ross 1991, 112). In particular, the AEA leadership quickly took steps to address the concerns of their critics. The moralistic *Statement of Principles* was dropped as early as 1888. By then, the organization was already trending toward nonpartisanship in order to remove barriers to membership of those of diverse affiliations and views. Ely resigned as Secretary of the organization in 1892, chased out by intellectual adversaries and allies alike who had come to consider his proselytizing an insurmountable obstacle on the road to professionalization (Furner 1975; Ross 1991).[2] The leadership chose Harvard's Charles F. Dunbar from among the traditional wing of the profession as its new President. Dunbar proved to be a good choice since he was a relative moderate on matters pertaining to the rift between the two schools of thought. To ensure balance in the leadership, a reformer in the Ely mold was chosen at the same time to succeed Ely as AEA Secretary. Henceforth, and despite the fact that the organization would welcome both traditional and reforming economists, it would represent, above all else, good economic practice as objective scientific inquiry freed from any explicit social ethics.

The maturation of the AEA as a professional organization in the 1890s was associated with the growing theoretical influence of the marginalist revolution. Alfred Marshall's *Principles of Economics* had appeared in 1890 and quickly influenced the leading American economists of the time (such as John Bates Clark). The adoption of marginalist theory had both professional and theoretical roots:

> . . .the preoccupation with marginal utility and marginal productivity analysis in the 1890's did not merely reflect the dissatisfaction with the unfruitful methodological and doctrinal controversies of the previous decade; it also reflected the economists' yearning for scientific status and prestige. This they sought to attain by dissociating themselves from the past, and by establishing economics as an independent scholarly discipline, from theological, ethical, historical, and sociological connotations and, above all, free from the taint of missionary zeal and political partisanship (Coats 1960, 566).

The turn toward objective deductivist science proved to be deeply consequential in the decades that followed. From the 1890s onward and despite challenges from various camps within and beyond economics, the center of gravity in the profession favored the promotion of a social science patterned on the methods of the natural sciences. The job of the economist was to explore systematically and without judgment the determinants of economic behaviors and outcomes, and to instruct others in the nature of these principles so as to promote better economic understanding and, ultimately, rational economic policy. AEA President Dunbar represented and articulated the emerging consensus.

> Dunbar granted that the economist, as a citizen, had as much right as anyone else to form opinions and try to get others to agree. "In the university," he added, "he is under other obligations; and there it is for him to decide, how far, with his habit of mind and his temperament, he can give expression to judgments lying beyond his proper sphere, and yet related to it, without injury to the severe neutrality of science which he is bound to preserve within that sphere" (Furner 1975, 121).

The increasing emphasis on objective science was connected to another important development: the rise of the modern university system in the United States and the associated migration of professional training into the new research university (Larson 1977; May 1980; Ross 1991). From the 1870s onward, the university extended its mission to incorporate professional training; this trend accelerated with the rise of graduate programs (first at Johns Hopkins University in 1876) and graduate academic certification. The monopolization of economic training by university departments affected the focus of economic research and the sensibilities of economic researchers. Economics (and other professional training) entered the university just as the university came to define its mission in positivist terms. "Thus," William May (1980, 207) argues,

> the university became the institutional matrix that shaped the professions and their ethics at approximately the same time that many faculty members began to exclude questions of values from the university's domain.

Henceforth, emphasis would be placed on abstract reasoning divorced from the political or ethico-spiritual agendas that had previously marked the field of economics.[3]

Important presumptions underlie the aspiration to objectivity. By the end of the nineteenth century, many prominent American economists had come to believe that the economy was an object of study little different from the natural world that lent itself to rigorous value-free investigation, both abstractly and empirically. Affected like other researchers by the positivist trend in the natural and social sciences (Ross 1991; Sullivan 2005), economists came to view the economy as comprising regularities that were reducible to universal attributes of human nature. Rightly or wrongly, Adam Smith was taken to have identified the entirely natural disposition of human agents to act in their own self-interest and to have begun to infer the implications for economic organization. That we might want human nature to be otherwise was beside the point: economists were to don the secular garb of the scientist and not the sacred robes of the clergy. This universal human drive led to patterns of behavior that generated the observed economic phenomena. The job of economics was to discover economic patterns and regularities and to trace these phenomena back to the operation of universal drivers. This became the primary domain of economic science as early as the turn of the century—to explore and discover how the economic machinery works, without judgment.

In this view, "positive" science was primary. One could not begin to consider what should be done—what kinds of economic policy governments ought to enact—unless and until the economic system as it is was fairly fully mapped. For instance, in 1900, economist Edward A. Ross expressed worry about "the premature discussion of ethical questions" that had "disturbed the development of our science." He added, "I think that the ethical aspects of our economic system should come after a rational, cold-blooded explanation of what is" (cited in Ross 1991, 179). In this way of thinking, economic policy was ultimately dictated not by wishful thinking—by how we would like things to be, as given to us by Ely's Christian or any other social ethics—but by the way that the economy actually works.[4]

By 1920, the fight over the appropriate methods for economics and what these implied about the status of ethical matters in the field were largely settled for the majority of economists (the efforts of dissidents like Thorstein Veblen notwithstanding; see Ross 1991). By then, the profession had come to focus intensively on the project of advancing objective economic science. The positivist conception of economics facilitated the pursuit of the influence that economists believed they deserved but had not yet achieved in economic affairs. In 1925, the *American Economic Review* (*AER*) published a lament by Frank Fetter about the insufficient influence of his profession in policy deliberation:

> In building a costly house, architects are employed; in making roads and bridges, engineers; in all the material arts and sciences the value of special training is recognized. But the work of fitting our economic legislation and policy to rapidly changing conditions is still entrusted to men with little or no economic training. . . Economics has not as yet attained the objective scientific character of the natural sciences. Yet its clearer analysis of terms; its deeper insight into the nature of the problems; its emancipation from the various errors which beset popular thinking on the more complex economic relationships. . .these give economics at its best a strong claim to scientific standing and to popular confidence (Fetter 1925, 16–17).[5]

The positivist understanding of economic science proved to be extraordinarily durable (Amy 1984; Nelson 1987; Bernstein 2001; Sullivan 2005; Ross 1991). Despite the dissent of a small corps of mainstream economists and various heterodox schools of thought over the past century, the model of economics as objective inquiry insulated from ethics continues to inform economic training and practice. Most important for our purposes, this conception of economic science has played an influential role in regard to how the profession thinks (and more often doesn't think at all) about professional ethics.

THE AEA AND PROFESSIONAL ECONOMIC ETHICS

Tracing what leading economists believe about professional economic ethics requires the work of the archivist since they have had so very little to say for public consumption on the matter. In her detailed account of the early decades of the AEA, which draws heavily not just on the published material of its founders but also on a wealth of private correspondence, Furner (1975) makes no mention at all of any discussion of professional ethics. And in his authoritative survey of the historical development of the American economics profession, Bernstein (2001) notes just one instance in which the AEA took up the matter. This he finds buried in the AEA's records rather than prominently placed in the pages of its journals. The case is instructive: in 1946, at a time when there was growing concern across the disciplines about the increasing involvement of the state in academic research through public funding for research programs, economist Joseph Spengler called on the AEA Executive Committee to examine

> the ethical rules or standards o[f] [the] profession." He wondered if the discipline needed "a Hippocratic oath to guard against government economists violating sound doctrine to follow [a] party line, or to insure sound ethical practices on the part of counselors and non-teaching economists[.]" While Spengler's suggestion went unheeded, the concerns to which it gave voice remained. A bit over a decade later, AEA secretary-treasurer James Washington Bell could receive an irate letter that declared "[s]ome U.S. economists are quacks—out-and-out fakers." The missive closed with a taunting question: "While the Unions are cleaning out their Hoffas and Congressmen are exposing nepotism,—what are *you* doing? (Bernstein 2001, 121).

Concerns of this sort were voiced much earlier, in fact. In June of 1921, George J. Eberle, an economist with the B.C. Electric Railway Co., wrote to the Secretary of the AEA urging an initiative that would provide for certification of professional economists in a manner similar to that found in engineering, law, medicine, accounting, and architecture. He also argued for the establishment of an organization within the AEA, or a collateral association, that would seek to "protect the practicing economist and assist materially in placing his work before the public on a high professional plane." The AEA rejected Eberle's proposals; the Secretary of the Executive Committee communicated its decision in a terse memo that read in part: "The committee was indisposed to establish such requirements, and voted to lay the motion on the table" (AEA Archives, Boxes 17 and 18). No further explanation was given.

Coats (1985) cites other instances in which the AEA leadership was forced to confront the need for a professional code of conduct and the related matters of professional certification and licensing of economists. These issues arose with some frequency during the 1920s and 1930s. Discussion centered on three issues:

. . .[economists'] responsibilities as advisers to government bodies and private organizations—a matter of obviously growing importance; the direct or indirect involvement of some economists in stock exchange speculation; and the issues of principle and practice arising from the acceptance of continuing research grants or retainers from private sources and vested interest groups (Coats 1985, 1710).

The last of these concerns was, then, attracting the attention of other academic bodies as well. The American Association of University Professors (AAUP) created a committee in 1930 to investigate the growing influence of business interests over academic practice. The committee called for a code of conduct to govern privately funded research, especially in engineering and economics, and laid down a set of rules to govern the acceptance of funds from business by universities and individual researchers. The committee urged academic institutions to refuse grants to fund research on any "specific question of actual or probable controverted public policy" and admonished the university professor to refuse retainers from outside interests to study controversial issues "if he is to retain his reputation for impartiality and retain the whole-hearted confidence of the public" (cited in Dorfman 1959, 209). Notably, Coats explains, no reference to this report ever appeared in the *AER*.

During the 1930s, the AEA received several inquiries about its code of conduct and requests to take up one matter or another pertaining to the ethical behavior of economists. Instances include a petition to the AEA from the business and economic faculty of the University of Arkansas in December of 1933 to adopt a "Plan for Improving the Professional Status of Economists," comprising among other things a certification process for economists to protect the profession and the public from damage wrought by unqualified practitioners, a "code of ethical practices for economists," and the institutional means necessary to police it (AEA Archives, Box 26). But by then, the profession had formed the habit of sidestepping such issues:

> [T]he executive committee, when pressed, viewed the investigation of such matters as beyond the range of its proper functions . . .The usual response to enquirers was that the AEA needed no special code of ethics because the canons of correct professional practice were too obvious to require specification (Coats 1985, 1710–11).

Throughout the middle of the century, the AEA received complaints about *AER* refereeing practices and standards (and related matters). In 1958, a plagiarism complaint was lodged against leading economists, including some associated with the *AER*, and was widely circulated among AEA members (AEA Archives, Box 96). This time, the Executive Committee had no choice but to investigate. AEA President A.F. Burns appointed the "Committee on Professional Ethics" to consider the charges. The committee filed its final report to the AEA Executive Committee in 1963; it reported that the "evidence did not offer a sufficient basis to question the integrity of those charged or to warrant further investigation" (*AER* 1963, 690).[6] The Executive Committee dismissed the complaint and terminated the Committee on Professional Ethics "with thanks for their work" (*AER* 1963, 690; Coates 1985, 1711). The report of the Executive Committee that appeared in the *AER* that year simply notes the disposition of the case without providing any discussion of the matter.

Over time, the profession's leading economists and flagship organization became more dismissive of professional ethics. The Executive Committee minutes indicate that calls for a code of conduct were submitted to the Committee in 1971, 1981, 1983, and 1994 (at least two of these coming from economist Joseph A. Hasson).[7] Each time, the matter was summarily dropped since, as we learn from the minutes, there was "general agreement that such a code was not necessary" (*AER* 1972, 478). When the matter came before the Committee in 1994, owing to yet another letter from a concerned economist, it received an even cooler reception than it had previously. As one attendee reported the story, a Board member addressed the matter this way: "Sure, we'll have a code—its first rule will be 'Don't predict interest rates!'" Everyone laughed, the joke was taken as sufficient attention to the matter, the conversation was terminated, and the meeting adjourned (McCloskey 1996, 107).[8]

After the 1994 meeting, the matter remained of how to respond to the economist who had petitioned the Executive Committee for a code of conduct. The Secretary-Treasurer, C. Elton Hinshaw, wrote to the incoming AEA President Victor Fuchs to advise him regarding the content of his reply. Hinshaw's letter (dated January 10, 1995)[9] is particularly useful since it summarizes carefully what he understands to be the reasons for the AEA's historic resistance to its establishment of a code of conduct. Hinshaw lists five arguments against the adoption of a code. First, the Association lacks the requisite expertise; second, the "Association would have to be extremely careful to insure that the rights of the accused were adequately protected in any mechanism established to adjudicate disputes"; third, implementation of a code would likely embroil the Association in litigation; fourth, the Association likely lacks "effective sanctions for those found guilty of violating the code," since the Association does not "license or accredit" or "even attempt to define who is an economist"; and fifth, there is no evidence that codes have had their intended effect in other professions that have adopted them. "In summary," Hinshaw concludes, "the Executive Committee seems to view these codes as hortatory with little real positive impact."

These arguments would warrant close attention were the profession ever to begin to move toward adoption of a code. Any one of these arguments might prove to be decisive in such deliberations. But what is most important about them for present purposes is that they represent objections to a *code of conduct*, and not to professional ethics. The letter spoke to the question of a code of conduct since that is what was sought by this and the other petitioners to the AEA Executive Committee over the past century. None sought the establishment of a tradition of inquiry into and debate over the myriad ethical issues that arise in the context of professional economic practice. This is most unfortunate: it reflects and contributes to the common error of conflating professional ethics with a code of conduct (see Chapters 1 and 6). There is no evidence that the Executive Committee has ever taken up the matter of professional ethics broadly construed.

In print, economists have had almost nothing to say about a code of conduct for economics (or professional economic ethics) and/or the related issue of licensure for economists (we will explore the connection between these two instruments in the next chapter). Promising leads evaporate upon closer inspection. For instance, in his essay "Occupational Licensure for Economists?" Nobel Laureate and Chicago School economist George Stigler (1980) treats the matter cited in the essay's provocative title only in passing before moving on to other questions. This is unsurprising given his view of the rather uncomplicated and disinterested role of the economist in public affairs, which he described in his Presidential Address to the AEA as follows:

> Economists generally share the ruling values of their societies, but their professional competence does not consist in translating popular wishes into an awe-inspiring professional language. Their competence consists in understanding how an economic system works under alternative institutional frameworks. If they have anything of their own to contribute to the popular discussion of economic policy, it is some special understanding of the relationship between policies and results of policies.
>
> The basic role of the scientist in public policy, therefore, is that of establishing the costs and benefits of alternative institutional arrangements (Stigler 1965, 1–2).[10]

Later on, we will examine the few exceptions to this general silence—recent instances where economists have begun to explore, at least obliquely, matters pertaining to professional economic ethics. These exceptions notwithstanding, the fact of the matter is that a century's worth of eminent economists, who have found it appropriate to explore with painstaking care so many other aspects of social organization (large and small), have simply ignored the question of whether their own profession has need for or would benefit from a body of professional ethics.

CONCLUSION

The historical origins of the AEA in the midst of the Progressive Era's complex and contradictory understanding of the nature of science and the proper role of the professional in addressing the most pressing social problems of the day surely contributed to its view of professional ethics.

Looking to shed the moralism of its recent past and to secure the public influence it felt it was due, the profession by the early-twentieth century coalesced around the need for hard-headed objective inquiry that provided little space for ethical consideration. In this regard, economics aspired to achieve the standing and methods of physics rather than medicine. As a consequence, there seemed to be little need to wrestle with the profession's ethical obligations. From that point forward, it became difficult for advocates of professional ethics to gain a foothold in the profession.

That said, virtually all other professions that matured during the same era adopted at least a code of conduct, and some adopted a full-blown body of professional ethics. Other forces must have contributed to what is now a century-long antipathy of the profession to professional economic ethics. A fuller account must advance other arguments about the nature of economics and the way that economists understand the world around them. It is noteworthy in this regard that Britain's Royal Economic Society displayed a similar reluctance in its formative years (and since) to take up the matter of professional ethics (Coats 1968). It is also noteworthy that today, most professional economic organizations around the world do not advocate professional economic ethics. This suggests that there might be something inherent in the economics profession—in the way that it theorizes its own work and the world about it—that precludes sustained attention to professional ethics. The next chapter explores just what and why this might be.

Notes

1 Exchange appears in Box 25 of the archives of the American Economic Association, held at Duke University. This and all AEA documents referenced here are available from the author.

2 Many economists who had shared Ely's enthusiasm for socialism had begun to reverse course, in part, as a consequence of the political reaction that arose in the wake of the class turbulence of the mid-1880s. John Bates Clark was among the first to undertake "an intense effort to rethink his position" when "the Haymarket riot sent shock waves through the upper and middle classes" (Ross 1991, 115). Even Ely repudiated his socialist commitments when he was brought up on charges before the regents of the University of Wisconsin in 1894 for allegedly "siding with labor, favoring socialism, counseling union organizers, and threatening to boycott a printer doing university business for not adopting a union shop" (Ross 1991, 117).

3 This is not to say that the aspiration to pure science unmediated by ideological presumptions was achieved. For instance, many prominent members of the profession—including Marshall, Pigou, Edgeworth, and Irving Fisher adhered to the "science" and endorsed the politics of the eugenics movement that achieved influence especially in the latter decades of the nineteenth and the early decades of the twentieth centuries in the United States and England (Peart and Levy 2007). According to Peart and Levy (Chapter 4), economists endorsed all three of the major policy proposals of the eugenics movement: positive inducements

to improve the quality of the genetic stock; negative inducements to reduce the fertility of the inferior classes; and immigration restrictions. Only in the mid-twentieth century, in the wake of the horrors of the Holocaust, did the profession (especially Austrian and Chicago economists) begin to rid economics of the presumptions of racial differences that informed the eugenics movement.

4 Progressivism entailed a contradiction that bedeviled the economics profession. Progressivism emphasized "civic ideals that seemed to require a moral and political integration of life that could only be achieved if modern citizens were educated to a high level of public participation" (the view of Ely and his supporters), but also the promotion of "scientific expertise and technical efficiency as the keys to the more advanced form of society" (the view of the economic traditionalists; Sullivan 2005, 101). See Nelson (1987) and the other references provided in this chapter for good accounts of the combined effect of these contradictory forces on the economics profession.

5 While expressing this confidence in objective economic science, Fetter was an active advocate of eugenicist policy.

6 The AEA publishes the minutes of the annual meetings of the Executive Committee each year in the *AER*.

7 For example, in 1974, Hasson wrote to AEA President Walter Heller, seeking an "Ethical Practices Committee within the Economics profession. It is long overdue!" Hasson referenced the fallout in the legal profession from the Watergate affair, citing that profession's "self-criticism" and its exploration of its failure to police itself properly. President Heller replied that "There is no question but that your objective is an entirely valid one. But for the American Economic Association to take on the responsibility for protection against unethical practices would probably go beyond its jurisdiction and capabilities" (AEA Archives, Box 124).

8 The meeting minutes include the following account of the discussion: "As to a code of ethics, the committee showed no enthusiasm. Someone suggested that the Association should propose that economists should not forecast interest rates. There appeared no sentiment to pursue the idea of an ethics code" (*AER* 1995, 463).

9 Letter provided to author by AEA Secretary-Treasurer John Siegfried and cited here with permission of Professor Hinshaw.

10 I thank Fátima Brandão for bringing this passage to my attention.

Chapter 5

Interpreting the Silence

The Economic Case Against Professional Economic Ethics

Insofar as economists have considered the subject, as a rule they have not been too friendly to the special claims of the professions ... They have been aware that there would be certain difficulties about the operation of free market forces in the professions, notably medicine, on account of uncertainty and asymmetric information (Arrow, 1963); but, on balance, economists have tended to regard departures from free competition in the professions as serving the purpose of a restrictive cartel ...

R.C.O. Matthews (1991, 738)

The silence of the economics profession on the matter of a professional code of conduct has been broken only when circumstances conspired to force economists to take up particular cases of alleged malfeasance. Even in these instances, leading economists failed to pursue the painstaking, hard-headed analysis that the profession takes to be its chief contribution to the social sciences. Yet, economists worked incessantly to professionalize economics and to solidify its standing and influence. What are we to make of this curious silence when all around economics, other professions have adopted codes of conduct and some have developed and sustained rigorous fields of inquiry into the ethical conduct of their work? Answering this question requires inference and speculation.

Two general resolutions to this puzzle present themselves. The first is an "economics exceptionalism" argument: it is the idea that in comparison with other professions, there is something unique about the economic practice and the roles played by economists that eliminate the need for professional economic ethics. A second, complementary explanation focuses not on the peculiarities of economic practice but on the unique way that economists reason about matters before them. I will argue that the economist's worldview engenders skepticism concerning the matter of professional ethics. The following discussion pursues these two explanations while offering supplementary arguments along the way. The goal is to build the strongest case that I can, drawing where appropriate on economic theory, to justify the economist's antipathy to professional economic ethics.

ON ECONOMIC EXCEPTIONALISM

The case for economic exceptionalism has three legs. The first derives from widely held views about the nature of economic knowledge and research that distinguishes economic practice from many other professions that serve the public good. We have already taken note of these views, which reflect the deep influence of positivism among economists from the late-nineteenth century to the present. For many economists, economics is understood first and foremost to be an objective science that entails the search for the laws that drive economic affairs. Economics entails the construction of parsimonious models of economic behavior and processes; the identification of testable hypotheses; rigorous collection and exploration of economic data; and more generally, a commitment to ideologically neutral scientific norms and practices. Coats (1991, 121–22) puts the matter this way:

> In the economist's case a central tenet of [professional] ideology is the conception of the neutral objective scientific expert which underlies the above-mentioned distinction between 'science' and 'art,' or between 'positive' and 'normative' economics, to use the current jargon (Hutchison 1964). In the economics community the academic ideal, namely that of the pure research truth-seeker, the detached non-partisan expert, outweighs any more pragmatic conception of professionalism or public service. . .".[1]

It follows that the ethical obligations appropriate for economic inquiry are the same as those that obtain across the natural sciences and have little to do with those that guide fields like social work, law, or medicine. These obligations are self-evident: the economist should presumably not plagiarize, falsify empirical results or allow personal biases to interfere with the interpretation of the data, and so forth.

Role Specification and Professional Economic Ethics

The second defense of economic exceptionalism requires more attention. In their professional work, economists occupy two types of roles. On the one hand, they undertake research and teach in universities. On the other, some economists promote social welfare through applied work beyond the academy. Prominent economists frequently leave the university (temporarily or permanently) to take up positions where they can work toward implementation of the findings of their science. As we saw in Chapter 2, applied economists hold thousands of positions in government, the multilateral agencies, think tanks, consulting, law and brokerage firms, investment banks, hedge funds, and beyond. In these roles, economists engage in practices that directly and indirectly alter the course of public and private decision making—often with staggering effects on economic flows and economic, political, and social outcomes. Surely here, beyond the academy and in the domain of the applied economist, one might think that there is a need for professional ethics to guide the work of these influential actors.

A closer consideration of the matter undermines this conclusion, however. A person who is an economist is many other things besides, and the assessment of his behavior in these other roles depends upon judgments that are unrelated to his professional status as economist. He may cheat on his taxes or beat his children, but the evaluation of the morality of these actions depends on judgments that pertain to his role as a citizen or parent, not as an economist.

These examples highlight the need to specify carefully the diverse roles in which a person acts before drawing conclusions about which norms apply in each domain of behavior. This lesson implies that it would be mistaken to presume that everything an economist does in the professional world ought to be subject to professional *economic* ethics since he performs some of his work not as an economist but as the occupant of some other professional role. Many professional economists teach, for instance—and the ethics of that practice ought to be (and generally is) governed by ethical standards that pertain to all teachers. The economics professor, just like the professor of history or anthropology, should not solicit favors from students in return for grades or establish a cult of personality rather than actually teach. These imperatives attach to the practice and responsibility of teaching rather than to the discipline taught; hence, they bear on the economics professor in his role as professor and not as economist per se.

This insight relates to the work of applied economists as well. When we inquire carefully into the roles that economists play, we find that the professional ethics that should govern (if there are any at all) derive from the noneconomist roles that economists occupy in these institutions and not from their expertise as economists. Most notably, economists do not typically occupy positions with the authority to direct economic strategies, flows, or outcomes. Instead, they typically produce economic knowledge that will be used by others. If they are working *as economists*, they are undertaking objective research that will provide those in authority with the information and analysis necessary to make good decisions.

Sometimes an economist rises to the position of actual decision maker— such as when she runs for and secures political office. But in cases of this sort, she then occupies a role which displaces that of economist, just as when she is also a citizen paying taxes, a parent raising children, or a professor teaching students. She is now also a senator or mayor or city councilor, and the ethical obligations she faces in her work come to her as a consequence of that role. In this domain, she no longer works as an economist even if (as we would expect) she uses her economic knowledge and expertise in fulfilling the obligations of her office.

The Moral Insulation of the Economic Advisor

We have to be very careful, then, in thinking about just what constitutes the work of the economist to which a body of professional ethics would pertain. And when we probe the various roles that applied economists occupy, we find that economists typically advise (directly or indirectly) rather than make strategy or policy decisions. They gather and examine data, they answer the specific questions put to them, and they produce reports that evaluate options. While the ultimate decision maker must wrestle with all sorts of difficult ethical challenges, the adviser—provided she comports herself in a manner that is consistent with the obligation to pursue truth and to report truthfully to those she advises—is spared ethical responsibility for the decisions ultimately made.

Dennis Thompson (1983; 1987) has produced the most insightful work to date on the matter of the ethical entailments of advising. He identifies three types of arguments that are associated with the idea of the moral insulation of the advisor. The first entails the idea of "null cause" (1987). In this view, an agent cannot be held ethically responsible for actions that she did not herself bring about:

> Applied to relations between persons, the idea is that one person is responsible for what someone else does only if the first person causes the second to do it. On this view, as long as an adviser merely advises, we would not normally say that he causes the advisee to decide one way rather than another. Since the advisee remains free to accept or reject the advice, we would not blame the adviser for anything the advisee did. Just as in the law a voluntary intervention by another agent—a *novus actus interveniens*—breaks the chain of responsibility, so in morality a subsequent voluntary decision by an official shifts the entire responsibility to him (1983, 547).

The second argument concerns intentions: an advisor can only be held responsible for what she intends and not for the unintended consequences of her advice. If the decision maker makes poor or opportunistic use of the advisor's counsel, she alone is to be held morally accountable. The advisor is morally insulated since (as per the null cause argument) she cannot be held responsible for the actions of another.

The third argument concerns the advisor's moral duty to fulfill the obligations of the role that she occupies.

> An adviser may claim that by the formal or informal expectations of his office he is bound to give advice in certain specific ways (such as providing merely technical analysis), and so long as he does so properly, he cannot be held responsible for anything other officials do with his advice (1983, 554).

Indeed, the advisor might sometimes be expected or even required to play the role of devil's advocate—arguing forcefully for a view that the advisor believes to be wrong-headed so as to better elucidate the options available to the decision maker. In the event that she proves to be persuasive, she can hardly be indicted for the poor decision ultimately chosen. Her ethical obligation is to fulfill the role as best she can—not to bring about any particular policy decision.

We should add to Thompson's arguments the view that is so central to the idea of economic exceptionalism—that advisors are mere technocrats "whose work is value free and apolitical" (Amy 1984, 581). Douglas J. Amy explains that by the 1960s, when economists came to play a heightened role in public affairs, the notion of the advisor as neutral technocrat was well established. We noted above the influence of positivism during the formative years of the American economics profession and its enduring presence in shaping economists' view of their profession. Amy emphasizes its continuing influence in conditioning the self-perception of the expert advisor:

> Positivism provided the intellectual underpinnings for the technocratic role of the analyst in government. Trained in positivist social science, analysts could draw a sharp distinction between normative questions and factual questions. In practice, this meant that analysts could focus on questions of means, while leaving questions of ends to policymakers. It was thought that politicians would set social goals, and analysts would give them technical advice on how these goals could best be achieved (Amy 1984, 581).

The positivist perception of advising has been widely shared by prominent economists who have served in government. Nelson emphasizes that positivism remained strong among applied economists late into the twentieth century, when he served on the economics staff of the U.S. Department of Interior: "Economists tend to view their professional role in the governing process as that of experts separate from politics, value judgments, and other subjective and normative factors" (Nelson 1987, 50). This view was shared by leading academic economists throughout the twentieth century as well. George Stigler argued the point concisely in this way:

> And there we have the answer to the question of how the economist can operate so extensively and so easily as a critic of policy when he is not in possession of a persuasive ethical system. The answer is that he needs no ethical system to criticize error: he is simply a *well-trained political arithmetician* (Stigler 1980, 152, emphasis added).

While the purported innocence of the advisor for the ends pursued does not in and of itself necessitate the conclusion that the advising professions need no professional ethics,[2] it certainly diminishes substantially the potential breadth and scope of any such ethics.

If these arguments are correct, they represent a rather strong case against the need for professional ethics to guide applied economists.[3] The applied economist does not bear the ethical burdens associated with the mantle of authority. That lies with others—with those whom the economist advises. In her role as economic advisor, she is to serve as a neutral technocrat who serves those with the authority to decide. When, instead, the economist is authorized to decide, her work as economist is trumped by the new role she has acquired. In this case, the ethical obligations she faces emanate from this new role, not from her status as an economist. Altogether, then, it appears that the applied economist faces the same, self-evident ethical obligations as does the academic economist. For the former as for the latter, "Pursue and disseminate the truth!" provides all the ethical guidance necessary for correct conduct.

Economics as a Nonprofession

The third leg that supports the case for economic exceptionalism is this: economics is not a profession. Hence, it makes little sense to pursue the matter of professional economic ethics.[4]

In order for the notion of profession to have meaning, there must be a basis for drawing a clear distinction between professional and nonprofessional occupations. This basis lies not just in the amount of study and training required nor in the level of expertise to which that training gives rise. Nor does it lie in the status or income achieved by people in the occupation, even though in common parlance, we tend to equate high income with professionalism. It derives instead from the explicit application of this hard-won expertise to the public good (and not just or primarily the pursuit of private interest), and from a governance structure that provides the occupation with substantial autonomy and self-direction.

A commitment to public service distinguishes many fields that rise to the level of profession from those that do not. Professional athletes achieve success only on the basis of sustained participation in grueling training regimes. Actors and artists can invest lifetimes honing their craft, while business managers may have particular skills that are acquired only through extensive classroom and on-the-job training. But none of these occupations achieves the standing of a profession since none carries with it an explicit obligation on the part of the incumbent to serve society rather than to pursue her own self-interest.

Economics is similar to other occupations that require substantial training for success but that do not define themselves in terms of a commitment to the public good over and above self-interest. Like business managers, economists may, in good conscience, pursue successful careers without giving a moment's thought to whether their work makes any social contribution whatsoever. Indeed, those economists who believe that their work makes a social contribution would be encouraged by their professional training to find a way to internalize that positive externality— perhaps by forming a firm that markets their research to those who would be willing to pay for it. Though these economists would theorize this arrangement as increasing the supply of socially beneficial goods and thereby serving the public interest, they would not be expected by those in their field to do it for that reason. Economists, above all others, presume and justify self-oriented behavior—how then could they view their own occupation as having a responsibility to the social good that conflicts with the pursuit of self-interest?

Professions tend to seek the right of self-governance even if they must collude with the state to secure this privilege. Professions take care to demarcate the set of practices that only their members can perform, and they enforce the boundaries around these practices through the establishment of standards, certification, or licensing. Professional self-governance also entails influence over the graduate programs that generate new members of the profession—sometimes through participation in accreditation procedures—and the postgraduate training and examination procedures that potential initiates must pass to achieve the right to practice in the profession.

If we take self-governance as a necessary determinant of a profession, then we find that occupations like medicine, law, engineering, and architecture pass muster, while business management does not. Though there are graduate programs in business, of course, and though those earning the MBA might have expertise not widely available to those who do not achieve the degree, business management does not represent a profession in the sense detailed here. There is no self-governance in this occupation. One needn't secure an MBA (or even attend college) to work successfully in many branches of business; nor is there any professional body that has sought the right to dictate who can and cannot enter the field. There is no licensing, exam, or certification process for those seeking to enter the business world in most of the positions available there.

Economics is like business and unlike medicine and law in this respect. The occupation does not self-govern in any way. It certainly does not attempt to control access to the trade. One can skim a first-year textbook (or not) and hang the shingle "Jane Smith, Economist" outside one's door. And if one can secure clients in need of economic analysis, one is a fully fledged economist—in exactly the same way that one would be a fully fledged "business manager" were one to secure employment in that capacity—even if one bases his business decisions on his favorite airport bookstore offering on how to succeed in business.

It should be emphasized that the objection to the idea of economics as a profession and to the need for professional economic ethics does not imply that economists face no ethical challenges. Like business managers, economists may confront difficult dilemmas in their work. These might be so frequent and severe as to warrant some attention during undergraduate and graduate training in economics, just as they do in business school curriculums. The objection, instead, targets the specific idea of the establishment of "professional ethics" for economics. Since economics is not a profession in the sense of recognizing social obligations as against self-interest, professional ethics are irrelevant; and since it is also not a profession in the sense of being self-governing, professional ethics are untenable since it is entirely unclear to whom a code should apply and virtually impossible for any professional body to enforce it. The latter problem has been well understood by members of the AEA Executive Committee over the years that have fielded and rejected calls for a professional code of conduct. We should recall one of the arguments given by Secretary Hinshaw against the adoption of a code of conduct (cited in the previous chapter). He wrote that the AEA likely lacks "effective sanctions for those found guilty of violating the code," since it does not "license or accredit" or "even attempt to define who is an economist" (Hinshaw January 10, 1995).

PROFESSIONAL ECONOMIC ETHICS: A NATURAL ANTIPATHY

We will examine critically (and indeed reject) the economics exceptionalism argument in the next chapter. For now, it bears mention that many other recognized professions that embrace professional ethics share many of the features of economics. But might there be other reasons for the refusal of economics to embrace professional ethics when so many other similar professions have thought it necessary to adopt it?

The answer is certainly "yes." Mainstream neoclassical economic theory provides us with a direct and powerful argument against professional economic ethics—one that is accessible to any student who has endured Economics 101. We have alluded to this idea in passing above: human actors are opportunistic, self-interested agents that seek in all cases to make those decisions that will accrue to their own benefit (and perhaps, that of their family and close friends; see Stigler 1980). If this is true of nonprofessionals, it is all the more true of those who have born extensive opportunity costs to secure professional training. These are rational maximizers with a vengeance: having sacrificed for years to secure a privileged position in the labor market, they are surely bound to take all steps available to ensure a proper return on their investments.

Noneconomists might think that this conception of the human actor would make professional ethics more urgently necessary since in this view, the professional (just like everyone else) is apt to undertake whatever actions are most likely to maximize his personal well-being. He might lie, cheat, and steal if he can get away with it to increase his income. And since professionalism entails a mastery of knowledge and expertise that is unavailable to others, including those to whom he will sell his services, the market for professional services is apt to be rife with fraud and deceit. Surely, the professional is in a position to exploit those he purports to help; and in the economist's view, he might be prepared to do just that.

But there's a rub. In and of itself, professional ethics—or even a code of conduct—is unlikely to improve the situation. There is little reason, after all, for a self-interested professional to sustain costs to act ethically in the absence of enforcement mechanisms, especially when clients are unable to evaluate his behaviour adequately. Indeed, it is not at all clear that he should do so or that we should ask this of him. Leland Yeager, in his Presidential Address to the Southern Economic Association, puts the objection concisely:

> Expecting people to act against their own economic interest tends to under-cut the signaling function of prices and the incentives of loss-avoidance and profit. How are people to know, then, when it is legitimate and when illegitimate to pursue economic gain? (Yeager 1976, 566).[5]

Making matters worse, the unscrupulous professional might be able to exploit the existence of a code to secure the unsuspecting trust of those to whom he sells his services, thereby extracting even greater fees (Matthews 1991). As Yeager put it,

> The more prevalent and well-based is the belief that people are generally decent and honest, the greater is the chance that culprits have to benefit from the presumption that they too have these virtues. They will enjoy a free ride on, while posing unfair competition with, the warranted credibility of other people (Yeager 1976, 569).

A voluntary code of conduct exacerbates this problem to the degree that it builds trust for the professional among an unsuspecting public. Those with good sensibilities do not need a code to behave well; those with deficient sensibilities will hardly be deterred by it from behaving poorly and may even profit from the reduced public vigilance that the code induces.

Professional Ethics and Licensure

We arrive rather directly at the conclusion that professional ethics (and especially a code of conduct) might serve the purpose of enhancing the status of a profession while providing no beneficial effect on the behavior of the professionals who purport to subscribe to it. What is necessary to change professional ethics from a fig leaf to a binding constraint is a set of incentives in the form of rewards and punishments that professionals would have to reckon with as they decide how to comport themselves in their work. The most common form of incentive in this context is professional licensure. Under this arrangement, a professional must secure a state-sanctioned license that qualifies the holder for professional practice. In this case, a professional who violates the code of conduct can be disciplined in various ways, including being deprived of the right to practice. In the legal profession, for instance, lawyers can be admonished and in the extreme, disbarred for violating the profession's ethical obligations. Other licensed professions operate under similar procedures with state boards authorized to impose sanctions on professionals who work within their geographic jurisdictions.

This argument implies that a profession should seek legislative reform that requires licensure or certification (by a state agency or quasi-public organization) that is both required for professional practice and can be rescinded when a professional runs afoul of the profession's legislated ethical principles. This simple formula seems to provide the public with protection since unethical behavior will lead to meaningful punishment of the errant professional. And this is precisely the avenue that has been undertaken over the past century by many other professions.

This formula holds little appeal for economists, however. Licensure establishes a monopoly that restricts supply, raises prices, and leads to a loss of social welfare.[6] In Milton Friedman's words,

> The most obvious social cost is that any one of these measures, whether it be registration, certification, or licensure, almost inevitably becomes a tool in the hands of a special producer group to obtain a monopoly position at the expense of the rest of the public. There is no way to avoid this result (1962, 148).

Licensure also limits the choices available to consumers and retards innovation. Rational insiders will not waste the time and energy to improve quality or pursue product differentiation when they can ensure a steady flow of income by increasing the vigilance with which they repel outsiders. Licensure provides an ideal means for doing so, especially since insiders will have an incentive to control the routes by which applicants gain access to the field. Licensure can also be exploited by insiders to discriminate against disadvantaged minorities who seek access to the profession. As a consequence of all this, licensure reduces labor mobility and diminishes the quality of services available to the public.[7]

The effects of government-induced monopoly are troublesome for economists, whether the license under review limits the number of taxi drivers or accountants. In professions whose chief output is knowledge, however, we run the far greater risk of diminishing experimentation and discovery. Where freedom of thought and the associated freedom to chart new paths that diverge from the mainstream or consensus view are at stake, licensure represents a particularly grave danger. Licensing economists would therefore risk a kind of thought control and policing that is antithetical to and corrosive of the intellectual enterprise.[8]

This prospect is frightening for intellectuals, many of whom choose careers in academia because they value freedom of thought so highly, but it is also perilous for the profession as a whole. At stake are intellectual pluralism and dissent—in writing, policy advocacy, and in teaching. It would be dangerously naïve not to anticipate the possibility that licensure would open the door to the sanctioning of unpopular views (or unpopular economists). Licensure might serve as a new bulwark by which those holding the majority view solidify their standing against their critics. And in this event, what is lost is the raison d'être of the profession and perhaps even its soul.[9]

The Consequentialism of Economics

Neoclassical economics is wedded to a consequentialist approach to the assessment of actions and interventions, such as economic policies (Sen 1987).[10] The tradition considers only what will be the consequences of agents' actions (rather than, say, the motivations that lead to the actions). Historically, the only consequence of note in evaluating outcomes has been the subjective states (the "welfare") of those who are to be affected by the action under review. Actions are explicitly not evaluated in terms of their inherent rightness or wrongness.

The consequentialist bias of neoclassical economics can serve as an imposing obstacle to professional economic ethics if the latter is taken to comprise a code that reflects a set of intrinsic judgments about professional behavior. In the consequentialist view, good behavior cannot be legislated once and for all since in the circumstances of a particular case, behavior that has been ruled out of court might in fact bring about the best outcome. Contra Yeager (see fn 5), lying, cheating, and stealing might in fact bring about the best result in a particular case. For instance, there might be cases in which truth telling by an economist might undermine a vitally important economic intervention.

Consequentialism dictates that the case for professional economic ethics must be secured on the basis of clear evidence that it actually improves behavior and outcomes in those professions that have adopted it, and that these benefits exceed the costs associated with its implementation. But where is the evidence for that? Such evidence is scarce—specification and measurement problems are terribly confounding in this area. Indeed, it is not at all clear how a knock-out empirical test could be designed and implemented. Absent persuasive data, economists have good reason to suspect that professional ethics actually yields harmful consequences to those who rely on professional services. The burden of proof, therefore, lies with those who advocate professional economic ethics, not with those who oppose it.

Ethics, Aperture, and Wasted Resources

As discussed above, economists typically aspire to an objective, value-free science of human affairs. But ethics is by nature a value-laden inquiry. Hence, there is no assurance that economists will settle on the right set of ethical principles or even that such principles exist. More likely, the pursuit of professional economic ethics would be fraught with the discovery of intractable conundrums that generate interminable debate. This is just what we see in other professions: professional ethics is a domain of persistent aperture and turbulence, not closure and equilibrium. This implies that in confrontation with professional ethics, economists will find themselves unmoored and adrift as they try to make their way in the world. Since we know in advance that adopting professional economic ethics is bound to raise these difficulties, why should we risk it when there is so much important and potentially beneficial economic work to be done right here, right now?

Consumer Sovereignty

Economics 101 also teaches us that it is imperious for economists to think that they should dictate the nature of the services that they will supply. After all, the adoption of a binding code by the profession amounts to the imposition of the ethical preferences of suppliers on the consumers of economic services. Shouldn't the individuals and institutions that contract for economic services be free to decide what they expect of the economists they employ? And shouldn't an individual economist who is willing to provide the services that a client seeks be free to do just that, unrestricted by whatever ethical constraints the profession has imposed? Shouldn't the consumer be sovereign in this relationship?

Fortunately, there is a mechanism at hand to ensure consumer sovereignty. If licensing to ensure ethical conduct is *unwise*—unwise because it represents an infringement on personal freedoms (including freedom of thought), promotes wasteful monopolies, and even if successful, imposes the value preferences of economists on others—it is also largely *unnecessary* since there is a far more powerful institution available that can ensure appropriate professional conduct. That institution is the market. Absent licensure, market competition will force professionals to make good on their promises to potential clients. But it will also force them to promise the right things—ethical behavior as defined not by a cartel of suppliers but by the consumers of economists' services. In Friedman's words, relying on the market "gives people what they want instead of what a particular group thinks they ought to want" (Friedman 1962, 15). Those economists who fail to do so will be outcompeted by other practitioners whose ethical conduct coincides with those values most precious to those they serve. If an entire profession takes a wrong turn, it will soon face competition from newcomers who see in the profession an opportunity for product specialization in the form of honest and ethical service. While unethical behavior remains a danger in the professions, then, market competition provides a powerful means for self-correction without the need for meddlesome actions by the state or by the profession as a whole.

Market power through government-induced monopoly—this, as every economics student learns, is among the most pernicious of threats to economic welfare and personal liberty. In almost every case, economists urge the government to rescind the action that restricts competition. This will allow outsiders to enter the market and will encourage insiders to refocus their attention on the needs of the buyer. In the case of the professions, this logic implies that the free market provides all the incentives and sanctions we need to ensure that the suppliers of services comport themselves in a manner that is consistent with the ethical principles that society takes to be fundamental.

CONCLUSION

We have here a strong case against the adoption of professional economic ethics. The economic exceptionalism argument tells us that economists are engaged in a largely value-free practice of scientific inquiry, regardless of whether they work in the academy or beyond. Their job is to follow the norms of good scientific practice, they are to map the way the world works so that others can choose policy options that reflect the economic principles that economic researchers have uncovered. Moreover, the applied economist largely exerts influence through advising. Provided the economic advisor follows basic commonsense ethical principles, she is spared ethical responsibility for any action taken on her advice. When she advances to the position of actual decision maker, the ethical obligations she faces derive from the new role she has assumed. Finally, we find that economics does not rise to the level of profession, owing to its refusal to make an explicit commitment to advance the public interest and its failure to seek or secure the right of self-governance. Hence, the pursuit of professional economic ethics makes no sense.

A second line of reasoning solidifies the case against professional economic ethics. Economists have good reason to believe that professional economic ethics would be at best inefficacious, and at worst, positively harmful. Professional ethics can improve the behavior of practitioners only when it is reduced to a code of conduct that is backed by sanctions; without these, professionals are not apt to give it much attention, and the field degenerates into a set of sanctimonious and forgettable platitudes. In the world of the professions, sanctions typically take the form of licensure and certification which permit the establishment of monopoly power. This the economics profession simply cannot countenance, given its deep antipathy to unnatural monopolies. It would be odd indeed—perhaps even *unethical*—for this profession to endorse a monopoly of—of all things—*economists*.

Fortunately, we have good reason to conclude that in a free-market economy, economists will behave just as ethical professionals should. They will act ethically because they recognize that failure to act in conformance with the client's ethical preferences will jeopardize their careers and waste the enormous investment that they made in their own human capital. Ethical behavior arises, then, as a consequence of economists practicing what they preach: acting rationally, which in this context entails satisfying the ethical preferences of those they serve. All this is to the good: given the market's ideological catholicity, it is not only efficient but also consistent with the preservation of freedom to let it administer rewards and punishments rather than to place that authority in the hands of a self-anointed professional "god squad" that may itself act on impure, unethical motives.

This concludes the economist's case against professional economic ethics. Is it compelling? I will present arguments in the next chapter that refute the most important of these claims. I will attempt to show that each of the arrows in the economist's quiver misses the mark. My goal in the chapter is not to secure the case for professional economic ethics—I will attempt that one chapter later—but only to show that the economist's dismissiveness of the matter is unwarranted.

Notes

1 Coats argues that this conception of the objective scientist attaches in the economist's mind even to the work of applied economists in nonacademic, policy-oriented institutions.

2 What if the official seeking advice is, say, a despot lacking constitutional or other legitimacy? Is the technocratic advisor insulated morally in this case for assisting the despot in achieving whatever goals he has set—even if those goals are explicitly abhorrent? Or what if the goals are innocuous but the means to achieve them are morally indictable?

3 As we will see in the next chapter, Thompson and Amy reject each of them.

4 This argument appeared in a referee report for this book, and although it was offered by a faculty member of a business school, it is one that is apt to resonate with many economists.

5 Yeager pulls back from the full implications to which this argument might lead, however: "I am referring, of course, to the pursuit of gain as such, not to the methods used. Lying, cheating, and stealing do not become right by being used in the pursuit of otherwise honorable ends" (Yeager 1976, fn 25). But why is this at all obvious? Yeager is wading in deep philosophical waters here—raising the matter of what has come to be known in professional ethics (and following Sartre) as the conundrum of "dirty hands"—apparently without realizing it. His view on the matter—that one should never commit an ethical wrong in order to bring about some greater good—is controversial. We return to the matter of dirty hands (and its relevance for economic ethics) in later chapters.

6 Friedman (1962) touched off substantial research in this area that extended through the 1980s. See Kleiner (2000 and 2006) for good recent reviews of the literature.

7 For opposing perspectives, see Leland (1979); Shapiro (1986); Kleiner (2000); and Law and Kim (2005).

8 This argument is in keeping with the general theme of Friedman's *Capitalism and Freedom*. For Friedman, licensure doesn't just represent a loss of economic efficiency. It also represents an unwarranted expansion of government authority and a consequent assault on personal freedom.

9 Coats argues that one other feature of economic knowledge may play a part in the resistance of the profession to professional ethics:

Skeptics may argue that it is not ideological distaste grounded in an inherited liberal moral philosophy that explains the reluctance to enforce strict controls over entry, a code of professional ethics or procedures for excommunicating those who fail to maintain acceptable standards of behaviour or performance. Rather, it is the wisdom of recognizing that that species of professionalism is simply unenforceable, perhaps even undefinable, in economics.

Underlying this situation is a troublesome epistemological question: exactly what do economists "know" (i.e., that other professionals do not)? (Coats 1991, 123).

10 I am indebted to economist Rob Williams of the University of Texas for drawing my attention to the relevance of consequentialism to the economic case against professional ethics.

Chapter 6

Breaking the Silence

A Rebuttal of the Economic Case Against Professional Economic Ethics

The professional . . . cannot be simply the client's tool or instrument. The professional is accountable to the client as to whether the former is serving the latter's best interests, but the professional is also accountable for the public purpose for which the profession exists.

William M. Sullivan (2005, 81)

One need not deny the value of all the insights that economists bring to bear against professional ethics in order to sustain a robust rebuttal. It is best to maintain some measure of the economist's hard-headed skepticism as we explore the matters before us. But we will see that economists' concerns are largely misplaced—they are presented as arguments *against* when they ought to be viewed as arguments *within* professional economic ethics.

PROFESSIONAL ETHICS VERSUS A CODE OF CONDUCT

The economist's perspective is deficient on a central point that relates to most of the arguments presented in the previous chapter against professional economic ethics. Economists have treated professional *ethics* as coextensive with and reducible to enforceable *codes of conduct*. This conflation derives no doubt from the fact that in many professions, the code of conduct represents not just the first but also the last word on their ethical obligations. Nevertheless, the error has prevented economists from giving the matter of professional ethics the attention it deserves and has led it down unproductive paths.

Properly understood, professional ethics engages all matters pertaining to the identity, character, and behavior of the professional; and to the institutions, rules, and norms that guide the profession as a whole. Professional ethics is not reducible to a list of commandments that oversimplify the ethical terrain that the professional inhabits (see Bourgois 1990). It comprises instead a broad set of searching questions and probing explorations ranging over professional practice, teaching, rights, obligations, motivations, and commitments. Most of its insights are not translatable into professional do's and don'ts.

It must be said that few professions engage professional ethics in a serious way. Medicine and law lead the way, of course, but to varying degrees, fields such as journalism, social work, and the sciences that undertake research involving human subjects (such as anthropology) do as well. So do some fields that comprise diverse professions, such as public administration and environmental stewardship. Each of these professions and fields nurtures professional ethics as an important aspect of professional training and practice. And each is populated by first-rate specialists who treat professional ethics not as a sidelight to their real work but as their primary professional commitment. Some fields sustain journals and newsletters that encourage ethics-based research and discussion and also enrich professional training with curriculum in ethical matters. Some of these professions have codes of conduct. But the important point is that these codes do not stand in for professional ethics. Rather, the codes of conduct represent working distillations of just some of the central principles that emerge in much more complex bodies of thought.

This is as it should be. Absent professional ethics as a tradition of inquiry, a code is apt to become just what many economists fear: a collection of platitudes that gets us not one whit closer to ethical practice and that might instead serve as cover for professional privilege.

Economists also err in presuming that codes of conduct necessarily have legislative force. This is not at all the case. In most professions, codes of conduct are aspirational rather than binding. Such codes lack the force of law—they are intended instead to promote awareness of professional responsibilities and commendable behavior. This is true of professional codes in academic disciplines such as sociology and anthropology and also in those fields that span academic and applied work, such as statistics. For instance, the Preamble to the Code of Conduct of the American Anthropology Association emphasizes that "The purpose of this Code is to foster discussion and education. The American Anthropological Association (AAA) does not adjudicate claims for unethical behavior" (AAA 1998).[1] Nor is the code of National Association of Forensic Economists enforceable. Recognition of the fact that a code need not imply regulation ought to put to rest the various anxieties expressed by the AEA leadership in the past concerning the legal implications of adopting a code.

These insights substantially weaken the economists' opposition to professional ethics. If professional ethics entails something other than a code of conduct, and if a code of conduct need not imply enforceable regulation, then discussion of ethics should not be reduced to a debate over the virtues and evils of the sanctions (such as licensing) necessary to police a code. Whether economics needs a code of conduct and whether it should be hortatory or binding are not simple matters that ought to be tossed around as off-the-cuff chatter during the closing moments of an

AEA Executive Committee meeting. They are complex issues that ought to be worked out and debated only later on, after the establishment of and within the yet-to-be constructed field of professional economic ethics. It may be that the economics profession (or at least certain branches within it) does in fact need a code and a mechanism for enforcing it, notwithstanding economic arguments in favor of consumer sovereignty and against monopoly power. But it is far better to presume in advance of careful investigation that this is an entirely open question. Were there to be a field of professional economic ethics to which highly trained economic ethicists contributed their energies, we would have a much better idea than we do now about how to answer that question.

An analogy might clarify the relevance of the distinction between professional ethics on the one hand and a binding code of conduct on the other. Many times over the past century, the AEA has promoted investigation into economics curriculum at the graduate and undergraduate levels (see Chapter 12). It has sponsored sessions at its annual meetings on matters of pedagogy and curriculum; it has created special and standing committees to explore these issues; and it has established *The Journal of Economic Education* where debates range from practical issues pertaining to curriculum, pedagogical strategies, and technologies to much broader and more esoteric and philosophical questions. Despite these initiatives, however, the AEA does not attempt to impose any sort of curricular standards; nor does it seek the right to accredit economics departments. It has never countenanced intrusions into academic freedom nor erred in conflating the examination of pedagogy with the institution of standards or rules.

The profession's approach to economic education provides a useful model for considering its potential involvement in professional ethics. It could do much to introduce, support, and sustain serious inquiry into professional ethical questions without purporting to have any particular expertise or obligation to legislate for the profession. It could recognize that just as pedagogical inquiry should be distinguished from pedagogical control, so should ethical inquiry be distinguished from ethical legislation. Professional ethics without (necessarily) a code of conduct—*investigation and education without legislation*—this is the appropriate avenue for improving the conduct of economists and for enhancing the responsibility and social value of the profession.

Since I am not advocating a professional code of conduct, we need not concern ourselves further with many of the economist's objections that we encountered in the previous chapter: the degree to which a professional code interferes with consumer sovereignty, the way in which licensing secures monopoly privileges, and so forth. All of these are fascinating and important arguments that would receive attention in the field of professional economic ethics. Economists' interest in such questions promises to yield a body of professional ethics in economics that is in some respects richer and more insightful than that which appears in other fields that have been inattentive to these matters. Indeed, economists might find themselves in a position to make important contributions to professional ethics across the professions.

What does it mean to be an ethical economist? What does it mean for economics to be an ethical profession? These are the kinds of questions that professional economic ethics would engage. The field would comprise new curriculum, journals, research, and textbooks; and new and lively controversies and debates. It would cultivate professional ethical capacities and sensibilities among those who face the extraordinary burdens associated with economic practice. And it would explore and implement new pedagogical methods that promote the training of the "ethical economist."

HUMAN BEHAVIOR AND PROFESSIONAL ETHICS

For most of the past century, neoclassical economics theorized the human actor as self-interested—as self- rather than other-regarding. This insight led economists to view professional ethics with suspicion, as we have seen. In this view, professional ethics provides cover for unscrupulous behavior while doing little to improve the quality of professional services. The corrective (if one is indeed necessary) lies not in licensing or other barriers to entry but in market competition where consumers dictate the contours of appropriate professional behavior. In a free market for professional services, suppliers will be forced to conform to consumers' ethical preferences.

Various heterodox traditions within economics—including social, feminist, institutionalist, and Marxist economics—have generated rich and compelling critiques of this conception of human nature. Recently, mainstream economists have added their voices to the dissent. Among others, Amartya Sen has argued that the conception of human behavior that underlies neoclassical thought undermines the power of economic explanation. In his words,

> Indeed, it may not be quite as absurd to argue that people always *actually* do maximize their self-interest, as it is to argue that *rationality* must invariably demand maximization of self-interest. Universal selfishness as *actuality* may well be false, but universal selfishness as a requirement of *rationality* is patently absurd (Sen 1987, 16).

Sen and other critics argue that human motivations are complex and diverse. They run from the pursuit of self-interest to the advancement of projects and the attainment of goals that may have no bearing on one's well-being or that may even imperil it. In fashioning our life plans, we are driven not principally by unmediated desires but also by our conceptions of higher purpose, the interests of others, and our beliefs about moral rights and wrongs.

These claims are now confirmed in the relatively new field of behavioral economics where economists explore human motivations. This research finds what investigators in other fields have known for some time: that people act on diverse sets of motivations and purposes that reach beyond and conflict with self-interest (Thaler and Sunstein 2008; Coyle 2007).

Experiments using "ultimatum games" provide compelling insight on this score. In ultimatum games, participants are given just one chance to divide among themselves a specified reward (such as a sum of money). One participant is empowered to make an offer of a share of the total reward to the other participant, while the second participant has just one chance to accept or reject that offer. The presumption of rationality predicts that those participants who are entitled to make offers will offer only negligible portions of the total amount, and those participants on the receiving end will accept whatever positive sum is offered to them since the rules of the game imply that their refusal of any offer leaves them with nothing at all. But evidence from the experiments indicates that subjects routinely act in ways that conflict with self-interest: participants offer too much, on the one hand, and reject offers that they take to be unfair, on the other. Subjects often choose to receive no reward at all rather than settle for what they take to be an unfair share. From this and other evidence, Sam Bowles (2008, 1601) concludes that

> Behavioral experiments that model the voluntary provision of public goods and relationships between principals and agents show that substantial fractions of most populations adhere to moral rules, willingly give to others, and punish those who offend standards of appropriate behavior, even at a cost to themselves and with no expectation of material reward.[2]

Researchers have found that in making choices that involve ethical matters, people take into account the expected behavior of others. In situations where there are high levels of trust people are often willing to act in ways that serve others even when those actions entail the imposition of costs on themselves and when there are no mechanisms to ensure repayment. This example highlights a more general finding: the milieu in which people act, including the quality and character of social interactions and the nature of the (formal and informal) institutions and the norms that exist, are crucial in shaping the motivations that find expression in human behavior. Coyle (2007, 220) sums up the findings this way:

> . . . social sanctions, communications, mutual expectations, and also how people's choices are framed all affect the extent to which we cooperate with each other as opposed to making self-interested, (boundedly) rational choices.

These findings bear on the matter before us. They imply that the economist's cynicism about codes of conduct and professional ethics more broadly is simplistic. The new research suggests that whether professionals regard professional ethics as an annoyance or as a valuable

guide for professional behavior would likely depend on a range of factors over which a profession can exercise significant control—such as the
weight that the profession places on professional ethics during professional training; whether the profession takes steps to acknowledge ethical
behavior among its members such as through the bestowing of honors
and awards; in the case of a code, whether the code is known to exist (and
perhaps the degree to which it is understood) by clients and the general
public; whether the profession takes care to recruit initiates with highly
developed ethical sensibilities; and whether professional ethics is debated
by leading figures in the profession and adjusted over time as new insights
emerge and as professional practice raises new quandaries on which the
existing ethics is found to be inappropriate, vague, or silent.

While it may not be the case that professionals are inherently more
public spirited than others, it is surely the case that they are as every bit
as complex in their motivations. Like others, their personal and professional identities, the motivations that they express in their work, and the
conceptions that they hold of their professional obligations to others (and
much else) are the result in part of ethical cultivation that is influenced
by the networks and relationships—by the professional milieu—in which
they find themselves. The milieu includes the presence or absence of professional ethics and the corresponding existence or absence of expectations for other-regarding behavior as opposed to self-regarding incentives.
Recent evidence from experimental economics demonstrates that the latter distinction is vital in shaping human behavior. From his review of the
evidence, Bowles concludes that incentives which appeal to self-interest
may fail when they undermine the moral values that lead people to act
altruistically or in other public-spirited ways:

> . . . economic incentives may be counterproductive when they signal that
> selfishness is an appropriate response; constitute a learning environment
> through which over time people come to adopt more self-interested moti-
> vations; compromise the individual's sense of self-determination and there-
> by degrade intrinsic motivations; or convey a message of distrust, disrespect,
> and unfair intent (Bowles 2008, 1605).[3]

Bowles infers from the evidence that "policies that appeal to economic
self-interest" often affect adversely "the salience of ethical, altruistic, and
other social preferences" (Bowles 2008, 1606). It is not surprising, then,
that a profession that teaches the ubiquity of self-interest narrowly defined
might have the effect of cultivating just this sentiment in its members, as
some recent research on economics teaching suggests (Frank, Gilovich
and Regan 1993). A profession that instead emphasizes the paramount
importance of service to others and self-sacrifice might have the effect
of cultivating those attributes in those who enter the field.[4] A profession committed to ethical practice would set for itself the mission of discovering means to achieve this end rather than presume *ex ante* that its
members lack the capacity for public spiritedness, or that (in noted economist Leland Yeager's memorable phrasing) expecting individuals ever

to act against their own narrow self-interest "strains and damages moral muscles" (Yeager 1976, 566). Like studying Mandarin, practicing piano or gymnastics, or pursuing other forms of rigorous mental and physical exercise, "straining moral muscles" under appropriate direction can strengthen rather than damage our most important human capacities.

ON THE ETHICS OF ADVISING

Is the applied economist morally insulated when she works as an advisor rather than as the ultimate decision maker? In Chapter 5, we encountered plausible arguments that have been offered to defend this idea. When we take proper account of the nature of the practice of advising, however, we find that all of them fail.

The first argument in defense of the moral insulation of advisors advanced above builds on the notion of "null cause": since the advisor's influence does not compromise the autonomy of the advisee (if she puts a gun to the head of the advisee she is no longer advising, after all), she cannot be held accountable for the decision ultimately made. Dennis Thompson (1983) rejects this view as simplistic:

> Such a view may be appropriate for ascribing responsibility to agents who act independently in causal chains that produce physical effects. However, it fails completely to capture the complexities of the process of advising, which involves interaction among agents and influence that differs from the causing of physical events (Thompson 1983, 547).

Thompson emphasizes that advisors necessarily make choices that bear subtly but powerfully on the influence they will have on those whom they advise. They must decide how to frame issues, how much weight to give to various arguments, what language and rhetoric to adopt, and much else. Recognition of these choices reveals the nuanced relationship between the advisor and advisee and illuminates how the advisor exercises "causal influence" over the decision-making process. Attached to this influence are ethical obligations that the ethical advisor needs to consider as she undertakes her work.

If we understand the advisor's choices to be consequential, important questions arise. How much emphasis should the advisor give to options that she finds wanting as opposed to those she prefers? To what degree and how does she take into account (or even exploit) the relative ignorance of the advisee, her knowledge of the advisee's biases and inclinations, and the forms of rhetoric that do and do not move him to action? To what degree is the advisor to be held accountable for her failure to discourage an unwise course of action that is being pressed by other advisors? And how many options does she put before the advisee? Experimental evidence indicates unambiguously that the framing of choice such as through the inclusion of irrelevant options systematically affects the choices made

(Thaler and Sunstein 2008). Knowing this, the advisor cannot pretend that choices over framing are practically or ethically inconsequential. All of these are difficult questions; all come into view only once we reject the simplistic idea of the advisor as having no appreciable effect on the ultimate outcomes that result from the decision of the advisee.

The second justification for the moral insulation of the advisor examined above claims that an advisor can be held accountable only for what she intends and not for any unintended effects of her interventions. Thompson again helps us to see the inadequacy of such a claim. Unintended consequences are sometimes predictable, probable, and/or significant. For instance, an advisor might have good reason to believe that her well-intentioned counsel will be exploited to achieve unjust or unwise objectives. In such cases, Thompson argues, she bears some responsibility for her actions.

When it is likely that an advisor's work will contribute to harm, the evaluation of her intentions becomes less salient in assessing her conduct. For example, sometimes advisors find themselves in institutional arrangements that are prone to bad decision making, perhaps because the environment induces pandering to authority rather than honest discussion or because the decision maker exploits debate among his advisors to give the appearance of open mindedness when, in fact, he is unalterably committed to a particular course of action, regardless of what the advisors have to say. Should the ethical advisor carry on in an institutional environment that is clearly deficient or corrupt, or should she dissent in ways that are intended to disrupt the dysfunctional institutional processes that generate poor outcomes? Does she blow the whistle or resign publicly to bring public attention to the situation (Allen 1977)? If she refrains from dissent, does she then share responsibility for sustaining the institutional dysfunction and contributing to the decisions that ensue? On the other hand, what if she has good reason to believe that quitting (or whistle-blowing) might worsen the situation, if only marginally? (Thompson 1983). What is her obligation *then*?[5]

The notion of role responsibility, which claims that an advisor is morally insulated provided she fulfills the roles assigned to her, also fails and for some of the same reasons. Advisors face choices among the roles that they play vis-à-vis the advisee. This choice is ethically charged since it may affect the decisions ultimately taken. Should the advisor accept the role of devil's advocate if she has good reason to believe that her doing so may increase the likelihood that bad policy will in fact be implemented (perhaps because she knows that she is the most able of the advocates where she works)? Does she have a *duty* to take on this role if she finds that the advisor advocating a view she opposes is not performing his job adequately? Alternatively, should she choose to play the role of dispassionate technocrat who simply states the facts as she sees them while refraining from advocating the view she finds most compelling? Thompson argues that neutrality will not suffice, especially when the advisor has reason to believe that her failure to advocate forcefully will lead to "some serious and irreversible harm" (1983, 556). Indeed, in Thompson's view, "advocacy itself becomes a duty of counselors, and the more advocates, the better" (1983, 557).[6]

In complex organizations, an agent may play several roles simultaneously. In taking on any particular professional role, then, an agent does not on that account transcend the ethical entailments associated with his other roles. Diverse roles may carry distinct and conflicting ethical obligations or norms. The obligations one faces as a consequence of an institutional role, for instance, can conflict with those that emanate from one's professional role (Wueste 1994). Role conflicts can be very difficult to identify owing to the sociology of the institution in which one works (May 1980). The ethical advisor must be attentive to them and manage them conscientiously rather than dismiss them through oversimplifications that deny their existence or significance.

Taken together, the discussion of intentions and role responsibility implies that advisors must pay close attention to the health of the institutional milieu they inhabit (see also May 1980). Their consideration of their own ethical obligations requires that they continually assess whether that milieu is properly calibrated so as to generate good outcomes. When it is not, it is no longer appropriate for the advisor to continue to play the role that she's been assigned (Allen 1977). As Thompson warns us, when the institution is found to be out of kilter,

> [the advisor] should abandon his normal role and seek to remedy the distortion in the process. If he fails to do so, he cannot, simply by appealing to the requirements of his role, disclaim responsibility for his part in the harmful decisions that the system produces (Thompson 1983, 558).

Finally, there is a

> general problem with appeals to role, as ways to limit the responsibility of an adviser: they tend to confuse the responsibility of persons and the "responsibilities" of a role, permitting the latter to absorb the former (Thompson 1983, 558).

Such appeals thereby validate ethical sleepwalking that takes cover in the claim that the advisor is "just doing his job." This form of ethical insulation cannot pass the muster of professional ethics since it can lead to extraordinary institutional misconduct which results in part from good service by the professional to the client (Adams and Balfour 2004; and see the epigraph to this chapter).

On Positivism and the Ethics of Advising

One matter remains in our evaluation of the moral insulation of the economist as advisor. Earlier we examined the positivist presumptions that have informed economic practice and especially the self-conception of economists since the flowering of Progressive thought at the turn of the twentieth century. We found that these presumptions served to stiffen the moral armor of the practicing economist since, just like the economic researcher, she is understood to engage in objective truth seeking. Working in this normatively simplified milieu, her ethical obligations are self-evident. She must commit herself to truth telling, which in this context entails the honest, unbiased reporting of what she finds. In this respect, she serves as an instrument of observation and analysis—a conduit for discovering and reporting on what is actually out there. Hence, and as we saw, the AER Executive Committee could act as if "the canons of correct professional practice were too obvious to require specification" (Coats 1985, 1710–11).

By now, many noneconomists have questioned the presumptions that guided the early Progressive reformers and, in particular, the positivist conception of the role of the advisor.[7] Comforting though it may be, the notion of the autonomous advisor who does nothing more than assemble the data and issue value-neutral reports to superiors does not square with the actual complexities of the advisor's role, as we surveyed a moment ago. Advisors face ethically laden and difficult decisions that arise from the complicated nature of their institutional locations. The choices they make as they negotiate these issues matter—they affect the course of events and so bear on those whom policy affects. Fortunately, according to economist Robert Nelson who served on the economics staff of the U.S. Department of the Interior for 18 years, this realization has been absorbed by at least some practicing economists as well. He reports that

> Economists coming into direct contact with government decision making have found that they cannot limit their role to that of neutral technicians; to do so would be to make themselves irrelevant and ultimately excluded. Instead, the more effective economists serve as active proponents for a way of thinking derived from basic economic training and for the policy conclusions it yields. Accepting the necessity and legitimacy of this behavior, Charles Schultze (1982, p. 62) has stated that an economist in government appropriately serves as a "partisan advocate for efficiency" and other economic principles (Nelson 1987, 50).

Some economists have advanced beyond this critique, finding that value neutrality itself is unachievable. In Nelson's words,

> As economists gained practical experience in government, they generally found that the criticisms of progressive political concepts were well founded. As Schultze put it, "political values permeate every aspect of the decision-making process in the majority of federal domestic programs" (Nelson 1987, 55).

Nelson concludes from his experience that economists who seek greater policy influence (as, in his view, they should) must "accept the fact that in many areas of policy it is probably necessary to be an entrepreneur and advocate for specific economic policies, rather than simply a neutral technical analyst" (Nelson 1987, 85–86).

These various insights have tremendous ethical import. If the economic advisor is not simply the "well trained political arithmetician" that Stigler claims she is, if she does not simply receive instructions without judgment from her superiors and hand back technical reports without any concern for the persuasiveness of her work, and if she does not simply accept the roles assigned to her with no proper interest in or responsibility for the actual policy decisions taken; if instead she exerts all sorts of influence in the way she frames issues; if she must and does exploit her gifts of technical proficiency, persuasion, wit, charisma, relationship building, trustworthiness, and more to secure what she takes to be good outcomes; if she always faces choices about which roles to play; if she always also faces the dilemma about what to do when the institutional milieu in which she finds herself is not working properly, so that her carrying on in her prescribed role is likely to lead to bad outcomes—then she must be recognized as facing ethical hazards to which she must be attentive (if she is to be ethical) and for which she must be properly trained. When a profession throws her into this milieu unarmed, suggesting that she needs nothing other than her common sense to navigate these waters since she will be entirely insulated ethically by her intentions or her role, the profession fails to meet its ethical responsibilities.

ECONOMICS AS A NONPROFESSION

Just two matters remain as we counter the case against professional economic ethics, and each can be handled quickly. The first is the idea that economics, like business management, fails to meet the requirements of a profession owing to its lack of explicit commitment to serve the public good and its failure to seek or enjoy rights of self-governance. Not least, it does not attempt to restrict entry into the field or define who is and who is not an economist.

This argument presumes wrongly that the identity, status, influence, and consequent ethical obligations of an occupation is established once and for all rather than evolving in response to changing historical circumstances. Economics has experienced dramatic escalation in its status and influence over the past 50 years across the globe, owing to new political and economic arrangements that have placed much greater demands on economists. We will explore some of these developments in later chapters, such as the increased influence of the World Bank and IMF in shaping economic flows and outcomes and institutions in the South and the transition economies. This enhanced influence carries strong ethical entailments whether or not the field recognizes them. Indeed, the failure of economists to account properly for these ethical obligations ought to be understood in part as a consequence of their profession's failure to engage professional economic ethics. It can't then also be taken as a license for the profession to continue to mislead its members into believing falsely that their work is ethically neutral.

It is noteworthy in this regard that the current global economic crisis is encouraging business school faculties and students to reexamine the failure of their field to engage professional ethics. In the spring of 2009, over 20 percent of the students graduating from Harvard Business School with the MBA signed onto "The MBA Oath," an ethical pledge that the students had crafted (MBA Oath Organization 2008). The authors of this pledge viewed it as the "first step in trying to develop a professional code not unlike the Hippocratic Oath for physicians or the pledge taken by lawyers to uphold the law and the Constitution" (Wayne 2009). In interviews with a curious (and incredulous) business press, the students emphasized the moral responsibility of business managers to serve the public good and not just the interests of shareholders. Indeed, the Oath commits its signatories to "safeguard the interests of my shareholders, co-workers, customers and the society in which we operate," to "develop both myself and other managers under my supervision so that the profession continues to grow and contribute to the well-being of society," and to refrain from "decisions and behavior that advance my own narrow ambition but harm the enterprise and the societies it serves" (available at http://mbaoath.org/take-the-oath/).

In speaking of business management as a profession, these students were tapping into what has been a long-standing minority tradition among business school faculty to redefine the field in just these terms— as a profession with attendant ethical responsibilities. During the 1950s, studies commissioned by the Ford and Carnegie Foundations cited the need for greater analytical rigor and argued for business to become "a true profession, with a code of conduct and an ideology about its role in society" (Holland 2009). This proposal was not adopted, of course, and indeed, in the following decades, business school curriculum came to be infused with Friedman's analysis that presented narrow self-interest in the business context as not just descriptively accurate but normatively appropriate (Friedman 1970; Dobson 2003). This argument was largely taken as warrant to side step wider ethical obligations altogether. According to Harvard Business School Professor Rakesh Khurana, "A kind of market fundamentalism took hold in business education. The new logic of shareholder primacy absolved management of any responsibility for anything other than financial results" (Holland 2009).

Today, in the midst of the global economic crisis, the idea that business management should aspire to the status of profession and recognize the attending ethical obligations is again attracting attention and finding expression in various new business school initiatives (Holland 2009; Wayne 2009). New curriculum reflects changing sentiments about the role of the business manager in society. It also reflects heightened awareness among business school students about their obligations as actors who will have an impact on the lives of others. These developments, tentative though they may be, suggest that the status of business management as a nonprofession is not settled. Instead, the self-conception of business management is contested today on precisely the grounds that it is held up as a model for defining economics as a nonprofession.

Are the particular claims that sustain the idea of economics as a nonprofession correct and relevant? Do economists recognize an obligation to serve the public good? I have no doubt that the commitment to the service of others is as high in economics as it is in other fields, even if the field paradoxically teaches the ubiquity of self-interest. There is limited evidence on this matter, however. Surveys of graduate economics students in leading universities reveal a desire to engage in public policy work as a motivation for entering the profession, though they quickly come to recognize that this work is not valued by their professors (Klamer and Colander 1990; Colander 2005a). Robert Nelson (2003) cites both the words and deeds of economists throughout the twentieth century in support of the view that economists have been obsessed with promoting the public good. He emphasizes the "missionary commitment" of leading economists to economic science as a means to promote human advancement and concludes that "Many—perhaps most—of them, I would submit, have chosen to enter the profession of economics because they had a basic commitment to economic progress as the essential route of the common good" (Nelson 2003, 5). For example, when William Baumol was asked why he had become an economist, he replied, "I believe deeply with Shaw, that there are few crimes more heinous than poverty" (Nelson 2003, 1).

Addressing the paradox that a profession that preaches self-interest is populated by altruists, Nelson cites an important tenet of Progressive idealism that held the professional to be aloof from the temptations affecting others. Nelson reports on the view of Paul Samuelson and other twentieth-century economists who believed that "the social obligation of an economic professional, like a member of a priesthood of old, would be to serve 'the public interest'" (Nelson 2003, 10). Hence, in this view, the economy that was understood to be populated by self-interested actors would be overseen and managed by economists who did not share this vice.

I do not expect this evidence to persuade those who are skeptical about economists' sensibilities. One could presumably design surveys of economists to ascertain their professional motivations and the impulses that drive them in their work. I would suggest, however, that if the intent is to assess the moral obligations of a profession, another question must be asked: given the nature of the work performed by those in an occupation—most importantly its significance for and impact on the lives of others—should those who work in the field recognize an ethical responsibility to service when pursuing that goal imposes costs on themselves?

And on that ground the case for economists facing ethical obligations is as strong as it is in most other professions (whether or not they or their professional associations recognize it). This is because the actions of economists today bear on the life chances of the world's population far more substantially than do the actions of the members of most other professions (see Chapter 7).

It is certainly true that economics has not sought self-regulation, and this reflects in large measure its reluctance to restrict entry into the market for economic services. The primary associations in economics have not wanted to serve as "guilds" in defense of the self-interest of its members; they have seen their role instead as promoting what Goode (1960, 906) calls the "ethic of science."[8] But it must be emphasized that this, too, is an inappropriate criterion for determining whether economics is in fact a profession that requires professional ethics. Holding up the failure to self-regulate as a decisive criterion reflects again the conflation of professional ethics with codes of conduct. Self-regulation (or in the instant case, its absence) would certainly matter practically were economics ever to decide to adopt a binding code of conduct to govern the behavior of its members, since in that case it would be necessary to decide to whom the rules apply. One could envision in that case a certification process (if not licensing) for economists—one that might entail educational requirements, apprenticeships, examinations, and the like. This effort presumably might be tied to processes to restrict the economics labor market to those who are certified either through public relations campaigns that convince prospective employers of the wisdom of hiring only certified economists or through political processes that restrict access to the labor market. The latter approach would indeed amount to self-regulation. But none of this is relevant to the establishment of professional ethics broadly defined as a field of inquiry into the ethical terrain on which economists work. Ethical guidance requires no governance whatsoever; hence, the refusal of economics to pursue self-governance has no bearing on its need for professional ethics. The two matters are simply orthogonal to one another.

CONSEQUENTIALISM AGAINST PROFESSIONAL ETHICS

At the risk of repetition, it bears emphasis that the attachment of economics to consequentialism in its assessment of economic strategies and policies might bear on the question of the need for a code of conduct for economics, but it has no bearing on the question of whether the field needs professional economic ethics. Consequentialism is one important approach to professional ethics, as even a cursory scan of the leading textbooks in professional ethics across the professions quickly confirms. It is certainly true that consequentialists often argue against inviolable ethical rules that are advanced on intrinsic grounds that ignore consequential reasoning, but these are arguments from *within* professional ethics about the kinds of ethical norms, rules, and standards for assessment that should and should not be adopted. They indicate that consequential reasoning has a place within professional ethics. And since economists are perhaps better trained in consequential reasoning than other social scientists, moral philosophers, or professional ethicists, we have good reason to expect that the involvement of economists in the application of economic logic to professional ethics will strengthen the field of professional ethics across the professions.[9]

CONCLUSION

My goal here has been to address and, where appropriate, to dispense with economists' criticisms of professional economic ethics—or better, the criticisms that it is safe to presume the profession would have made had it taken the time to consider this matter rigorously. I leave it to my colleagues in economics to decide if I have been fair in this attribution and in the rebuttal. I have tried to demonstrate that these objections are largely off point and otherwise unpersuasive.

I have claimed the following. First, economics is not exceptional in ways that make professional ethics in this field unnecessary or unwise. Second, professional ethics in and of itself has no necessary connection to a code of conduct or certification and/or licensing. Whether any of those is necessary or useful in some or all branches of economics is a matter yet to be explored in the field of professional economic ethics. Third, the fact that applied economists generally do their work as advisors does not shield them from ethical dilemmas or responsibility. Instead, taking on the role of advisor places the economist in an ethical minefield. The practice of advising is terribly fraught, not least since it generally occurs within dense social networks that affect the outcome of the advising process. As much as other professionals, economic advisors face difficult challenges of a professional ethical nature, yet they face the additional handicap that these are obscured by the outdated positivist ideology of the neutral advisor. An economic advisor who believes that he does not face ethical challenges, after all, is apt to make some very bad ethical decisions. Fourth, the argument that economics is a nonprofession and so does not need professional ethics, in part, because it doesn't recognize its ethical obligations to service is circular: it is likely that the profession's failure to consider explicitly its obligations to service stem from its refusal to recognize the need for and cultivate a tradition of professional economic ethics. The relevant question is whether economics faces ethical obligations by virtue of the impact it has on others. Moreover, the refusal of economics to self-regulate relates to practicalities associated with the adoption of a binding code of conduct, not to the more important question of the need for professional economic ethics. Finally, the consequentialist orientation of economics can and should find expression within professional economic ethics, but it has no bearing on the question whether there is a need for this field of inquiry.

I have not attempted to refute the consequentialist claim that the pursuit of professional economic ethics would waste resources that would be better put to other uses. Later on, I will try to make the case that the absence of professional economic ethics matters—I will argue that members of the profession have pursued courses of action that would not be tolerated by any imaginable body of professional economic ethics, and that the consequences of their so doing were severe. Beyond this, I cannot demonstrate that professional economic ethics will have a payoff that balances the costs. The truth of the matter is that we cannot begin to say where inquiry into professional economic ethics will lead. What we can say is that there is a strong ethical obligation facing the profession to take the risk of this exploration. This obligation stems from the extraordinary influence that economics enjoys today over public affairs—over economic policies, opportunities, constraints, flows, and outcomes. And with this argument, we make the transition to the positive case for professional economic ethics. This is the subject of the next chapter.

Notes

1 In statistics, the case is much the same. When the International Statistical Institute adopted its first code of conduct, the resolution that enacted the decision began as follows:

> After due consideration and deliberation the General Assembly adopted the following resolution on August 21, 1985: 'The General Assembly of the International Statistical Institute,
> 1. recognising that the aim of the Declaration on Professional Ethics for Statisticians is to document shared professional values and experience *as a means of providing guidance rather than regulation*, adopts the Declaration as an affirmation of the membership's concern with these matters and of its resolve to promote knowledge and interest in professional ethics among statisticians worldwide; . . .' (International Statistics Institute, August 1985; emphasis added).

2 See also Coyle (2007) and Ariely (2009).

3 See also Bowles (1998), Bowles and Hwang (2008), Frey (1997), and other sources cited in Bowles (2008).

4 How else to explain the behavior of journalists who put themselves in harm's way to cover wars and natural disasters, or who go to prison for contempt of court rather than reveal a confidential source?

5 The essays in Westin (1981) explore many of the most important questions that arise in the context of whistle-blowing.

6 Applbaum (1999, esp. Ch. 9) examines the thorny debate over the responsibility of the public servant to dissent when she believes the superior's course of action is misguided. At one pole in the debate is the "obedient-servant ethic" that holds "facelessness and nameless" to be "bureaucratic virtues" and that believes that "one's own beliefs about the good are never good reasons for action."

At the other is the "political realism ethic" that holds that "the job of an official is to press a substantive agenda as forcefully and as skillfully as she can" (Applbaum 1999, 214–15). This debate also relates to the "many hands" dilemma which we will examine in Chapter 8.

7 Julie Nelson (2009) calls this way of thinking a "folk belief" that has prevented economists from recognizing the inescapable value-laden nature of their work.

8 This choice, too, undermines the claim that the profession is self- as opposed to other-regarding since it has refused to take self-protective steps that would benefit insiders at the expense of outsiders.

9 Amartya Sen argues that the consequential reasoning found in economic theory stands to contribute much to ethical theory more generally (see Sen 1987, 71ff).

Chapter 7

The Positive Case for Professional Economic Ethics

The relationship between expert and layperson is grounded on an epistemic inequality. The expert knows more than the layperson about matters within the scope of her expertise. And if the layperson appeals to the judgment of the expert, he usually does so because he acknowledges the superiority of the expert's judgment to his own. Thus, the epistemology of the expert-layperson relationship can be focused on the concept of rational deference to epistemic authority. This rational deference lies at the heart of the particular form of power that an expert has and is also the center of the particular form of vulnerability that each of us, as a layperson, is in.

John Hardwig (1994, 86)

The positive case for professional economic ethics moves from recognition of the obligations that attend professionalism in general to the specifics of economic practice. I will demonstrate that a series of altogether uncontroversial claims about economic practice necessitate the embrace of professional economic ethics.

THE PROFESSIONAL COVENANT

What is a professional? The features that are most commonly cited in the expansive literature on professionalism are captured well by ethicist Daniel E. Wueste:

> (1) . . . centrality of abstract knowledge in the performance of occupational tasks. (2) . . . social significance of the tasks the professional performs—professional activity promotes basic social values. (3) Professionals claim to be better situated/qualified than others to pronounce and act on certain matters. This claim reaches beyond the interests and affairs of clients. Experts believe that they should define various aspects of society, life, and nature . . . (4) . . .professionals claim to be and have been recognized as being governed (in their professional conduct) by role-specific norms rather than the norms that govern human conduct generally . . . (5) . . .most professionals work in bureaucratic institutions (Wueste 1994, 11).[1]

Against this set of criteria, economics certainly warrants the status of a profession. Economics requires substantial expertise based on abstract knowledge which, economists believe, gives them authority to "pronounce"; the work has tremendous social significance; economists enjoy substantial autonomy in much of their work; and most economists work in bureaucracies. Economists have also emphasized over the past century a commitment to the public good (see Chapter 4). What does the professional status of economics imply?

Monopoly over hard-won professional expertise complicates the ethical life of the professional. On the one hand, it provides her with rights, privileges, prestige, and income that are often far greater than those typically enjoyed by people outside the professions. Indeed, many professionals have a degree of autonomy (even in bureaucratic settings) and economic security that exceeds that available to members of other occupations. Consider in this context university professors who take for granted important rights, protections, and control over their intellectual output though they do not enjoy the protections of licensing. On the other hand, expertise can generate substantial influence over the lives of others in spheres of life that are of tremendous "social significance." Sometimes clients engage professionals to help them solve complex problems that they confront, and in such instances, the professional's intervention generally affects their decision making and sometimes the course of their lives. At other times, professionals work in the background where they design and implement interventions that we may not appreciate or see (Hardwig 1994), but that may be just as consequential as those of the professionals whom we explicitly consult.[2]

In the view of professional ethicists, the rights, privileges, prestige, and influence that attend professionalism carry important ethical obligations. William May, one of the most insightful contemporary theorists of professional ethics, captures these obligations in what he calls the "professional covenant."

> The professional's covenant, in my judgment, opens out in three directions that help distinguish professionals from careerists: the professional professes something (a body of knowledge and experience); on behalf of someone (or some institution); and in the setting of colleagues. This summary definition highlights three distinguishing marks: *intellectual* (what one professes), *moral* (on behalf of whom one professes), and *organizational* (with whom one professes). These distinguishing marks call for three correlative virtues—practical wisdom, fidelity, and public spiritedness (May 2001, 7; emphasis in original).

The three correlative virtues are normatively laden and complex. Practical wisdom (*phronesis*) comprises technical expertise, to be sure, but it encompasses much more. It entails an ability to discern what one must know and what are useful ways of knowing, what puzzles and problems deserve examination and the expenditure of resources, and how best to apply knowledge in the service of others. Fidelity concerns not just the obligation to tell the truth to others, important though this may be, but also the more difficult obligation of the professional to be truthful to herself in situations where it can often be difficult to distinguish between justifications for action that are self- and other-regarding. Some strategies that are best for the professional are also good for the client, but sometimes the client is best served by strategies that are difficult and perhaps risky for the professional to pursue. Fidelity also requires candor about the limitations of expertise—one's own and that of one's profession (cf. Hardwig 1994)—since hubris can induce professional conduct that yields devastating harm to others. Public spiritedness requires a willing embrace of the goal of advancing the well-being of others even when no one is watching (or paying). Like practical wisdom and fidelity, public spiritedness must be cultivated by the profession so as to attract into its ranks those with the right predisposition and to reinforce the application of this virtue when circumstances are least conducive to its sustenance.[3]

The idea of a covenant that attaches to the work of some occupations but not others might seem quaint or romantic to economists, owing to our tendency to theorize the world in hard-headed terms—like personal preferences, human capital, and voluntary exchange. In the economist's view, a professional, like a nonprofessional, performs a service for a fee, full stop. May and other ethicists urge us to recognize that the professional positions we occupy require considerations that economic concepts do not adequately illuminate. What makes for good professional conduct is not reducible to what sells. Indeed, the covenant may require the professional to refuse to sell when what the client seeks will be injurious to him or to others. Good professional conduct emanates, instead, from recognition of and judgments about our deepest obligations to each other.

THE ESCALATING CASE FOR PROFESSIONAL ECONOMIC ETHICS

We are now in position to build an "escalating case" for professional economic ethics. The argument cites features of economic practice that I take to be uncontroversial. This case escalates in the sense that while the first feature examined here on its own warrants professional economic ethics, each successive feature strengthens the case. While establishing the case for professional economic ethics, the discussion will also begin to orient our thinking about just what might be some of the principles that would receive attention in that yet-to-be launched field of inquiry.

Central to all that follows is this fundamental point: *when economists act, they act on others in consequential ways.* There is a gap between the subjects and objects of economic practice—between those who design economic interventions and those whom the interventions target. This point would be too obvious to make but for the fact that it represents the foundation of the case for professional economic ethics. When economists assess, propose, and advocate; when they warn, advise, and counsel; and when they make the myriad other decisions that their work requires, they alter the life circumstances of those who populate the economy, sometimes decisively. Economists' influence is not an unintended by-product of their work: it is rather the whole point. Economists hope to make interventions that improve the functioning of the economy and public policy and that enhance the quality of life.

Intellectual Monopoly and Influence over Others

The first step in the escalating case for professional economic ethics is this: *economists enjoy authority and exert influence over others by virtue of the intellectual monopoly they hold over a body of knowledge that is vital to social welfare.*

The relationship between the economist and the community that her work targets is marked by important asymmetries. Economic theory today is intimidating and inaccessible to the untrained. Even otherwise well-educated people are largely ill equipped to make sense of the language of the field, overtaken as it has been by abstract reasoning and mathematical formalism. The economist's expertise is mysterious and opaque to outsiders.[4] This is true in polities where many citizens are exposed to undergraduate level economics, let alone in communities where few receive economic training. This asymmetry in expertise generates another—in the relative influence of economists over economic affairs. Economists today enjoy *authority* in an area of tremendous social significance.

I stated a moment ago that each step in the escalating case suffices on its own to sustain the need for professional ethics. We should linger on this first step for a moment, then, to consider its ethical import. The influence that economists enjoy by virtue of their expertise in a field that is vital to social welfare entails important ethical questions.[5] First, when economists are in a position to advise or legislate for others, what *kind of policy* should they advocate? Is it policy that promises efficiency, fairness, economic security, sustenance of community, or something else entirely? Second, and more germane to the matter of professional ethics, what should be the *role of the targeted community* in policy design and in selecting the values that inform it? Should it have a meaningful say? Should its values and aspirations influence or even dictate economic policy making? It might seem obvious that since the community and not the economist will have to live with the effects of an economic intervention, perhaps for generations, it ought to enjoy the ultimate authority to decide which course of action to adopt and how. This is the view taken in several other professions where practice affects the lives of others decisively and where principles like "prior informed consent" recently have come to have salience (see Chapter 8). In this view, economic interventions that are imposed by the economist would be deemed illegitimate on that account;

and so, then, would be the economic practice that generates them. This view implies further an obligation on the part of the economics profession to cultivate economic decision-making capacities and procedures in the communities that economists serve. It also has implications for the matter of whether and under what circumstances an economist would be warranted in advising an authoritarian regime where those who will be affected by an economic intervention are deprived of meaningful opportunity to decide their own economic fate.

I want to emphasize, however, that these conclusions are by no means obvious. If they were, there would be little need for professional economic ethics. One could instead argue plausibly for an alternative view in which the economist is understood to face a difficult ethical duty to do what is best for the community, even when this entails a course of action that the community opposes or abhors. In this view, the economist might be counseled to keep the targeted community at a distance in order to insulate herself from the pressures that might otherwise emanate from special interests. Perhaps her unfamiliarity with many aspects of the targeted community is necessary to ensure the neutral application of objective economic science. This view foregrounds the heavy burden that attends professional practice—from medicine, to social work, to engineering—the burden that originates in expertise, in "knowing more" than those whom the professional serves. The child doesn't want the inoculation; the parent and doctor insist nevertheless on grounds that the child is not fully competent to decide. So it is with economic practice. In this view, the ethical economist must be prepared to use her influence to bring about the policies that the community would endorse or should endorse were it to understand the full ramifications of the case at hand.

Credible arguments can and have been advanced in favor of each of these two contending perspectives. Which is the correct view, then—the rights-based view that emphasizes the autonomy and integrity of the community—or the consequentialist-based view that privileges, instead, the expertise of the economist? In adjudicating among them, rhetorical shortcuts and common sense will not suffice for a profession that aspires to ethical practice.

A third question, which is both difficult and important, is this: how should the economist comport herself publicly as she undertakes her work? The question concerns the *attitude* and *virtues* that it is appropriate for the economist to exhibit—toward the community she is to serve and toward her practice. Should she express certainty in her science and her prescriptions, or should she cultivate professional humility and emphasize publicly the limitations to her science while expressing doubt about the efficacy of the analysis and interventions that she has to offer, as May (1980), Hardwig (1994), and other professional ethicists insist?[6]

This last question deserves careful attention since its salience in economic practice may exceed its salience in other professional practice. It may be that by presenting policy prescriptions to a targeted community with more confidence than the economist, in fact, feels, she may enhance substantially the credibility of the policy she proposes within the community and thereby increase its chances of success. This judgment is sustained by the insight that credible policies are more apt to induce behaviors that promote the objectives that the policies seek (see Kydland and Prescott 1977). In economic affairs, beliefs can be self-fulfilling.

This reasoning may compel the conclusion that sometimes the economist is warranted not just in exaggerating the benefits of a policy intervention but also in actually *lying* to the targeted community about her degree of confidence in that intervention. The challenges facing the Fed and U.S. Treasury officials (and their counterparts abroad) over the past year, when the world confronted financial crisis, illuminates the point. Government economists not only have had to design economic interventions but also to induce sufficient confidence in these interventions among financial market participants and other economic actors if they were to succeed in quieting economic anxiety and promoting the restoration of lending, investing, hiring, and spending. They might have had little chance of success in this mission had they expressed publicly and candidly their private reservations about the interventions they were enacting.

Thinking about such cases might lead us to conclude that sometimes the economist is ethically required to lie when the stakes are sufficiently high, and his role puts him in a position to alter events through his public statements. Many take it for granted that this is the case. In the view of former World Bank economist Liaquat Ahamed, "What [government economists] have to say about the economy affects its outcome," he notes. "As a consequence, they have little choice but to restrict themselves to making fatuously positive statements which should never be taken seriously as forecasts" (cited in Maslin 2009). Philosopher Stuart Hampshire, discussing the conflict among ethical principles that emerges as a consequence of the fact that humans occupy multiple institutional roles, cites this example: the "Chancellor of the Exchequer is not required to respond honestly to questions about a future devaluation of the currency" (cited in Wueste 1994, 3).

If the economist can (or must) lie in some contexts, then, by exaggerating her level of confidence and overstating what she knows, might she also be licensed or required to lie in other ways that achieve the same objective? For instance, should she misreport data when she is certain that doing so will contribute to a policy's success by enhancing its credibility? Most economists would recoil against the practice, to be sure. But what is the ethical difference between the two cases (if, indeed, there is one)? Why is outright dishonesty in reporting one's level of confidence in pursuit of policy credibility appropriate, but dishonesty in the reporting of data that is likewise intended to enhance credibility, inappropriate? These are terribly difficult questions to answer, especially for a profession that lacks any tradition of professional economic ethics.

The foregoing is intended to demonstrate that even at this level of abstraction, before considering other factors that complicate the work of the economist, we encounter an important normative problem: *what ethical principles and virtues should guide economic practice in situations where the economist, by virtue of her intellectual monopoly, enjoys the authority to alter the life circumstances of others?*

This is a question that will not go away. Even in some imaginable hyper-participatory democratic society populated by well-educated citizens, there will be spheres of life where members of the economics professions must act on others, not least owing to the division of labor that complex social organization requires (Hardwig 1994). Divisions of labor stem from but also necessarily reinforce gaps in expertise between professionals and those they serve. We therefore need to get the ethics of this situation straight so that economists have appropriate guidance as they exercise their authority and so that communities targeted by economic policy have appropriate standards against which to hold economists accountable.

Institutional Power

The second proposition in the escalating case for professional economic ethics is this: the influence that comes to the economist by virtue of intellectual monopoly has been substantially augmented by historical developments and institutional changes of recent decades that have transformed the applied economist from peripheral advisor to central decision maker, and at the extreme, to social engineer. In short, *the economics profession today enjoys "institutionalized" power.*

In recent years, economic institutions have come to achieve enormous influence over economic affairs. The judgments of economists often are codified in decisions with binding force, such as regulations and other legally sanctioned edicts. For instance, most countries by now have undertaken central bank reform that establishes central bank independence. Historically, it was routine for central banks to be accountable to political authority; today, most banks have been freed from direct political control.[7] As a consequence, central bank economists now enjoy more direct influence over economic flows and outcomes than in the past.

Over the past several decades, other economic institutions have achieved increased significance. Multilateral economic agencies such as the IFIs have acquired substantial new authority in directing economic affairs across the globe. This new authority has arisen in part as a consequence of historic developments in the developing world and in the transition economies. From the early 1980s onward, many developing countries faced dire circumstances owing to escalating levels of external debt. Burgeoning debt exacerbated the dependence of the debtor nations on the IFIs since they were the only multilateral institutions available to intervene in a crisis of this scale. In the early 1990s, the collapse of communism in Central and Eastern Europe created new opportunities for IFI influence. The transition countries actively sought international assistance in restructuring their economies. Suddenly, leading economists confronted a historical opportunity to alter world economic affairs. Their influence was augmented by pledges of assistance from developed countries. In this context, economists at the IFIs, international consulting firms, and a raft of think tanks came to wield a kind of institutional influence with which economists have largely been unacquainted over the previous century of economic practice.[8] Economists were now able to influence what policies would be enacted in the transition countries, where aid would flow, to what purposes it would be put, how it would be managed, what conditions would be attached to it, and much else besides (Wedel 2001). With this authority came the power to affect the life chances of hundreds of millions of people.

Over roughly the same period, economists also came to acquire institutional power through their growing role in private for-profit firms. Financial liberalization (which entailed, *inter alia*, the elimination of capital controls and privatization of financial institutions) and the integration of the world's financial markets presented new opportunities for massive financial gains. The complexity of the new global financial markets and assets (such as derivatives and collateralized debt obligations) that liberalization promoted called for the kind of modeling expertise that some economists possessed. Along with statisticians and mathematicians, economists found new entrepreneurial opportunities in the world's leading hedge funds that promised both enormous incomes and substantial economic influence. Long-Term Capital Management may be the most well known of cases where high-profile economists (including Nobel Laureates Myron Scholes and Robert C. Merton) became deeply involved in international financial markets.

As a consequence of these developments, economists face relatively new challenges as they attempt to do good work. One is the problem of "double agentry" or conflicting loyalties in which the economist finds himself serving competing interests—those of the institution that employs (and may protect) him and the diverse communities that the institution is intended to serve (May 1980, 217). These developments also have provided the economics profession with a depth of influence on human affairs that neither it nor most other professions have ever enjoyed in the past. Some economists today *govern*—they don't just advise and counsel. Economists govern today not just by virtue of their monopoly over economic expertise, though that source of influence is indeed significant. They also govern by virtue of the institutional power that is now at their disposal. This power provides economists with both indirect and direct means of influence over economic interventions. Indirectly, economists' decisions in consulting firms and hedge funds alter the environment and practices of private and public actors, with extraordinary effects on individuals, communities, and nations. Directly, leading economists at the world's most important multilateral agencies sometimes engage in what can only be considered social engineering.[9] Economists can sometimes influence decisively which public enterprises ought to be privatized (and how that should be accomplished), what subsidies and price supports should be terminated, and what trade and environmental policies should be enacted. In this activity, they are not shy about activating the levers of influence available to them as a consequence of the institutional positions they hold.

In short, economists today sometimes find themselves in the position of central architects of economic policy and institutions. Their institutional influence has grown most dramatically in the developing world, where the gap between the subjects and objects of economic practice could hardly be greater. This influence intensifies the ethical dilemmas and challenges that economists face as they do their work. *What does it mean to be an "ethical economist" in this complex environment where one's expertise and position combine to yield institutional power?* I hope it is by now clear that the answer to this question is not obvious. The economists who now govern need professional ethics to help them manage the awesome power that they enjoy. And so do the communities whose fortunes are affected by economic practice.

Unevenness and Anticipated Harms

The third step in the escalating case comes directly from Econ 101: *economic interventions typically affect distinct groups of people differently.* Some people are harmed by economic interventions that are understood to be beneficial in the aggregate. The most widely known example appears in trade theory, which purports to show that when tariff protections are removed, the economy as a whole (usually) benefits. In the aggregate, consumers are now richer, owing to the efficiency gains from specialization. But trade theory also emphasizes that under the best of circumstances, some people will be made worse off by trade liberalization. Those who work in industries for which a country does not have a comparative advantage will experience a loss in employment opportunities and income.

Mainstream economic theory demonstrates that policy changes often are of this sort—they yield net benefit in the aggregate while hurting some members of the economy. This fact would seem to create a dilemma. Should economists advocate for and enact policy that will harm some people for the so-called good of society? Most economists hurriedly answer "yes" (as would most utilitarians). While the affirmative answer to this question might in fact be warranted in at least some cases, *the rush to that answer* certainly never is.

The field of public health is instructive in thinking through this matter. Would a health practitioner be warranted in proposing or implementing a medical intervention that benefits the community at large but that harms some of its members, perhaps severely? The answer might very well depend on the circumstances. Consider the case of quarantining against their will nonsymptomatic community members who have been exposed to a pathogen during an epidemic in order to prevent the spread of the disease. Now compare that case with another—one that involves the termination of the life of one person in order to harvest organs that will save the lives of several others. These two cases are very similar in crucial respects: both cause severe harm to unwilling victims for the benefit of others. Yet, we might want to make a distinction between them; we might find it more appropriate to endorse the quarantining of potentially infected persons, even if it increases the chances that some who are isolated involuntarily will become ill and perhaps die by virtue of their being corralled with the infected, than to endorse the taking of a life to harvest organs.[10] Posing the two cases side by side induces a moment of hesitation and discomfort in which we are encouraged to think carefully about the ethical complexities of the matters before us.

Economists might argue that this comparison is off point. After all, the harm from trade liberalization is only temporary: in the long run, those displaced by imports will likely be able to find new employment that offsets their losses. But we can revise the medical example to make it more comparable with trade. Is a doctor (always or ever) warranted in pursuing interventions that are likely to make some people seriously but only temporarily ill, in order to benefit others? Can the doctor extract a person's kidney (without her consent), for example, in order to save the life of another, if the chances are very good that the donor will survive the procedure? Again, we have reason to hesitate. There is something disturbing about the idea that we can violate a fundamental right or impose serious harm on one to benefit another, even if that harm is only temporary. And that moment of hesitation, when we take the time to think through the ethical implications of harming one for the benefit of another, provides reason for hope for ethical medical practice.

Economists, on the other hand, do not often hesitate. It is second nature for us to advocate policy that benefits some while harming others. Think of the standard textbook treatment of minimum wages or rent control. Both are to be eliminated for the good of society although some will suffer as a consequence. Economists often dodge the ethical matter of imposing harm altogether by insisting that those made worse off by an economic policy intervention should be compensated for their losses through side payments (Bhagwati 1994). In the event of full compensation for the losers, the argument runs, no one suffers from a policy change. This provides a simple and neat blackboard solution to the ethical problem.[11]

The historical record indicates, however, that those displaced by free trade are rarely compensated fully and that many never fully recover. Economists know this better than anyone (Rodrik 1997). We must inquire, then, into how this knowledge affects the ethics of the situation. If an economist knows that some will indeed suffer lasting harm, are they still ethically warranted in advising or instituting the policy that will generate the harm? Does it matter who in society will suffer—is there an ethical difference between the situation where those who stand to lose are the best off in society and the situation where the victims are the worst off? Does it matter how much greater are the potential aggregate gains than the potential losses? And does it matter to what degree those who will be harmed are consulted prior to the intervention? Is their level of support for or (more likely) opposition to the intervention ethically relevant? Should the economist take into account the reasons for their support or opposition, or should these be dismissed as tainted by self-interest? On these ethically fraught matters, economists tend to stumble. But what they do not do, often enough, is take the time to think the matter through.

Historically, economists have acted as if the ethics of the situation simply requires them to keep a ledger of winnings and losses and to use these findings to advocate for those policy changes that yield net benefit in the long run.[12] But economists would likely not countenance such simple mindedness in other professions that affect the lives of others. Most would avoid (and would likely also ethically indict) a doctor who was so cavalier about the potential harms inflicted on some patients for the betterment of others. What is it about economics, then, that constitutes and justifies this enormous ethical difference from other professions that confront harm? Perhaps the answer would be discovered in the field of professional economic ethics, were it to exist. Or perhaps we would learn instead that, in fact, economics is much more similar to other professions like medicine in terms of its central ethical dilemmas—and that economists have been far too quick to impose costs on some for the benefit of others.

Uncertainty, Risk, and Unanticipated Harms

The fourth proposition in the escalating case concerns the epistemic condition facing the economist—the degree of knowledge and certainty that obtains in economic practice. Until now, we have largely presumed an Econ 101 version of the world in which economists have sufficient knowledge of the context in which they operate and the effects of their actions; they therefore know that the intervention they recommend will succeed, and they know what will be the precise consequences of this intervention's success. In the world of Econ 101, there is no risk of failure; even the harms associated with an economic policy are presumed to be known in advance by the economist who advocates the measure. This is what David Colander calls the "economics of control" approach to policy since it presents the economist as having his hand on the levers that drive the economy (Colander 2005c). It yields an extraordinarily aggressive approach to economic policy—one that does not countenance the possibility of failure.

The fourth proposition disputes these claims. It is this: *the economist operates in a world of uncertainty and epistemic insufficiency—where interpretive practice necessarily infuses the processes of knowing, error is inevitable, unintended consequences are the norm, ignorance is rife, and human subjectivity is not a temporary disability but an ineradicable condition of our being and acting in the world.*

I take it to be uncontroversial that despite the advances made in economic theory over the past century, the economist today does not know with certainty and cannot control whether any particular economic intervention will succeed; nor does she know with certainty what harms may be caused by the intervention, even if it proves to be successful by some criterion or other; nor does she know with certainty the harms that will befall the targeted community should the intervention fail; nor does she know the normative commitments of the targeted community, and so on. There is a degree of ignorance here; there is uncertainty on many levels, and as a consequence, there is risk of policy failure. In Fritz Machlup's view, this is the typical context of most economic policy making. Machlup makes the point by distinguishing between the analytically tractable world of the blackboard and the messiness of real life where "most things are unknown and almost everything is uncertain" (Machlup 1965, 7). Inevitably, these features are most common in situations where the stakes are greatest and the threats are most grave, such as economic restructuring, climate change, and the like (Weitzman 2009).

Do uncertainty and ignorance entail ethical substance that was absent from the previously discussed context of perfect information? The answer, of course, is that they do. Now, economic practice is fraught with normative responsibilities of the policy maker to the targeted community that were absent from the previous case. The economist (no matter how proficient she is in her craft) now runs the risk of causing substantial, unanticipated harm. The ethical economist must take account of this potential harm: to factor it into her calculations somehow or other when advocating any particular intervention.

How should she do this? What new burdens does she carry as she undertakes to serve communities who are at once in need of her attention and liable to be harmed as a consequence of her interventions? Potential for unanticipated harm hardly implies that the economist should fold up her tent and go home. The professional must keep in view that doing nothing itself entails risks of severe harm. As Sharon Welch (2000) reminds us, risk is something that must be confronted ethically—it is not something that can be avoided—and so we are not ethically warranted in turning our backs on the needs of others whenever risk presents itself.

The greater the risk of unanticipated harm and the greater the potential impact (for better or worse) of the professional, the more urgent is the need for careful attention to the ethical questions attending professional engagement. Economics achieves high scores in both dimensions: in many cases, the economic practitioner confronts a high degree of uncertainty, which implies a high risk of harm, and the extent of that harm can be quite severe.

Influence Without Control

Earlier, I argued that economists sometimes occupy the position of social engineer where they enjoy substantial influence over policy choices and institutional design as a consequence of the institutional power they hold. The present consideration of uncertainty and risk allows us to add nuance to the previous discussion. Even the most influential economists who have institutional power generally do not "control" economic policy formation, let alone economic outcomes. In all institutional contexts (from democratic to authoritarian), the world of policy making and governance involves competing interest groups with their own particular aspirations, visions, and resources that they use to promote, block, or hijack policy interventions. In this milieu, economists represent just one input into a complex mix of forces that ultimately yields policy outcomes. It is therefore naïve to impute to economists effective control over economic affairs. Under the best of circumstances, economists face the risk that their interventions will be exploited by other actors for their own purposes, and in such cases, the ultimate outcome is not apt to accord well with economists' intentions.

Later on, I will explore one case in which economists exerted enormous influence—the case involves radical market liberalization in the South and in the transition economies during the 1980s and 1990s. And so it is important to note in the present context that even in this case, economists did not enjoy the extent of influence to which they aspired (as they themselves have lamented; see Chapter 9). Political scientist Rachel Epstein (2008) demonstrates through comparative study of postcommunist transition economies in Central and Eastern Europe that the success of the IFIs in driving the economic reform process depended on a set of factors that were largely beyond the control of these institutions or their economists. In particular, Epstein finds that IFI success in advocating reforms depended upon the level of uncertainty among domestic policy actors regarding the reforms, the perceived status of the outside experts and the need of domestic actors to secure their "social approbation," and the perceived credibility of the policies that the IFIs proposed.

Epstein's findings should remind us that economists are but one input into the policy-making process. They are hardly the only efficacious actors; indeed, they are not usually the most important or powerful of the actors who shape policy. Moreover, in those rare instances when economists exert actual control over the policy-making process—where they really do engage in social engineering—they cannot control policy implementation or the economic outcomes that these policies induce. There is slippage here owing to all sorts of uncertainties, and this slippage can be acute. These insights imply that harm may result not just when economists fail to get their way but also when they are able to implement the precise policy regimes that they have sketched out on the blackboard.

Recognition of the complexity, uncertainties, and risk that attend economic interventions and what they imply about limits to economists' control bears directly on the matter before us. These insights do not weaken, in the least, the case for professional ethics; instead, they relate to its content. A useful professional economic ethics must address not just or primarily the ethics of practice in cases where economists exert extensive control, since such cases are rare.[13] It must speak primarily to the ethical challenges that arise in the far more complex contexts where economists *enjoy influence but lack control*. In these contexts, the economist intervenes as best she can to shape the policy-making and implementation processes while anticipating that her intervention might yield damaging social, political, and economic outcomes. A robust professional economic ethics must emphasize her limited capacities and explore the ethical implications of the constraints and dangers she faces as she acts in the world with influence but without control. The ethical economist recognizes that though she is just one factor in the chain that connects policy deliberations to policy and economic outcomes, she is not thereby spared ethical complicity. Following Welch (2000), we might look to professional economic ethics to elaborate an appropriate "ethic of risk" that can enable responsible economic practice in a world that the economist cannot control.

CONCLUSION

Here, then, is the escalating case for professional economic ethics. First, economists enjoy influence over others by virtue of their intellectual monopoly over subject matter of tremendous social significance. Second, economists today also achieve institutional power that enhances their authority and influence, and they sometimes acquire the powers associated with social engineering. Third, economic interventions generally yield anticipated harms as well as benefits, and those who suffer these harms are often uncompensated. Fourth and finally, economists operate in a world of epistemic insufficiency. They do not know with certainty what will be the effects of their interventions, and so there is risk of unanticipated harm. Although they are key players in economic policy making, they usually exert influence without effective control in that domain.

Each of these propositions is uncontroversial. In my view, each proposition on its own suffices to establish the need for professional economic ethics. Certainly, when taken together, the four propositions strengthen the case.

Those who occupy positions in which they can so significantly alter the life chances of others necessarily traverse dense ethical thickets.[14] Should the economist be guided by consequentialist precepts—evaluating policy and other economic interventions by reference to their effects—or by deontological precepts—by reference to their inherent rightness or wrongness? Should respect for individual rights be taken as one among many desirable means and end states (Sen 1992), or should they be taken as inviolable side constraints (Nozick 1974)? How should these and other normative principles be balanced in the ensuing policy? Should the normative commitments of the economist or of the target community govern? And in this connection, should the community's actual normative commitments be determinative, or should the economist advocate interventions that reflect the refined and sanitized commitments that (she presumes) would emerge in this community were it to undergo a painstaking process of reflection about values, goals, and so forth—perhaps undertaken by rational agents deliberating in a Rawlsian original position? Finally, how should the economist take account of the myriad ineradicable uncertainties that attend economic practice?

These are among the questions that the economics profession should engage but largely does not. Economists are left to manage on their own, as best they can. They need help. Neither they nor those affected by their work are well served by a profession that presumes that the ethical challenges attending its practice are too obvious to warrant serious attention. At the risk of repetition, I would suggest that where the lives of others are at stake, and where even the most competent and well-meaning economist can do substantial damage, the profession's failure to engage professional economic ethics is simply inexcusable.

Fortunately, other professions that share critical features with economics have engaged many of these challenges. What might economists learn from these professions? What are some of the principles or lessons that might emerge in the field of professional economic ethics, and how would these affect the behavior and performance of economists? The next several chapters explore these questions.

Notes

1 See also the useful discussion in Sullivan (2005) and Goode (1960).

2 Of the defining features of professionalism that Wueste identifies, only the fourth—recognition of role-specific norms that can dominate over the ethics of "what it means to be a decent human being," or "what Paul Camenisch calls 'ethics plain and simple'" (Wueste 1994, 1)—might not apply to the economics profession. In this regard, economics may not be an outlier, however. Alan Goldman (1980) argues that, in fact, most professions are not warranted in holding themselves to role-specific ethical obligations that conflict with the imperatives associated with general morality.

3 William Sullivan employs the concept of "civic professionalism" while reaching complementary conclusions about the ethical entailments of professionalism. He speaks of "the values of the academy [abstraction, technical expertise], the values of professional practice [practical ability], and the ethical-social values of professional identity [integrity, purpose]" (2005, 28). Sullivan worries that contemporary professional training emphasizes the first over the second and especially the third set of values, to the detriment of professional practice.

4 There is an important ethical question whether, in fact, economics needs to be or should be so impenetrable. Building an inaccessible façade is one way

in which professions can enhance their monopoly power, influence over, and autonomy from those they purportedly serve—all of which violate the professional covenant. May (1980, 210) concludes that the professions face an ethical obligation to "instruct" those they serve in order to reduce the knowledge gap that separates the two parties and thereby empower clients to decide on alternative courses of action.

5 Hardwig (1994) explores carefully the ethical entailments of "expertise." One of his most important claims concerns the obligation of the expert to be truthful regarding the limits to her expertise. We will revisit this matter when we explore the content of professional economic ethics in subsequent chapters.

6 Although I will not explore the matter here, I should note that Hardwig (1994) also examines the ethical obligations that bear on those who rely on professional expertise. These "clients" should not "generate pressure on experts to pretend to know more than they do, to overestimate the relevance of what they know, or to feign consensus within the community of experts where there is none" (1994, 96). Ethical professional conduct requires a reciprocal arrangement which entails appropriate conduct on both sides of the exchange.

7 Central bank independence is justified on the grounds that economic practice is so complex that it must be left to the experts, and that independence allows central bankers to pursue good economic policy free from short-term political considerations.

8 Some economists enjoyed substantial influence in the nineteenth century, when the so-called "money doctors" designed financial systems, particularly in colonized countries (see the essays in Drake 1994).

9 Most economists certainly do not ever come to enjoy such substantial influence. Most economic work entails much more mundane analysis, reporting, and consultation. Social engineering by economists occurs only when a constellation of forces conspire to position the economist as central decision maker. We will return to this matter later in this and in subsequent chapters.

10 One might argue that what distinguishes the cases is the fact that in the case of the isolation, the victims of the policy—those who will ultimately become ill by virtue of their isolation—are unknown when the policy is implemented, while in the other case, the person who will be put to death for his organs is a known individual. But our concerns would hardly dissipate if there were to be a lottery to determine who among us was to become the unwilling organ donor.

Alternatively, one could argue that the former case involves what Nozick (1974) calls "innocent threats"—those who pose a risk to others owing to no fault of their own—while the latter does not. Because those who are potentially infected pose a risk to others, the argument runs, their rights might be violated legitimately. This is perhaps true, but see Nozick (1974) for a discussion that illuminates just how difficult are the ethical issues that arise in cases that feature innocent threats. In any case, in economics, those who are harmed for the good of society rarely fall into the category of threat, innocent or otherwise. They are better analogized with the involuntary organ donor in the case presented in the text.

11 Usually, the demonstration merely shows that a policy adjustment is Pareto improving in the sense that the winners *could* fully compensate the losers while still enjoying net benefit. Jagdish Bhagwati (1994) claims that this demonstration is insufficient to sustain policy reform. In his view, the losers must actually be compensated for their losses.

12 Nelson argues that were economists to take full account of short-run adjustment costs to policy changes, they would hardly be able to take positions on most policy matters (Nelson 2003). He associates the economist's privileging of long-run outcomes over short-run adjustment costs with the theological nature of contemporary economics. The goal of the economist, in this account, is to deliver for society "heaven on earth" through the elimination of economic privation (see also Nelson 2010; and Kanbur 2001).

13 Central bankers represent an important exception. They exert control in a meaningful sense over the range of economic policy instruments and interventions within their jurisdiction. Moreover, some central bankers (such as Alan Greenspan) come to enjoy such a degree of authority over certain kinds of legislative matters that it becomes difficult to draw the line between influence and control. That said, central bankers at best only control policy interventions and not the economic consequences of those interventions.

14 The fact that economic interventions affect the lives of hundreds of thousands or even millions strengthens the case for professional ethics. Paradoxically, however, we seem to have the cognitive ability to embrace professional ethics in cases where the individual professional acts upon the individual client but not when the individual professional acts on many more.

Part II

THE CONTENT OF PROFESSIONAL ECONOMIC ETHICS

Chapter 8

Learning from Others

Ethical Thought Across the Professions

As to diseases, make a habit of two things—to help, or at least to do no harm.

Hippocrates

Many professions share features of ethical significance with economics. Medical practitioners and researchers, lawyers, engineers, public administrators, and other professionals act upon others in consequential ways and occupy positions in which they can cause substantial harm. The professional ethics traditions that have emerged in fields such as these would therefore be relevant to the economics profession were it to begin to establish its own ethical framework.

The following discussion surveys principles, questions, and issues that have emerged across various traditions within professional ethics. Since this book is not in itself an economic ethics textbook, the presentation here (and in later chapters) will be selective and suggestive rather than exhaustive or definitive. I identify several potential areas of productive importation from other professions into what I hope will be a new field of professional economic ethics.

PROFESSIONAL ETHICAL PRINCIPLES

Four ethical principles are codified in the "principlism" that emerged within bioethics in the 1970s: nonmaleficence, autonomy, beneficence, and justice (see Beauchamp and Childress 1989; Wolpe 1998). Today, these principles recur across the professions. Each of these principles is contested, as is principlism itself as an appropriate foundation for professional ethics (see Evans 2000). The interpretation and application of the principles vary across the professions, reflecting the wide diversity of professional practice. The four principles are also supplemented (and constrained) by others that comprise professionals' duties to their profession and peers, clients, research subjects, the public, other species, and artifacts. For instance, some professional codes emphasize the connection between competence and professional responsibility. Codes urge professionals to continue their professional development throughout their careers, to seek assistance of other professionals when appropriate, to refuse assignments for which they are insufficiently prepared, and to be candid with clients about their own professional limitations. Many also emphasize honesty in all professional activities. The "fundamental canons" of the American Society of Civil Engineers now includes the principle of sustainable development; codes in anthropology and archeology emphasize the duty of researchers to publish scientific findings in a timely manner and to preserve archeological resources (while anthropology extends the reach of moral consideration to the animals that anthropologists encounter in their work). Many professions also emphasize the duty of the professional to refuse employer or client directives that violate the provisions of their codes.

A full treatment of professional economic ethics would require an engagement with all of these issues. Here I will examine the salience of just two principles: nonmaleficence and autonomy. These are the most well established of professional ethical principles; moreover, they bear directly on professional economic practice.

Nonmaleficence

The most widely recognized principle within professional ethics is a concern for harm that professional practice may cause others. It is understood across the professions that potential for harm carries ethical entailments which any satisfactory body of professional ethics must address. The nonmaleficence that appears within principlism expresses the medical professional's obligation to wrestle with potential harm—to avoid causing harm when it is possible to do so and to ameliorate its impact when it is not.

Two fields in particular provide guidance for economics in this connection: medical and environmental practice. Medical practice (comprising research and treatment) has engaged the question of harm systematically, and its insights have achieved influence across other professions.[1] Environmental practice has adapted the nonmaleficence principle to interventions with uncertain, complex, and long-lasting effects that bear on large groups of people—all of which are features of many economic interventions.

Medical Practice

In medical practice, there is an asymmetry between the expertise of the physician and the patient which can yield for the physician appreciable *de facto* decision-making authority in establishing a treatment regime. Often the patient is relatively ignorant about the complexities attending his illness or the available treatment regimens (let alone the relative skill of the physician), and resource pressures associated with the provision of health care in the contemporary setting often prevent the doctor from taking sufficient time to train the patient in the relevant matters. Moreover, the doctor must often make decisions while the patient is incapacitated in ways that preclude meaningful participation of the patient in his own care.

In medical ethics the nonmaleficence principle is captured most elegantly in the admonition, *Primum non Nocere*, or "First, do no harm."[2] This principle comprises interrelated epistemic and normative components. Regarding epistemic matters, the principle presumes that the physician's knowledge about health, illness, and treatment is necessarily incomplete; that her judgment is fallible; and that her technical skill is imperfect. It presumes as a consequence that risk is inevitable—that the strategies a physician adopts might very well induce adverse as well as beneficial effects. The normative content follows: cognizant of these dangers, the physician is to conduct herself in a manner that does not worsen the patient's situation. In a world of perfect information, this ethic would be unnecessary. It would likely be replaced by a beneficent directive such as "Whenever and to the degree possible, heal the patient." But in a world of uncertainty, the directive "heal the patient" would be much too dangerous since it implies that the doctor possesses a kind of knowledge and consequent capacity to intervene correctly in every situation so as to bring about a favorable outcome that, in many cases, she simply does not have.

Environmental Practice

In the field of environmental protection and policy making, the "precautionary principle," though contested, is now advocated by many environmental ethicists and reflected in national and international environmental law. Writing in *Scientific American*, David Appell (2001, 18) argues that

> Although there is no consensus definition of what is termed the precautionary principle, one oft-mentioned statement, from the so-called Wingspread conference in Racine, Wis., in 1998 sums it up: "When an activity raises threats of harm to human health or the environment, precautionary measures should be taken even if some cause and effect relationships are not fully established scientifically." In other words, actions taken to protect the environment and human health take precedence. . . In this context the proponent of an activity, rather than the public, should bear the burden of proof (Montague, 1998).

Like "First, do no harm," the precautionary principle is rooted in recognition of fundamental uncertainty and risk, and of the gap between professionals and those who will be affected by their actions. If anything, the level of uncertainty in the environmental field is greater than in the medical field (and indeed, some of the uncertainties in medicine stem from environmental factors that bear on health). How will the elimination of habitat upon which a particular species depends affect the broader ecosystem in the near and distant future? What will be the long-term effects of climate change? How will the introduction of a new biogenetic technique bear on plant and animal life 10, 20, or 50 years hence? These questions are vexing not just because mapping the complex causal environmental pathways is so difficult but also because environmental impacts endure over long periods and depend on initial and subsequent conditions that can at best only be approximated. Moreover, the precautionary principle stems from recognition that today's decisions will bear not just or principally on us but on others. Ethicists emphasize the rights of and injuries caused to future generations; some also add into their ethical calculations the nonhuman species that suffer the effects of environmental imprudence. In the environmental field, then, there is no escape from the fact that those making consequential decisions are not coterminous with all those who will bear their consequences. Finally, the effects of many environmental policy decisions are irreversible.

As in medicine, the principle that emerges to address risk of harm is prudence: the precautionary principle requires that environmental decision makers act so as not to harm when the consequences of interventions are uncertain. Decision makers are to take care to protect and to prevent unintended consequences of otherwise beneficial projects. They are to aim for less than what could perhaps be achieved in order to diminish the chances that they will commit substantial errors that harm others who are not present or otherwise unable to decide for themselves.

The fields of medicine and environmental policy share two key features that are ethically salient: they entail social relationships in which some are empowered to make decisions that affect the rights and well-being of others, and they entail fundamental uncertainty and risk. In both fields, we find an ethical commitment to a principle of action that emphasizes prudence, or the imperative to avoid or minimize harm.[3] Hereinafter, I will refer to the broad class of directives that appear across professions that emphasize harm avoidance as the "prudential principle" except when I am referring to those fields (like medicine or environmental practice) that have specific nomenclature.[4] The question to be addressed in later chapters is what might economists take from the broad convergence among professions around the prudential principle.

Autonomy

On its face, a principle that calls attention to harm avoidance appears benign—indeed, ensuring that professional practice is benign is very much the point. But deeper consideration yields implications that trouble many ethicists. Is a doctor warranted in withholding information from a patient about the nature of his condition in order to avoid causing worry, for instance, when worry will be of little help (or may cause substantial discomfort) to the patient? Imagine that the patient is terminally ill: should the doctor tell him this if he believes that this information will interfere with the quality of the patient's remaining days or the effectiveness of his treatment? Should the doctor instead conspire with family members in a scheme that allows the patient to believe he is doing well so that he might live with hope and comfort right up until the moment of his death?

This example reveals two features of the nonmaleficence principle in medical practice that are empirically and ethically suspect. First, the principle presumes that the physician knows best in matters pertaining to treatment. But is this a safe assumption? While the doctor might have a better grasp of the physiological aspects of a patient's condition, there are other features of the situation that are ethically salient and which the doctor cannot know as well as does the patient. The doctor does not have access to the patient's deepest convictions or aspirations. Perhaps the patient would change the course of his life and pursue some vitally important project that he has always postponed were he to know that his life is about to end. In this case, the doctor's actions to protect the patient's welfare by withholding information may deprive the patient of one last opportunity to live his life as he sees fit. Driven by an imperative to avoid harm, the doctor may, in fact, cause significant irreversible harm while she protects the patient from emotional distress.

Second, the nonmaleficence principle presumes that legitimacy of paternalism, or the doctrine that it is right to limit the freedom of an agent *for his own good* (Goldman 1980; Thompson 1987; Buchanan and Brock 1989). Paternalism implies that the doctor is authorized to make those decisions that are in the best interest of the patient even when those decisions might conflict with the judgment that the patient would make were he to be fully cognizant of his situation. The principle countenances practices that are inappropriate in other contexts whenever these practices are apt to shield the patient from harm. The case of lying that we just considered is one example.[5] More generally, paternalism might allow the doctor to constrain the decisions or behavior of an altogether rational patient for his own good.

What is ethically troubling about paternalistic interventions? Paternalism denies something that Kantian and other contemporary philosophers take to be fundamental: it denies the agency and compromises the integrity of those whom the professional serves.

> To deny an adult the right to make their own decisions, however mistaken from some standpoint they are, is to treat them as simply means to their own good, rather than as ends in themselves (Dworkin 2005).

Paternalistic interventions discount the vital interest of an agent in living his own life as he sees fit, for better or worse (Mill 1859). They separate the authority for life planning from the agent whose life is to be lived, shifting this authority to a guardian that is taken to have greater wisdom about the agent whose life it now directs.

It is not my purpose here to adjudicate the debate over the legitimacy of paternalistic interventions (in general or in economics). The purpose, instead, is to highlight the demands placed on the ethical professional of another principle that now finds a place of privilege in medical and other developed bodies of professional ethics: the Kantian principle of respect for the autonomy and integrity of those whom professionals serve. Today, professional ethics tends to embrace the fundamental idea that the professional is to comport herself in a way that recognizes the agency, autonomy, and integrity of her clients and others who are affected by her actions.

The recent shift toward respect for autonomy appears with particular clarity in the ethics of medical practice and research. An early version of the Hippocratic Oath included the following passage:

> I will follow that system of regimen which, according to my ability and judgement, I consider for the benefit of my patients, and abstain from whatever is deleterious and mischievous (available at http://www.geocities.com/everwild7/noharm.html).

Nowhere does the Oath (nor the broad Hippocratic tradition—see Shuster 1998) recognize the autonomy or will of the patient. Neither does "the prayer of Maimonides, Percival's Ethics, or the early codes of the [American Medical Association] or the World Medical Association (Veatch 1984)... Outside agents—including the patients themselves—were simply not deemed qualified to participate in the formulation of ethical behavior within the profession" (Wolpe 1998, 39; see also Wolf 2002). In Hippocrates' own words,

> The art of medicine has three factors, the disease, the patient and the physician. The physician is the servant of the Art. *The patient must cooperate with the physician in combating the disease* (cited in Shuster 1998, 974; emphasis added by Shuster).

Now consider this passage from the Yale Physician's Oath, drafted during the 1990s by medical students and the University Chaplain:

> I will respect the moral right of patients to participate fully in the medical decisions that affect them. I will assist my patients to make choices that coincide with their own values and beliefs (available at http://info.med.yale.edu/education/osa/milestones/commencement04/oath.html).

The Yale Physician's Oath carries forward the beneficence obligation of the physician to place the highest value on patients' health and welfare: "The health and dignity of my patients will be my first concern." Moreover, the Oath recognizes the physician's agency: the doctor is not to sacrifice her authority to the whims or flights of fancy of the patient. But the physician's authority to undertake a treatment regimen is now substantially constrained by the need to engage the patient as a partner in the treatment plan. This passage places paternalistic strategies in ethical doubt: consent secured on the basis of lies or partial truths can hardly be considered valid or informed. The Oath codifies a presumption that the patient and not the physician should decide how much and what kind of information he will receive, for instance, and his demand to be fully informed must be honored no matter how damaging that information may be to his physical or psychological health.

The contemporary trend toward recognition of autonomy in professional ethics is associated with the fairly recent challenges in political philosophy to the doctrine of "utilitarianism." The challenges have been advanced by Kantian and other scholars who advocate ethical systems grounded in individual rights and freedom (Wolpe 1998). In brief, utilitarianism is an approach to social evaluation that seeks to maximize the aggregate well-being of a community. In this approach, the intervention is best that promotes the greatest human happiness, satisfaction, or other psychic aspect of well-being. Under utilitarianism, a doctor is expected to take those steps that she believes will lead to this outcome, all things considered. She would certainly be authorized to substitute her judgment for that of a patient who seems bent on pursuing a course of action that will induce harm to himself (or to his family and friends). On this account, an ethical physician is apt to be a paternalist.

Many philosophers and ethicists today argue that utilitarianism is insufficiently respectful of autonomy since it discounts the right and interest all persons have to envision, direct, and manage their lives according to the commitments and values that they have reason to cherish (Rawls 1971; Williams 1973; Nozick 1974; Sen 1987). Critics argue that something fundamental to human existence is violated when others are licensed to watch over us and dictate action that they take to be in our best interests. In this view, there is something imperious about professional ethics that amplify rather than dampen the professional's aspiration to direct the affairs of others. Contemporary professional ethics grapples with this matter—and with the ensuing tension between the duty to avoid harm and the rights of those whom professionals serve.

The imperative to recognize the agency of others spread widely across professional fields during the latter decades of the twentieth century. One example must suffice. In 1989, at the Second International Conference on Ethics and Development, sponsored by the International Development Ethics Association, the majority of attendees signed the "Merida Declaration," which states in part:

In the face of the profound inadequacies of modernization development strategies, WE PROPOSE:

1. To intensify the search for and study of an alternative for social transformation, supported by at least the following ethical principles:
    - The absolute respect of the dignity of the human person, regardless of gender, ethnic group, social class, religion, age, or nationality. . .
    - The affirmation of freedom, understood as self-determination, self-management, and participation of peoples in local, national, and international decision processes . . . (Crocker 1998, 338).

It is notable that although this Declaration engages the matter of professional practice toward particularly vulnerable communities, it is altogether silent on the matter of the prudential principle while emphasizing the right to self-governance of those targeted by development interventions.

Prior Informed Consent

Recognition of autonomy is reflected today in the widespread requirement that professionals secure "prior informed consent" before acting on others, especially but not only in experimental contexts.[6] Prior informed consent requires that "The information disclosed should be accurately comprehended, the recipient should be competent to decide, and the decision should be made freely" (Wolf 2002, 136). In medical practice, this requires the physician to discuss treatment options with a patient in a way that the patient can understand and to secure permission (without coercion) to pursue one course or another. In research, prior informed consent establishes an obligation on the part of the researcher to brief potential research subjects fully so that they are aware of what will and could happen to them in the course of experimentation.

Like the prudential principle, prior informed consent is subject to dispute among ethicists across the professions. Its application is complicated even in the simplest of cases where professional interventions target individuals one by one.[7] Matters become more difficult still when an intervention affects large groups of people. Yet in such cases, the principle is finding a footing in professional ethics and, recently, also in public policy. For instance, the precautionary principle that we considered a moment ago encompasses not just prudence but also prior informed consent. As Montague (1998) argues,

> The process of applying the Precautionary Principle must be open, informed and democratic and must include potentially affected parties. It must also involve an examination of the full range of alternatives, including no action (Montague 1998).

These aspects of the precautionary principle relate directly to the relationship between the professional and those upon whom she acts and demands that to the degree possible, those who will bear the effects of a policy intervention be empowered to participate meaningfully in the decision whether to implement it. Pollan (2001; 94) emphasizes this point as well:

> [T]here is a sense in which the [precautionary principle] is "antiscientific," if by scientific we mean leaving it to scientists to tell us what to do. For the precautionary principle recognizes the limitations of science—and the fact that scientific uncertainty is an unavoidable breach into which ordinary citizens sometimes must step and act.

Simple enough to say, of course, but what does it require when a large number of people will be affected by a proposed intervention? Is there a violation of fundamental rights if each and every individual in a community is not given the opportunity to sign off on an intervention before it is undertaken, as libertarians might conclude? Consent by each and every agent is generally impossible in cases other than localized interventions that affect a small number of identifiable people. In other cases, where the pool of affected individuals is large and/or dispersed, we need to search for legitimate procedures that authorize some to give consent on behalf of others.

These matters are now arising with some frequency in the environmental field. Two recent international agreements, the Rotterdam Convention on the Prior Informed Consent Procedure for Certain Hazardous Chemicals and Pesticides in Trade (the PIC Convention) and the Cartagena Protocol on Biosafety, which is associated with the Convention on Biological Diversity, incorporate procedures by which parties must secure prior informed consent before undertaking certain actions that could affect the well-being of others. Under the PIC Convention,

> A government is required to notify FAO [the Food and Agriculture Organization] when it bans or severely restricts a pesticide . . . FAO then passes the notice to designated national authorities (DNAs) in other countries. When exports are expected, the exporting country is required to ensure that the importer's DNA gets a copy of (or reference to) the original notice to FAO about control action, with a specific alert that an export is planned . . . Importing countries must establish internal procedures and authorities for handling information, advise FAO about the acceptability of a pesticide, and ensure that actions taken with regard to an imported pesticide are not more restrictive than those for the same pesticide produced domestically or imported from another country (Wolf 2000, 494).

In a similar way, the Cartagena Protocol incorporates "advance informed agreement" provisions to regulate trade in living modified organisms (LMOs). Like the PIC, the Protocol places a substantial burden on the initiator of the action—on the party seeking to export potentially hazardous material to another country. Both treaties require the approval of a body in the receiving country that is certified as having the capacity to make appropriate judgments. Safeguards also exist to protect the population in those countries that lack sufficient capacity to ascertain risk. In the case of the Cartagena Protocol,

> Developing countries or economies in transition that lack a domestic regulatory framework for deciding whether to import an LMO commodity may notify the clearinghouse that its decision to first import a commodity requires a risk assessment (most likely at the expense of the exporter) (Wolf 2000, 497).

These international agreements are relatively new, and so it is premature to ascertain their long-term effectiveness or to anticipate the ways in which their prior informed consent mechanisms may evolve over time.

My purpose here is simply to demonstrate that professional ethics in a field that shares much with economics (including the extent of uncertainty of an intervention, the risk of harm, and the numbers of people affected by an intervention) has begun to think through what the ethical imperative of prior informed consent requires of practitioners and to show that this thinking has begun to find expression in public policy. These are promising leads for economics as it begins to flesh out its own professional ethics.

ETHICAL QUESTIONS AND PROBLEMS FROM ACROSS THE PROFESSIONS

Professional ethics entails more than a list of key principles.[8] It also encompasses questions that arise in professional work and complicate the ethical life of the practitioner and the ethical obligations facing the professions. We encountered one of these in Chapter 6 when we examined the ethical responsibility of the advisor. We found that the advisor is not ethically insulated simply by virtue of the fact that she may not be the ultimate decision maker. The following discussion explores several other pressing questions that professional economic ethics must engage.

The Problem of "Dirty Hands"

Is the professional warranted in doing wrong in order to do right? Is he justified (always or ever) in violating some compelling ethical norm when some other, presumably more important ethical objective or outcome is at stake? Following Sartre (1960), the question is whether it is ever appropriate to dirty one's hands in pursuit of some objective that is held to be paramount.[9] We examined one example of the "dirty hands" dilemma above: it concerns the question whether it is ever right for a medical practitioner to lie to a patient in order to promote his health (or prevent his anguish). Truth telling is widely regarded as an ethical imperative across the professions since it is now regarded as central to the recognition of the autonomy and integrity of those whom the professional serves. Does autonomy imply, then, that the professional may never lie to those he serves, no matter how small the lie or how important the objective that the lie will secure? Or is he to be forgiven for violating the obligation to truth telling when his objective is to do better for the client than he otherwise could? Indeed, is a professional indictable for ethical simple mindedness if he always tells the truth, no matter the stakes, even if his doing so will sometimes redound to the detriment of those the professional purports to serve (see Bok 1989)?

This question is difficult, to be sure, and it is also of direct relevance to economics. Returning to another example broached in the previous chapter, what should we think about the economist who believes (or perhaps knows) that exaggerating the confidence that she has in the policy she recommends will do much to enhance its credibility and, consequently, its likelihood of success? What if she believes that full disclosure about alternative policy options will run the risk that those she counsels will make what is by her lights the wrong choice? Is she warranted in describing the preferred policy as the only choice available and using her authority to prevent full consideration of alternatives? Is she warranted in failing to speak truthfully or make a full disclosure in service of a higher objective—the promotion of the economic welfare of the community she serves? Or is her obligation to truth telling paramount despite the consequences it might have for others?

Since economists occupy ethically complex environments where they may be encouraged or required to compromise some ethical imperatives in order to achieve important objectives and where they can have an immense impact on the lives of others, there is a pressing need for the profession to think systematically about the question of dirty hands as it relates to the diverse aspects of economic practice.

The Problem of "Many Hands"

Sometimes, organizations pursue courses of action that cause grievous harm although all of the individuals in the employ of the organization appear to be acting appropriately when judged by the norms of their professional and/or institutional roles. Ethicists refer to this as the problem of "many hands" (Thompson 1987). Professional ethics must consider carefully whether and how to assess the culpability of each of the agents who contribute (perhaps unwittingly) to "administrative evil" (Adams and Balfour 2004) and ascertain the responsibility of the professions whose members are apt to find themselves in this situation.

The historical touchstone for this problem is, of necessity, the Holocaust (Arendt 1963). Here is a case of horrific wrongdoing to which many otherwise dedicated, conscientious professionals contributed. The sanitation engineers who designed and built systems to process the human waste generated in the concentration camps so that local waterways would not be contaminated; the railroad managers who maintained and operated the trains that transported the human victims to the camps; the bookkeepers, doctors, economists, scientists, merchants, and lawyers whose work, in one small way or another, conspired to enable a complex killing machine—many of these people conducted themselves exactly as their institutional and professional roles would have seemed to require. Yet, without their complicity, the evil that unfolded could not have occurred. What are we to make of situations like this in which each participant could say with some plausibility that he was simply "doing his job"?

The question of many hands is of particular relevance today since professionals are routinely ensconced in bureaucracies rather than self-employed. This is particularly true of applied economists, the large majority of whom work in complex institutions such as government and multilateral agencies and private sector organizations that they do not typically

direct. In environments of this sort, it is not enough for the ethical economist to focus on her own conduct. She must also concern herself with the
goals and conduct of the organization she serves (May 1980). She must
evaluate carefully the degree to which the organization actually promotes
the social good. And when she discovers that the institution is causing
harm or violating rights, she must investigate whether and how she can
induce reform. Moreover, the professional ethics of her profession must
provide her a moral (and perhaps legal) foundation for resisting indictable
organizational practices.

Confronting institutional wrongdoing can be very difficult. The pressures to conform may overwhelm the isolated professional who is sur-
rounded by other reasonable people who do as they are told. The sensibility
to recognize and intervene against institutional evil is something that cannot be presumed; it must be cultivated by a profession that is widely
understood by its members to place a high value on courageous, ethical
behavior. The profession must help its members to distinguish those circumstances where it is appropriate to subordinate one's own concerns
and judgments to those of authority from those where doing so represents
a violation of one's professional responsibilities (Applbaum 1999, Ch. 9).
How does one balance the virtues of humility and loyalty with the virtues
of autonomy and individual responsibility? The profession has an important role to play in this regard—in part, by cultivating awareness among
its members of the challenges and obligations that they face.

Conflict of Interest

Successful professionals often are well paid for their services. They can
prosper by enhancing the welfare of others. But they also can find themselves in situations where they can prosper by placing their own interests
above those of the organization or the clients they serve. Professionals
sometimes form relationships that they can exploit for their own purposes, while a monopoly over important expertise presents them with
opportunities to take advantage of their clients. For instance, an unscrupulous doctor can order unnecessary tests, perhaps at a clinic in which
she has an equity interest, since the patient is generally unable to make an
independent judgment about the need for the procedure.

Professional ethics in all fields explores the conflicts of interest that
practitioners confront. What kinds of conflict of interest typically arise
in this or that profession? What is an ethical practitioner to do when she
encounters such conflicts? How ethically troublesome are instances in
which there is the appearance of conflict when no real conflict exists?
What kinds of training, rules, norms, consultations, or other mechanisms
should the profession establish so that it can assist its members who find
themselves on uncertain ethical ground?

These questions bear with particular force on economic practice.
Practicing economists sometimes gain access to privileged information

that would allow them to place lucrative bets in financial markets. Economic consultants can pander to the whims of unsophisticated clients and thereby inflate their billable hours beyond what a project actually requires. Absent careful thinking by the profession, it is not clear that well-meaning economists will recognize when the circumstances in which they find themselves represent a conflict of interest or know what to do about it when they do recognize apparent or real conflicts.

An adequate field of professional ethics must encourage practitioners to avoid conflicts of interest that fall below the radar of formal rules. This is because many institutions that employ professionals do not police conflicts of interest aggressively (or at all), and because the nature of expertise and the degree of specialization within many professions make it difficult for outsiders to recognize them when they exist. A recent report by the Inspector General of the Department of Health and Human Services of the U.S. government found that

> 90 percent of universities relied solely on [medical] researchers themselves to decide whether the money they made in consulting and other relationships with drug and device makers was relevant to their government-financed research,

while "half of universities do not ask their faculty members to disclose the amount of money or stock they make from drug and device makers" (Harris 11/9/2009, A17). Eric Campbell of Harvard Medical School claims that universities often fail to police federal conflict of interest rules out of fear of losing their "star researchers" (Harris 11/9/2009, A17). At the time of this writing, the U.S. Congress is investigating the laxity of medical school enforcement of their conflict of interest regulations, and this attention might very well yield more stringent reporting rules. But it is also likely that conflict of interest will remain an area where formal rules will never suffice to eradicate wrongdoing. Rules must be augmented by increased emphasis within the professions on self-policing by professionals that are imbued with a sense of integrity in their work.[10]

Corruption

Conflicts of interest can bleed into outright corruption. Professional ethics engages this matter as well in hopes of providing professionals with encouragement to avoid corruption and the skills for thinking through how to manage complex situations in which they become aware of corruption within their institutions or among their peers.

The appropriate response to corruption seems simple enough. When a professional encounters corruption, she is to hold herself apart from the illicit activity, report the offense to the relevant authorities, and let the chips fall where they may. But as in other cases (such as truth telling), an adequate body of professional ethics does not provide inflexible rules; instead, it cultivates ethical sensitivity and awareness. Imagine, for instance, the following plausible scenario. An economist works for a non-governmental organization (NGO) that is doing vital work in a desperate community that receives no aid from other organizations. The NGO relies on donations from funders who would not be apt to continue their funding were they to learn that some funds are siphoned off by the local project manager for personal expenditures. What is the economist to do if she learns of a transgression of this sort? Perhaps the theft is trivial relative to the organization's budget (or is that irrelevant?), and the good that the organization does is apt to be jeopardized were the manager to be exposed. Is it ethical under these circumstances to tolerate the corruption—or might ethical conduct require some other approach?

Development economists often operate in contexts in which corruption is tolerated. In some contexts, corruption may facilitate development projects that a community desperately needs (see Griffiths 2003). Cases like this raise the matter of dirty hands since they may involve the economist in unethical and/or illegal practices for the achievement of some overriding, socially beneficial objective. The economist in this situation is likely aware of the economics literature on the harms of corruption (e.g., Mauro 1997; Svensson 2005), yet he might ascertain that in the particular context in which he finds himself, there is no practical option but to submit to corrupt practices. His refusal to do so might imperil a project and the lives of those whom the project serves. On the other hand, he likely cannot know in advance with any certainty just what consequences (good or bad) will result from exposing the corruption. How should he then decide what to do? More generally, when is an economist obligated to refuse to tolerate corrupt schemes, even if this refusal necessitates the termination of vital economic interventions and, as a consequence, causes suffering and might cost lives? When, instead, is he morally justified in tolerating corruption to ensure the viability of a necessary intervention? Indeed, when is he not only justified but morally obligated to dirty his hands in this way? When is an insistence on professional fastidiousness cowardly rather than virtuous?

I regret to say that I do not have answers to these questions. Unfortunately, neither do most other economists. I do know that a profession that takes the view that it has no role to play in helping its practitioners to think carefully and act ethically in complex cases of this sort is failing its members and the communities they serve. Such a profession surely must share the blame for any harm that befalls its own members or the public when its practitioners mishandle the corruption that they encounter.

Whistle-blowing and Resignation

When an economist concludes that it is right and appropriate (all things considered) to resist practices that involve dirty hands, the administrative evil that originates in many hands, conflict of interest or corruption, this decision in turn raises difficult practical and ethical questions. How should one intervene in order to stop such practices? Should one quietly report the activity to someone in the institution who is in position to fix the problem and then wash one's hands of the matter? What if that avenue is unlikely to produce the appropriate result but might lead to retaliation? Is it then appropriate to make a public condemnation of the wrong and to name the guilty parties (Bok 1980)? So it might seem. But in the view of some ethicists there are difficult hurdles that must be overcome before whistle-blowing can be considered ethically warranted. Is there no other way to right the wrong—ways that might be less damaging to the institution and its mission? Can the whistle-blower be certain that her interpretation of events is correct—and how certain need she be, when the evidence of wrongdoing is largely hidden? Should she take pains to ensure that her motivations are honorable rather than grounded in envy, the desire for retribution against those who have wronged her, and/or the desire to damage rivals in the organization so as to further her own career? Since the institution or person she targets is apt to suffer a damaged reputation once the whistle is blown, what steps is she ethically required to take before resorting to such an extreme act?

Taking account of these complexities leads us to see that there may be times when whistle-blowing is not the appropriate course of action to take to respond to suspected wrongdoing. It may be that the ethically appropriate course of action, instead, is to resign one's position so as to remove oneself from an ethically compromised situation that one does not have the ability to change (Allen 1977; Henderson 1977). But when is this an appropriate course of action, and when, instead, is it professionally irresponsible or cowardly? What if the professional believes correctly that resigning will worsen rather than improve the situation, since the person who replaces her is apt to act in ways that facilitate the wrongdoing? Is she then obligated to carry on in her professional role, doing what (little) she can to minimize the adverse effects of the abhorrent practices (as a utilitarian might conclude)? What can economics learn from other professions that have grappled with these questions and have provided insights into ethical conduct in such challenging circumstances?

CONCLUSION

Economics shares much with other professions. Its practitioners influence the lives of others, often substantially, yet their practice is fraught with uncertainty and risk of harm. Fortunately, other professions have given careful thought to the ethical implications of these features of professional practice. For these reasons, economics can learn from other professions as it inaugurates the study of professional economic ethics. The prudential principle, respect for the autonomy and integrity of those the profession serves, beneficence and justice, the matters of dirty hands, many hands, conflict of interest, corruption, whistle-blowing and resignation—these and many other matters are relevant to the world of the economist. Careful attention to them just might help the profession do better for its members and for the publics its members serve. We don't know this to be true: but it is certainly irresponsible for the profession to continue to operate as if it were self-certain that its practice is beyond the reach of professional ethics.

One way to assess the strength of the need for professional economic ethics is to examine the actual performance of the profession in some of the most important economic interventions of recent times. To this end, the next two chapters present case studies of the contribution of economists to two historic economic initiatives: market liberalization in the developing and transition economies during the 1980s and 1990s, and the campaign to prevent more stringent financial regulation in the United States and beyond in the face of financial market innovation. We will find that in these contexts, the profession has not performed terribly well in meeting rather obvious ethical imperatives.

Notes

1 Though I do not explore the field here, public health ethics may prove to be particularly useful to the field of professional economic ethics. Like economics, public health interventions target groups rather than individual clients and often take the form of public policy measures. Like economists, public health professionals face ethical difficulties such as potential conflict between the rights of the individual as opposed to the interests of the group, the applicability of principles like prior informed consent to group settings, the meaning and significance of the dictate to avoid harm when some harm may be inevitable, etc. See Beauchamp and Steinbock (1999) for an introduction to public health ethics. I return to many of these themes below.

2 This principle appears in Hippocrates' *Epidemics*, Bk. I, Sect. XI (tr. by W.H.S. Jones; Loeb Classics edition).

3 The principle appears in the ethics governing several academic professions as well. For instance, see the "Code of Ethics of the American Anthropological Association" (available at http://www.aaanet.org/committees/ethics/ethcode.htm).

4 Hence, I will use the term prudential principle when I am abstracting from the specifics of any particular profession and want to focus instead on the broader issue at stake—namely, harm avoidance.

5 As recently as the 1970s, American physicians were debating whether it was necessary to inform terminal patients of their diagnoses (Wolpe 1998, 47).

6 The shift toward prior informed consent within medical research occurred largely as a consequence of the atrocities committed by German physicians in concentration camps during WWII. The Nuremberg Trial publicized the violations of human rights that occurred in the context of medical experimentation on unwilling subjects. The American judges at the trial formulated the Nuremberg Code, the first precept of which reads in part: "The voluntary consent of the human subject is absolutely essential" (cited in Shuster 1997, 1436). In 1964, the World Medical Association adopted the Declaration of Helsinki which specifies "Ethical Principles for Medical Research Involving Human Subjects." The Declaration has been amended repeatedly since, most recently to address concerns related to

the conduct of medical trials in developing countries. See Faden and Beauchamp (1986) on the history and theory of prior informed consent.

7 How can the professional be sure that the client or research subject understands the level of risk that the intervention will impose, for instance, when perhaps the professional is unsure of the extent of risk? Moreover, how does the professional convey meaningfully to a research subject the practical significance of a .01 percent increase in the chance of morbidity or the extent of discomfort or pain that might occur as a consequence of participation in a research project? And how can the professional ensure that consent is not predicated on misplaced trust by the research subject in the researcher (Corrigan 2003)? See also Rhodes (2005).

8 Indeed, virtue ethicists and others discount entirely a principle-based approach to professional ethics (Rachels 2007).

9 On the problem of dirty hands, see Walzer (1973), Goldman (1980), Thompson (1987), and Winston (1994).

10 Frustration with the performance of medical schools to police themselves has led the American Medical Student Association to introduce its own procedures for rating medical schools in terms of their monitoring of conflicts of interest involving their staff. In 2008, the Association gave Harvard Medical School (and many others) a grade of "F" on its *PharmFree Score Card* for its failure to provide sufficient disclosure of its faculty's connections with pharmaceutical companies (see http://www.amsascorecard.org/institutions/112). In response to pressure from students and the U.S. Congress, Harvard Medical School agreed to launch a review of its ethics policies in 2009 (Harris 3/27/2009). Recently, the School announced new rules that limit the outside pay of its senior officials that also serve on boards of pharmaceutical or biotechnology companies and that prohibit the receipt of speaker fees from pharmaceutical companies by its employees (Wilson 2010). One prominent economist I interviewed in connection with this book cited the example of the activism of medical students and argued that disclosure of outside private funding for and compensation of all economists should be required by the profession.

Chapter 9

Economists as Social Engineers

Ethical Evaluation of Market Liberalization in the
South and Transition Economies

It is helpful to imagine cavemen sitting together to think up
what, for all time, will be the best possible society and then
setting out to institute it. Do none of the reasons that make you
smile at this apply to us?

Robert Nozick (1974, 313–14)

Establishing a tradition of professional economic ethics entails costs and
risks. If it can be shown that economists have managed competently the
ethical challenges that they have faced in their work without the burdens
associated with professional ethics, then we might conclude that the profession should carry on without it. Here we will explore this question by
focusing on the most important project to which economists have contributed over the past several decades—the advancement of market-oriented
economic reform in the developing world and in the former socialist (or
transition) countries. This initiative has had extraordinary consequences
for much of the world's inhabitants, including, in particular, the most
vulnerable communities across the globe.

Since the prudential and autonomy principles are so central to professional ethics (see Chapter 8), we will restrict our ethical evaluation of
economists' involvement in this case to these two principles. Have economists intuited the applicability of and adopted these principles in their
work, despite the absence of professional economic ethics?

The evidence suggests they have not. Over the past several decades, the
most influential economists in academia, government agencies, consulting
firms, and the IFIs have disregarded the salience of these two principles
in their work. This is unsurprising: it indicates that reliance on technical
expertise and common sense is insufficient to ensure ethical professional
conduct.

The extensive involvement of so many of the profession's leading
figures in the case examined here suggests that any ethical failures that
we discover attach to the profession, rather than simply or primarily to
individual economists. This is not a case of individual renegade economists

breaking ranks with their peers and doing obvious wrong; it is rather a case of celebrated economists acting fully in accord with the predominant norms and expectations of their profession.[1] Reform must therefore also come at the level of the profession. It must cultivate norms and sensibilities that will prepare economists to do better in navigating the ethical fog that attends economic practice.

MARKET-BASED DEVELOPMENT IN THE SOUTH AND TRANSITION ECONOMIES

In the case of market-based reform, we confront an odd paradox: how is it that members of a profession that has exhibited such an ambivalent attitude toward government intrusion into the lives of citizens could avail themselves so enthusiastically of the levers of institutional power made available to them by historical events to redesign social, political, and economic institutions across the globe—often over the heads, and despite the opposition, of those who would bear the effects of these interventions?

The relevant historical facts are well known. During the 1980s and 1990s, the United States and other leading national governments, along with the IFIs, economic think tanks, and consulting firms pressed hard to transform the economies of many of the world's poorest countries and to do it abruptly. What came to be known as the Washington Consensus project entailed the extensive replacement of state direction of economic flows and outcomes with (presumably depoliticized) market mediation of economic affairs. The reform required privatization of state-owned enterprises and resources and the enhanced protection of property rights, deregulation of vital sectors of the economy, internal and external financial liberalization, trade liberalization, and the establishment of macroeconomic discipline. Economists expected the transformation to market mediation to spark a virtuous cycle of increasing efficiency, growth, and prosperity.

Economic reformers found support for this project from luminaries in the academic economics community. From the University of Chicago to MIT, most influential economists celebrated rapid and comprehensive economic transformation in the developing and transition economies. In the words of Lawrence Summers, "there was a striking degree of unanimity" on the desirability of such reform (cited in Murrell 1995, 164).

In all of the institutions that envisioned, planned, and implemented market liberalization, the central roles were played by economists. In the academy, economists engineered the theoretical models that demonstrated the gains to be had from comprehensive market liberalization; beyond the academy, economists (often the same people) crafted the economic blueprints embodied in the Washington Consensus and facilitated their implementation. Academic and applied economists worked hand in glove to bring about a historic transformation of the economies of many of the world's poorest and most vulnerable countries. Indeed, although economists surely did not exert control over events (see Chapter 7), it is not at all clear that such a transformation could have occurred in the absence of such a strong push from a profession that appeared to have the requisite expertise and degree of consensus necessary to legitimate it. Armed with a monopoly over technical knowledge and backed by the power of the institutions they served, economists advanced a historically unprecedented social, political, and economic transformation. The staggering breadth and depth of the institutional changes that economists secured can only be adequately comprehended with the concept of social engineering. Authorizing this engineering was a supreme confidence in the regime that they proposed.

I should emphasize that I will provide no evidence that places into doubt the view that economists were driven by the goal of advancing social welfare in countries that were badly in need of their assistance. It is important to remember that many of these countries faced difficult and, in some cases, even desperate economic circumstances—unmanageable fiscal imbalances coupled with monetary crises; widespread corruption; staggering poverty; and dismal economic, political, and social prospects. In the case of the former socialist countries, there was also a widespread if inchoate aspiration to some sort of market economy. Many of these countries needed professional expertise, and one might argue plausibly that the economics profession bore an ethical burden to involve itself in addressing some of the problems that these countries confronted. The question before us is not whether these economists were well meaning or technically competent but whether they comported themselves in a way that could pass the muster of professional ethics.

My central claim is that they did not. I will advance the thesis that the advocacy by economists of economic transformation in the South and in the transition economies was unethical—*not* when judged by any particular political ideology or social ethics, but when judged by a yet-to-be delineated professional ethics. This is a very strong argument, and it is of course difficult to sustain. Why shouldn't we presume that had the field of professional economic ethics existed, it would not only have justified economists' involvement in the transformation but also dictated that economists use their influence to advance it? The indictment therefore must succeed in demonstrating that the way in which economists advocated market liberalization could not possibly meet the standards of professional ethics—not of any *particular* body of professional ethics that I might care to offer, but *of any imaginable, viable professional economic ethics*. This is what I propose to do. I will do this by showing that the ways in which the profession advocated market liberalization flouted the prudential and autonomy principles that are at the heart of professional ethics.

Though this is a very strong thesis, I will advance it only tentatively. There is no cause for embarrassment here: strong theses can be (and generally ought to be) advocated tentatively just as weaker theses can be advocated forcefully. I will offer a *prima facie* case that deserves to persuade only to the degree that an equally strong case cannot be put up against it. I ask that the case be read in this way because, as should by now be clear, the adjudication of questions pertaining to the ethics of economic conduct is terribly fraught. It requires sustained inquiry into abstract principles, concrete situations, and perhaps, personal character. A comprehensive examination of the conduct of the economics profession in the case at hand would entail a detailed study of what, precisely, economists advised; the constraints they faced; the terms in which they advocated for one course of action over another; and much else besides. I do not have the space here to provide the depth of analysis that this examination requires. We should expect that a vibrant body of professional ethics would comprise investigations of just this sort. The following discussion therefore represents an argument to be tested against subsequent ethical and empirical investigation rather than a conclusive proof of the thesis on offer.

The Maxi-Max Principle, Utopia, and Economic Practice

The case of market reform in the South and transition countries is one in which economists enjoyed substantial authority over those to whom they provided expertise (and those who would be affected by what they proposed).[2] Economists sought to take advantage of the intellectual influence and institutional power they enjoyed to induce developing- and transition-country policy makers to reorient their economies toward market direction of economic flows and outcomes. Historical conditions conspired to provide economists with a degree of influence that few other social scientists have ever enjoyed.

This is also a case where uncertainty and risk reached extraordinary levels. Economists typically advocated an abrupt, wall-to-wall transformation to market liberalization "as fast as possible." Paraphrasing Stanley Fischer, Peter Murrell summarizes the prescription as proceeding

> as fast as possible on macroeconomic stabilization, the liberalization of domestic trade and prices, current account convertibility, privatization, and the creation of a social safety net, while simultaneously creating the legal framework for a market economy (Murrell 1995, 164).

This summary statement reminds us that the project to achieve market liberalization was nothing short of a *revolution*—or, if one prefers, an *experiment*—one that sought to displace, all at once, deeply embedded social, economic, political, and cultural institutions and associated social norms in order to bring about goals that economists took to be desirable. The breadth, depth, and speed of the policy prescriptions were nothing short of staggering, with Russia privatizing over one-third of its industry in just 27 months (Murrell 1995, 174). How, then, could there *not* have been substantial uncertainty and risk?

A strong theoretical case for market liberalization can be found in the neoclassical economic thought that dominated the field of economic development during the 1980s and 1990s.[3] This case focuses on the manner in which market mediation generates economic efficiency owing to the incentive structure that it entails (World Bank 1995). This case is well known, and I will not rehearse it here. Instead, I want to draw attention to one aspect of the case for market reform that has been ignored by its proponents and its critics and that bears on professional ethics. It concerns the decision rule that economists implicitly adopted in advancing the reform. I want to suggest that the neoclassical case for a radical and abrupt transition to market liberalization was based implicitly on what libertarian Robert Nozick and others call the "maxi-max" principle.

The maxi-max principle is a decision rule. When confronting a set of available policy options, each with a probability distribution of potential payoffs, the maxi-max principle directs the decision maker to select the policy option that "has of its many possible consequences one which is better than any possible consequence of any other available action" (Nozick 1974, 298). Selection under this rule is driven entirely by a comparison of the best possible outcomes promised by each of the potential courses of action. This principle is extraordinarily aggressive since it considers just the one desideratum of maximum possible payoff in policy choice. It is, therefore, a thoroughly utopian decision rule. Maxi-max recognizes risk explicitly, since it characterizes each policy option as a probability distribution of payoffs. But it then dismisses the matter of risk entirely in policy selection.

Imagine a choice between investing $100 in a low-risk asset that promises a 2 percent return and investing the entire amount in tickets for a lottery that promises immense reward on the infinitesimally small chance that the investor hits the winning number. The maxi-max principle directs the investor to buy lottery tickets exclusively since, in the unlikely circumstance that the investor wins, he will be better off than had he invested in the safer alternative. Even in cases where the difference in potential payoffs among the options is small but the range of risks is great, maxi-max directs us to seek the highest possible return without attending to expected values or any other procedure that incorporates probabilities or risk.

Economists do not speak of maxi-max in their policy work; nor do leading textbooks explore the influence of maxi-max in economic reasoning. Yet I contend that this rule guided development policy in the cases before us. The Washington Consensus prescription was advanced on very simple grounds: that its potential payoff to the targeted societies was greater than that of any other regime, full stop. At its best, a liberalized market economy was taken to be superior to all other systems, also at their best (which, from the perspective of late-twentieth-century neoclassical thought, could not be very good). A liberalized market regime was taken to promise Pareto improvements over any alternative arrangement.

While the abrupt transformation from a state-led to a market-mediated economy was understood to generate harm to many agents in the short run, the ultimate gains yielded to the winners were expected to be more than adequate to compensate fully the losers while leaving net benefit. No other contending regime could promise this result.

The Evidence for Maxi-Max

What grounds might there be to conclude that the maxi-max decision rule guided economists' behavior when, in fact, no one spoke its name? Let us consider the kind of practitioners, work and rhetoric that one would expect to find in a field that embraces maxi-max. The field would be dominated by Adam Smith's "men of system" (see Chapter 1) who produce policy briefs that advocate unequivocally for a preferred course of action rather than explore its virtues and drawbacks in a systematic way. Their policy prescriptions would seek rigid fidelity to the field's abstract theoretical insights rather than pragmatic reform that entails compromise with these insights. The influence of maxi-max would also be reflected in a relative silence in policy advocacy about the myriad possible alternative strategies that are available at any given time and *a fortiori*, about the relative merits of each (such as their achievability in particular contexts). Hence, we would not expect to find in maxi-max advising a balanced assessment of the probability distributions of their possible payoffs (positive and negative) under any particular set of conditions nor a detailed examination of their respective robustness in the face of the unknown features of the environment in which they will be implemented. Next, while maxi-max warrants recognition and the amelioration of adjustment costs in the event of policy success, it does not call for rigorous attention to and planning for adjustment costs in the event of policy failure. Finally, a field committed to maxi-max would not be apt to give much consideration to the level of certainty that one can reasonably have regarding all of its salient aspects in advance of policy implementation. Instead, we would expect the field to generate partisan legal briefs that advocate the policy proposal that promises to maximize potential gains in terms that are meant to persuade rather than to investigate critically or elucidate candidly.

Other decision rules generally yield distinct policy choices. One type of "minimax" decision rule requires selection of the policy option that promises to minimize harm in the event of policy failure; another seeks policy that minimizes variance in a policy's effects (Brock, Durlauf and West 2007); and a third requires selection of that option that maximizes the benefit (or minimizes the harm) to those who are most disadvantaged (Rawls 1971). Another alternative is an "expected value" decision rule that weights the respective potential payoffs of contending policies by their probabilities and endorses the policy that scores best in these terms. In contrast, a "robustness" decision rule would search for and advocate the policy that has the greatest chance of positive payoffs under a wide range of possible background conditions, reflecting the recognition that background conditions are generally unknowable in sufficient depth in advance of policy implementation (see Chapter 11). All of these decision rules would direct us to buy bonds rather than lottery tickets, though in more complex cases they are apt to yield diverse decisions. These (and other) approaches can also be combined into more fully specified decision rules. For instance, the conjoining of robustness and the third minimax rule just described yields a decision rule that requires the search for a policy option that promises to maximize the benefit (or minimize the harm) to the most disadvantaged under the widest range of background conditions.[4]

Which, if any of these decision rules, was in evidence in the profession's advocacy of free-market reform in the South and the transition economies? A fair reading suggests the predominance of maxi-max decision making in the case before us. This was a period of tremendous confidence at the highest levels within the profession about its technical competence, the maturity of its science, its grasp of the complexities it confronted, and its ability to chart a pacific course from state-led to market-mediated economic affairs in the developing and transition economies.[5] Throughout this period, neoclassical economic theory was taken to provide the insights necessary to identify the best possible economic regime, while historical conditions (of crisis and transition) provided economists with the authority and institutional influence necessary to construct this regime in places where it was most badly needed. These forces combined to generate an uncompromising utopian spirit that believed in the kind of massive structural change that the Washington Consensus endorsed. In this context, there appeared to be little need or sufficient time to attend to questions of uncertainty or the robustness of alternative policy regimes. Instead, widespread fidelity to market liberalization bred a suspicion of those advocating a more prudent or gradual approach to economic transition. In Ravi Kanbur's words, "'Give them an inch of nuance, and they will take a mile of protection,' seemed to be the mindset and stance" of the reformers (Kanbur 2009b, 4). The opportunities that economists faced were historic but also fleeting, and the exigencies of the situation were dire. Together, these circumstances induced the promotion of structural reform on a grand scale. The general presumption in the profession was that radical reform would succeed, and that in success it would promote a far higher level of social welfare than any other contending type of reform.

Maxi-max is revealed in the scholarship produced by the most influential academic economists during the 1980s and 1990s about economic reform in the developing and transition economies. The essays compiled in the two-volume collection edited by Olivier Blanchard, Kenneth Froot, and Jeffrey Sachs (1994) are emblematic. They provide insight into the thinking of the leading figures in economic development regarding the strategies necessary for successful transition away from state direction of economic affairs. The volumes include essays by the editors and other luminaries such as Stanley Fischer, Lawrence Summers, Andrei Shleifer, Rudiger Dornbusch, Simon Johnson and many others. One might expect to find here substantial disagreement among the contributors about the challenges represented by the transition economies, the policy approaches that are best suited to address them, and about the preparedness of the economics profession to intervene effectively in this uncertain environment. Given the imponderables of transformation on the scale contemplated, one might also expect to find substantial hand wringing about the risks associated with structural reform, the likely consequences that will befall the inhabitants of these countries in the event of failure, and the measures necessary in advance of the reform to insulate these inhabitants from ensuing trauma. But what one finds instead is an extraordinary degree of confidence in the consensus view about the required reforms. "At the center of this consensus," Peter Murrell argues in his extensive investigation of these papers, "is a confidence in the ability of economic technocrats to design feasible, if painful, solutions to the central problems of reform" (Murrell 1995, 164).

By the early 1990s, severe strains in several transition economies (along with much of Latin America and Africa) were visible, and it was apparent that economists had substantially underestimated these effects (UNICEF 1993; Calvo and Coricelli 1993; Eberstadt 1994; Murrell 1995; see also Stuckler, King and McKee 2009). Rather than reflect on possible mistakes in the presumptions that were guiding economic policy interventions, however, the papers reveal a tendency to blame others. "To the extent that failures are perceived and autopsies performed, the diagnosis usually centers on the political sphere . . . Sometimes socio-political systems simply get in the way of sensible economics" (Murrell 1995, 164). A decade later, leading economists continued to advance this explanation for failure. Discussing the failures of the privatization process in Russia, Sachs (2005, 147) argues that "Most of the bad things that happened—such as the massive theft of state assets under the rubric of privatization—were directly contrary to the advice that I gave and to the principles of honesty and equity that I hold dear."

For Murrell, the papers in these volumes largely suffer from a set of methodological and normative problems, one of which is of particular relevance. Most of these economists fall prey to the tendency to conceptualize the country they investigate and advise as a *tabula rasa* that is available to the technocrat for design according to the precepts of the theory he carries with him (cf. Hirschman 1980). Perhaps above all, the commitment to maxi-max is revealed in the utopian spirit of these economic revolutionaries. In Murrell's words,

> [T]he standard reform prescription . . . begins at the endpoint, an idealized market, phrasing everything in those terms, ignoring the crucial question of how reforms engage existing society. The project of the economist is to

grasp the tabula rasa and design a new system, to match events against the yardstick of that design, and to diagnose as failures any deviations from design (Murrell 1995, 177).

Others have identified the technocratic impulse in evidence here with the modernism that informs mainstream and also many heterodox approaches to economics. Drawing on James Scott's *Seeing Like a State*, Suzanne Bergeron argues that though economic reform efforts are driven by the "best of intentions," they are "frequently overshadowed by what Scott calls an ideology of high modernism: 'envisioning a sweeping, rational engineering of all aspects of social life in order to improve the human condition'" (Bergeron 2006, 31). For Bergeron and other critics, economists' utopian projects represent the outcome of a growing presumption throughout the twentieth century that economists have sufficient expertise to manage economic affairs. That some aspire to do so through an activist state that pursued socialist planning or Keynesian managerialism while others insist upon market-mediated restructuring is peripheral to the shared presumption among economists that the economist could "make legible" and therefore assert control over economic affairs. Time and again, this overconfidence seduced the profession into the overreaching associated with utopianism, which brought in its train consequential error and harm.[6]

John McMillan views the interventions in Russia in complementary terms. He draws usefully on Karl Popper's distinction between two kinds of reform—"utopian" and "piecemeal" social engineering. The former involves working off "a grand blueprint for society: 'it pursues its aim consciously and consistently,' 'it determines its means according to its end,' and entails searching for, and fighting for, its greatest ultimate good." Popper was deeply distrustful of such initiatives, of course, as was Adam Smith before him (see Chapter 1). In contrast, Popper endorsed "piecemeal social engineering" which entails "tinkering with parts of the system"; it involves "searching for, and fighting against, the greatest and most urgent evils of society" (McMillan 2008, 510–11).[7] McMillan concludes that the Russian shock therapy as envisioned and advanced by Sachs and others—which Sachs himself described as "a rapid, comprehensive and far-reaching program of reforms to implement 'normal' capitalism" (cited in McMillan 2008, 511)—was deeply consistent with Popper's utopian model of social engineering. Unfortunately, "The consequences of Russia's shock therapy corroborated Popper's dismissal of grandiose schemes" (MacMillan 2008, 511). In contrast, MacMillan argues that China pursued a somewhat more pragmatic, piecemeal approach to reform from the 1980s onward that generated successes without the extent of social dislocation experienced by Russia.

Given the strength of the consensus among prominent academic economists, many of whom played significant roles in shaping transition policies through their work for government, consulting firms, and think tanks, it is hardly surprising that applied economists, likewise, advocated market liberalization on terms consistent with the maxi-max principle. Through the 1980s and 1990s, the IFIs advanced the case for radical market reform in the South and transition economies with purpose and urgency on grounds that these reforms were the best avenue available to promote social welfare. While the IFIs paid some attention to the need to ameliorate the adjustment costs associated with economic transformation, the overriding presumption guiding these institutions was an unwavering belief in the efficacy and ultimate success of the prescription. No other regime could promise the efficiency and ultimate prosperity of the liberalized market economy. The IFIs went to great lengths to project the message; far less effort was made to convey the caveat that the promise of the reforms depended vitally on the assumption that they would in fact succeed.[8]

Recognition of the attachment to maxi-max helps us to understand how technically adept economists could fail to anticipate their inability to control political processes upon which the reform efforts depended. For instance, Anders Åslund attributed the failure of Russian privatization to "extraordinary rent-seeking" rather than any defect in the plan he had helped to devise (Angner 2006), while as we noted above, Sachs (2005) attributes this failure to the fact that Russian officials took actions that flatly contradicted his advice. Sachs also blames the suffering associated with the adjustment costs of structural adjustment in the former Soviet Union on the unwillingness of the Bush Administration to heed his calls for assistance (in the form of debt cancellation and emergency loans; see Pilkington 4/5/2008).

There may be some truth to Åslund and Sachs's interpretations regarding what went wrong, of course. What is so disconcerting, however, is the extraordinary naïveté with which they and other influential economists approached their work—a naïveté which was reflected in their failure to anticipate just how fraught and imperfect would be the privatization processes in which they so eagerly involved themselves and the consequent ways in which things could go so badly. In place of a balanced assessment of the imperfections of the political contexts in which they worked, leading economists succumbed to the temptations of utopianism, as presciently described by Robert Nozick:

> [U]topians assume that the particular society they describe will operate without certain problems arising, that social mechanisms and institutions will function as they predict, and that people will not act from certain motives and interests. They blandly ignore certain obvious problems that anyone with any experience of the world would be struck by or make the most wildly optimistic assumptions about how these problems will be avoided or surmounted (Nozick 1974, 328–39).

The Ethical Illegitimacy of Maxi-Max

The claim that market liberalization at its best promises far more than any alternative regime, also considered at its best, is deeply contested. Its validity depends first and foremost on the choice of the normative metric used to make the assessment but also on a wide range of other theoretical and empirical choices that are brought into the evaluation. The claim has been disputed within and beyond economics for the better part of three decades (see DeMartino 2000), and by now, some former proponents have begun to express doubt. But the point I am advancing here is rather different: it is that the defense given of the abrupt transition to a liberalized market economy depended on the presumption that it would, in fact, succeed. It is a defense that ignored the inherent risk of economic policy making, and the limits to economists' control. Partly as a consequence, it also ignored the potential harm that would attend policy failure. All of this is consistent with the maxi-max decision rule which does not treat the possibility of policy failure as a salient feature of policy choice. It need not factor in the well-being of those who suffer the consequences of its failure because under this decision rule, that information is irrelevant.

A maxi-max decision rule makes for inept policy making, to be sure. It is a decision rule that is apt to yield avoidable, damaging failures. Nozick (1974, 298) reports that

> Everyone who has considered the matter agrees that the maxi-max principle . . . is an insufficiently prudent principle which one would be silly to use in designing institutions. Any society whose institutions are infused by such wild optimism is headed for a fall or, at any rate, the high risk of one makes the society too dangerous to choose to live in.

Maxi-max yields an attitude to policy making that is hubristic and ideological rather than humble and pragmatic. But is its application by professionals *unethical?* Indeed it is. The maxi-max principle is entirely inconsistent with the two principles that we found earlier to be central to professional ethics: the prudential principle that directs the professional to avoid harm and the autonomy principle that requires the professional to respect the agency, integrity, and self-governance of those whom the professional targets for assistance.

Maxi-max could not be more distant from the ethical imperative of professionals to take care to avoid preventable harm to those they serve. Especially in cases that involve complex and novel interventions—where outcomes cannot be known in advance with any degree of certainty—maxi-max imposes extraordinary risk on the targeted community on grounds that *if* the experimental intervention is successful, the community will be better off than it would be under any other possible intervention. Maxi-max does not consider how much worse off the community would be under any other available intervention. It does not consider whether, in the event of failure, the community would fare better under an alternative. It is a rule that promotes the pursuit of perfection at the expense of the good, even if perfection is hardly attainable and if the costs of failure in its pursuit are grave. As economists know better than anyone, maximum reward generally requires maximum risk. Yet in their embrace of maxi-max the profession did not hesitate to impose such risks—even on extraordinarily vulnerable communities.

Matters are worse still for maxi-max, however. The principle also runs afoul of the imperative to respect the autonomy of those whom the professional serves. It ignores the ethical imperative to respect the right of self-determination. It explicitly does not call for "prior informed consent"; indeed, under this principle the views of those affected by policy are irrelevant. In the cases before us, the economists advocating market reform pursued this utopian ideal even when many of the intended beneficiaries were committed to alternative economic arrangements. Indeed, the greater was the opposition of a country's inhabitants and/or political leaders to market liberalization, the greater was the pressure that was brought to bear by the profession to secure it (Stiglitz 2002).

Maxi-max authorizes the professional to insist on a particular intervention over and against any opposition. Maxi-max eliminates the need to ask of those targeted by an intervention whether they would prefer a more cautious approach. It presumes that those receiving professional assistance would always want to take a chance at being as well off as possible—that they would always prefer buying lottery tickets rather than take safer bets buying bonds—or that they *should* want to take this chance, if in the event, they (irrationally) do not. What we find here, at best, is unvarnished paternalism of a sort that is deeply contested today within many bodies of professional ethics. Absent entirely is the respect for autonomy and integrity of the community that the economist targets in her work. We see this violation most obviously in cases where economists have advised authoritarian governments, where there is no opportunity for citizens to give informed consent to economic reform. But we find it also in the transition economies where, as we have seen, economists pressed nominally democratic governments to pursue the economic revolution as fast as possible, *before* citizens and interest groups could mobilize to influence economic affairs (see Chapter 1). Such disregard for public participation—for the integrity and autonomy of those whose lives are affected by economic reform—could only be justified on grounds that the economists knew best and that they were licensed to follow a maxi-max decision rule in their work.

The foregoing ought to give us pause as we consider the conduct of the economics profession in advancing the Washington Consensus. I submit that the profession's interventions were driven by an implicit embrace of a maxi-max decision rule. I offer the thesis that the conduct of the profession was unethical when judged by the standards of any viable professional ethics. The profession flouted two of the most important principles that have achieved standing across the professions: the imperative to avoid harm and the imperative to respect the autonomy and integrity of those the professional serves. I should add here that while professional ethics varies across the professions in many ways, no profession endorses anything like the maxi-max principle. Indeed, it is hard to imagine how any profession with a well-defined body of professional ethics possibly could.

Reverse Discounting

One further point warrants our attention in connection with the utopianism of the market liberalization project. Economists are familiar with the thorny ethical problem of the intergenerational distribution of burdens. Economic theory and practice calls for discounting the future in order to make economic values comparable over time. Among other things, this allows economics to undertake benefit-cost analysis of projects with enduring effects. Economists understand that the selection of a discount rate is terribly consequential since the larger the discount rate, the greater is the privileging of the interests of the present generation over those of the future (Dorfman 1993).

In the cases we are considering here, however, economists imposed a *negative* discount rate without attending to the enormous ethical questions that this practice raises. Economists advocated policies that imposed substantial costs on those living in the present for the purported benefit of those who would inhabit the future. In the event these costs included widespread depression of living standards, substantial increases in morbidity and mortality rates and reductions in life expectancy, deterioration in child care and increases in juvenile crime rates and alcohol abuse in several countries that were subjected to radical economic reform (UNICEF 1993; Angner 2006; Stuckler, King and McKee 2009).[9]

Reverse discounting is a common feature of utopian projects, but it has no place in professional ethics. Utopians are often prepared to impose severe hardship and cash in the lives of those who presumably cannot be saved today for the benefit of those who will populate an ideal social arrangement in the future. "Utopia is where our grandchildren are to live," quips Nozick (1974, 298). Utilitarianism also allows for the trading off of lives (though not negative discounting). In the words of a leading advocate of utilitarianism:

> If it were known to be true, as a question of fact, that measures that cause misery and death to tens of millions today *would* result in saving from greater misery or death hundreds of millions in the future, and if this were the only way in which it could be done, then it *would* be right to cause these necessary atrocities (J.J.C. Smart 1973, 63; emphasis in original).[10]

The influence of utilitarianism in mainstream economics may help to explain why economists who were involved in the transition were prone to accept a calculus that involved the trading off of lives. Or Robert

Nelson (2003) might be correct in arguing that the tendency of economists to overlook extreme short-run costs reflects the abiding theological roots of economics, which place exclusive emphasis on the achievement of "heaven on earth" in the long run (see also Kanbur 2001). In contrast, rights-based approaches to social ethics that privilege the autonomy and integrity of human agents object strenuously to the simplistic counting and trading off of lives that utopian and utilitarian thought embraces. Rights-based perspectives insist that the decision whether to impose sacrifices on the present generation for the benefit of future generations must be authorized by the present generation—not imposed upon it by experts who are driven by a maxi-max or utilitarian decision rule. This is the fatal flaw in arguments that defend the extraordinary suffering imposed on inhabitants of developing and transition countries in the 1980s and 1990s by reference to the level of per capita income or growth in those countries today. Respect for the rights of those whom economists serve allows for that kind of calculus only by those who will endure the suffering—not by the economic advisor who consults models that place exclusive value on the long run and in so doing, discounts actual lives today for the promise of a better tomorrow.

CONCLUSION

I will simply restate my thesis here. The advancement of radical economic restructuring across the developing world and the transition countries by economists with the authority to engineer it was unethical—not by the standards associated with any particular social ethics but by the standards associated with a yet-to-be crafted professional ethics. This would have been true even if market liberalization were to exhibit all the virtues attributed to it by neoclassical thought and to promise higher potential rewards than any other possible regime. Its advocacy by economists was unethical because it reflected a decision rule that is entirely inappropriate. Whenever the outcome of any professional intervention is unknowable in advance, great weight must be given to the prudential principle. Moreover, whenever professionals are in a position to alter the life chances of others, they must respect the autonomy of those whom they will affect—not least by securing their prior informed consent. But in the instant case, economists employed a maxi-max decision rule: one that conflicts directly with the prudential principle and dismisses the autonomy of those they hoped to serve.

It must be emphasized that it is certainly possible that economists who viewed market liberalization as desirable for the developing and transition countries could have advocated such reform in entirely appropriate ways. Professional ethics does not dictate to the economist whether she should embrace market- or state-mediation of economic affairs (or any particular balance between the two). It does not require of us that we all become libertarians or socialists, clear-eyed Republicans, or warm-hearted Democrats. It addresses instead the manner in which the economist conducts herself as she does her theoretical and applied work. It addresses her relationship to her work, her profession, and those she serves.

Notes

1 In this book, I have concentrated on the role of professional ethics in ensuring that virtuous people do good work; I have therefore avoided consideration of the role of professional ethics in policing professions to ensure against illegal or patently unethical behavior. In keeping with that focus, I will not explore here the scandal involving Andre Shleifer at the Harvard Institute of International Development, which led to legal action by the U.S. government against Shleifer (for conspiracy to defraud the U.S. government) and the Institute (for breach of contract). The defendants paid over $30 million to settle the suit, and Shleifer was fired from the Institute (though not from the University). In the wake of this scandal, Harvard closed the Institute (McClintick 2006). What is notable about the case for present purposes is not that an economist was accused of wrongdoing, but that the profession provides no forum for examining the particulars of the case. From the perspective of the ethical obligations of the profession, the case marks a lost opportunity to advance the ethical sensibilities of its members. It leaves the impression that if Shleifer did in fact act unethically, this was simply a matter of personal failure and therefore of no relevance to the profession.

2 In treating all the instances of market liberalization as one case, I am of course taking liberties that would not be permitted in a comprehensive ethical examination. One can imagine and hope for comparative studies in the years ahead that explore the case of each country's reforms separately, to see what can be learned about how distinct economists comported themselves under similar conditions. Ascertaining what is ethical economic professional practice stands to benefit as much from detailed studies of concrete events as it does from consideration of first principles.

3 Economics had begun to evolve away from the neoclassical orthodoxy by no later than the 1990s, due to the proliferation of new methods and theoretical insights (Coyle 2007). But in the case before us, policy was driven by un-reconstituted neoclassical thinking about human rationality and the efficiency of market dynamics. We return to this theme in the next chapter.

4 This discussion of decision rules should not be taken to imply that rational or ethical advising (or decision making) needs or should follow rules. Decision making can eschew decision rules entirely and embrace inelegant procedures for adjudicating policy on a case-by-case basis.

5 Among prominent mainstream economists, Dani Rodrik and Richard Freeman represent important exceptions to the rule. According to Freeman, ". . . economics does not have sufficiently compelling theory or empirical knowledge to answer questions about the institutional design of advanced capitalist economies, much less economies in transition" (cited in Murrell 1995, 164).

6 Of the various heterodox economic traditions that challenge the epistemic claims and managerialism of mainstream theory, one deserves particular mention. Over the past two decades, a poststructuralist approach to political economy has begun to emerge. Advocates of this approach view economic theory as an intervention in the world with material effects that bear on economic relations, processes,

and outcomes rather than a neutral mapping of the economy. Poststructuralist political economy is by now extraordinarily diverse and can be found among feminist, Austrian, and Marxian schools of thought. Besides the work of Bergeron (cited in the text), see Resnick and Wolff (1987); Gibson-Graham (1996); Ruccio and Amariglio (2003); and Burczak (2006).

7 Hayek's distinction between "taxis" and "cosmos" is similar to the one that Popper draws here. As Ted Burczak explains,

> A taxis is a constructed order, rationally designed to serve a particular purpose. . . A cosmos, in contrast, is an evolved or 'grown' order. A cosmos forms spontaneously, not as a result of human intention. . . According to Hayek, one of the fatal conceits of modern social thought is the tendency to treat a cosmos as if it were a taxis (Burczak 2006, 40–41).

8 What evidence would suffice to contradict my claim that economic prescription in these cases was informed by the maxi-max decision rule? Disconfirming evidence would include sustained attention in academic and applied work (including especially the public reports and policy briefs of the IFIs and leading consulting firms and think tanks) to the uncertainties attending reform and to various alternative policy strategies combined with comparisons of their respective risks and robustness in concrete cases under a wide range of background conditions, etc. In my review of relevant reports, policy briefs, and public statements by leading economists, I have found little attention to these matters. Rather, one finds emphasis placed on the promised payoff from proposed policies, often combined with the claim that no alternatives to Washington Consensus reform exists for developing and transition countries. Throughout the period, for instance, IMF officials argued consistently for the urgent adoption of market discipline on grounds that no other course of action was possible for developing countries.

Two representative examples will have to suffice here. Speaking in the wake of the Mexican financial crisis in October of 1995, IMF Managing Director Michel Camdessus argued that "*As is well understood* in Latin America, the countries of the region *have no choice* but to maintain their access to international capital markets if they are to achieve their potential for economic growth and development in the period ahead" (emphasis added; http://www.imf.org/external/np/sec/mds/1995/mds9513.htm). Referring to proposed IMF policies in a speech given during the East Asian financial crisis in 1998, IMF Deputy Managing Director Stanley Fischer said, "What these programs promote is things that many years, *many centuries of experience* suggest are necessary for an economy to operate well" (emphasis added; http://www.imf.org/external/np/tr/1998/tr981029.htm). The italicized text is important: in both cases it serves to suggest the certainty of the policy prescriptions on offer and to forestall debate about alternative policy strategies. This rhetorical strategy is employed consistently by academic and applied development economists throughout the period, even as they grappled with unique and challenging historical events upon which, contrary to Fischer's claim, previous centuries of experience shed virtually no light.

I do not mean to suggest through this discussion that individual economists have not attended to matters such as policy robustness and the risks of policy failure in their work (see Chapter 11). I am suggesting, instead, that the fact that such work did not predominate in the theoretical and applied work that influenced the comprehensive, systemic reform that we are discussing here reveals the depth of the attachment of the field of economics to the maxi-max decision rule.

9 Not that all reformers accept that these outcomes were linked to market liberalization. In reply to critics, Jeffrey Sachs argues that the reform programs were successful but that the social and demographic deterioration cited in the text resulted instead from missteps in social policy (such as the abandonment of an antidrinking campaign in Russia) and bad diet (Ahuja 2009). In response, Ahuja (2009) replies, "short of adulteration with poison, diet cannot explain sudden shifts in death rates." In the face of mounting evidence on the impact of privatization on mortality (Stuckler, King and McKee 2009), Sachs continues to claim that the link between privatization and deaths in these countries is "zero." See also Sachs (2005) for a defense of his reform efforts in Poland and Russia.

10 Though, to his credit, Smart immediately qualifies the argument by encouraging prudence of those who would pursue utopian schemes: "one would have to be *very sure* that future generations would be saved still greater misery before one embarked on such a tyrannical programme. One thing we should know about the future is that large-scale predictions are impossible" (Smart 1973, 64)—an epistemic point that economists, especially in the developing world context, have often forgotten. I should emphasize that the failure of economics to give full consideration to short-run adjustment costs is a consequence of its utopianism, not its utilitarianism, since utilitarianism requires a full accounting of all effects of interventions—short and long term.

Chapter 10

Global Economic Crisis and the Crisis in Economics

As I see it, the economics profession went astray because economists, as a group, mistook beauty, clad in impressive-looking mathematics, for truth . . . the central cause of the profession's failure was the desire for an all-encompassing, intellectually elegant approach that also gave economists a chance to show off their mathematical prowess.

Paul Krugman (Sept. 6, 2009, 37)

This mania was the product not only of a story about people but also a story about how the economy worked. It was part of a story that all investments in securitised mortgages were safe because those smart people were buying them . . . To a remarkable extent we have got into the current economic and financial crisis because of a wrong economic theory—an economic theory that itself denied the role of the animal spirits in getting us into manias and panics.

Robert Shiller (May 12, 2009, 16)

The global economic crisis that began to unfold during the summer of 2007 with the emergence of difficulties in the subprime mortgage market and that spread rapidly in late 2008 has brought unwanted attention to the economics profession. The crisis has encouraged economists to scrutinize their profession's behavior in the decades preceding the crisis. In this critical examination, they've been joined by Wall Street insiders and economic journalists who often accord economic titans inordinate respect. The list of critics includes Nobel Laureates Joseph Stiglitz, Paul Krugman, and Paul Samuelson along with Robert Shiller, Simon Johnson, Dean Baker, Barry Eichengreen, James Galbraith, and many others. By and large, prominent economists including those whose jobs entailed anticipating and heading off economic instability were caught off guard by the crisis. Critics allege that the profession is implicated deeply in the crisis through its stubborn advocacy of theoretical models that discount entirely the possibility of financial turbulence. The mainstream of the profession worried far too little about the behavior of actors in real markets and the diverse ways that deregulated asset markets could spin out of control. Few recognized that lending practices were imprudent and that the consequent escalation in home prices in the United States might be unsustainable. Even worse, armed with the insights of orthodox neoclassical theory, leading economists used their authority to staunch government oversight or regulation of the myriad new financial assets that proliferated during and since the 1990s, which few people within or outside of financial markets understood. They believed naively that markets would do what government regulation could not—impose discipline on market actors without interfering with the economic efficiency that financial innovation would promote.

The discussion here of the culpability of the economics profession in the global financial crisis will be brief since its advocacy of financial deregulation in advanced economies which contributed to the crisis was of a piece (theoretically and politically) with the market liberalization project in the South and transition economies considered in the previous chapter. Relatedly, the ethical failures of the economics profession in the two cases are similar. In both contexts, the profession exhibited excessive confidence in its expertise, which led it to embrace the utopian maxi-max decision rule in circumstances where doing so was far too dangerous. In the instant case, leading economists advocated unequivocally for government permissiveness in response to the dynamic situation in financial markets without giving serious attention to the range of alternatives that might have promised lower rewards but at much lower risk. The deregulation prescription was derived from a simplistic body of theory that abstracted too readily from the complexities of human behavior and the consequent dynamics of liberalized asset markets. Moreover, the profession continued to apply this theory even while some economists were discovering, through experimental techniques and historical analysis, that asset market participants do not act in accordance with the tenets of neoclassical theory and that developed, highly liquid markets can spawn bubbles and crashes. Economists ignored these insights and so did not attend to the risks associated with their policy prescriptions, the costs to diverse groups were the prescriptions to fail, and the ways that governments across the globe could and should prepare for these failures. Instead, they advocated for their "one big idea" (Tetlock 2005) without regard to the potential effects of this adventurism.

FINANCIAL LIBERALIZATION AND MAXI-MAX

From the 1980s onward, mainstream financial economists pressed for financial liberalization in the global South and in the developed economies (Grabel 1996). This prescription involved privatization and deregulation within the financial sector, removal of capital controls, an increase in permissible leveraging, and increasing dependence on banks to assess their own riskiness, etc. (Johnson 2009). In the context of the United States, financial liberalization involved rescinding long-standing restrictions on financial institutions that were intended to prevent conflicts of interest and systemic risk. For instance, the repeal of the Glass-Steagall Act in 1999, at the urging of leading economists, eliminated the firewalls that had historically separated commercial from investment banking. The institutional interlinkages and financial innovations that followed outstripped the regulatory apparatuses that were in place to police them.

Economists not only pressed for the removal of existing financial regulation but also resisted new government oversight of the financial assets and market contracts that proliferated from the 1990s onward. In the face of concern by members of the U.S. Congress regarding subprime and collateralized lending practices and other financial innovations, Federal Reserve Chair Alan Greenspan consistently reassured policy makers and the public about the sufficiency of market mediation to discipline financial markets. In 1998, Greenspan blocked the efforts of Brooksley E. Born, head of the Commodity Futures Trading Commission (CFTC), to regulate derivatives markets. Having succeeded in that battle, Greenspan then pushed Congress to "strip the C.F.T.C. of regulatory authority over derivatives" (Goodman 2008). During the Clinton Administration, he found an ally in Treasury Secretary Lawrence Summers who used his influence in the White House to oppose financial regulation. These economists believed that the new assets shifted risk to those agents most willing and best able to bear it; that on balance, financial innovation which allowed for extensive and sophisticated hedging strategies served to make financial markets more complete, robust, and safe; and that most steps by the government to stiffen financial regulation would cause harm to the economy while failing to reduce risk. While financial activity became more complex, Greenspan became ever more confident. In 2004, he argued that "Not only have individual financial institutions become less vulnerable to shocks from underlying risk factors, but also the financial system as a whole has become more resilient" (Greenspan Oct. 5, 2004).

Greenspan's faith in the market stemmed in large measure from his conception of the ways in which market mediation generates the trustworthy behavior upon which it depends. Referring nostalgically to an earlier period in U.S. history, when government intervened far less in economic affairs, Greenspan (May 15, 2005) said:

> Trust as the necessary condition for commerce was particularly evident in freewheeling nineteenth-century America, where reputation became a valued asset. Throughout much of that century, laissez-faire reigned in the United States as elsewhere, and *caveat emptor* was the prevailing prescription for guarding against wide-open trading practices. In such an environment, a reputation for honest dealing, which many feared was in short supply, was particularly valued. Even those inclined to be less than scrupulous in their personal dealings had to adhere to a more ethical standard in their market transactions, or they risked being driven out of business.

In this cosmology, burdensome government intervention is unwise not just because it stifles economic innovation but also because it undermines trust among market actors by diminishing the return to reputation (see Zak 2008). It is also unnecessary not only because the market induces ethical behavior even from rogues, but also because market actors face a disciplining mechanism far wiser, more compelling, and more efficient than that provided by any government regulators.

In the case for financial deregulation, just as in the case for market liberalization in the South and transition economies, the utopian maxi-max principle guided prominent economists on one of the most important policy matters of the day. Greenspan resisted government regulation on the grounds that liberalized financial markets promised greater rewards than any alternative regime. Greenspan's mastery of the art of equivocation before Congressional hearings was legendary. He routinely strung together meaningful sounding phrases while giving away nothing of value to his interrogators. But on the question of financial regulation, he was a model of lucidity. Greenspan's unequivocal advocacy of financial liberalization gave the impression that this was a no-brainer—that it would be foolish to forego the free lunch that legislative reticence promised. In his view, no other policy regime could yield the benefits that would flow from financial liberalization, there was little doubt that these benefits would indeed materialize, and the policy entailed little appreciable risk to the economy. There was simply no need to consider other options, their respective risk profiles, or the damage that each would induce in the event of its failure. In possession of an available first-best policy option that was fully expected to succeed, all of that seemed beside the point.

THE ALLURE OF THEORETICAL ELEGANCE

Up until the crisis, Greenspan was regarded widely as among the most successful Chairs of the Federal Reserve in U.S. history. For many, he exhibited an uncanny ability to read economic trends and to devise interventions that kept the economy on track over an extended period of time. His success stemmed in part from his refusal to commit to any particular monetary (or other) rule in conducting bank affairs (Andrews 2005; Mankiw 2006). Instead, he was renowned for gathering relevant data from all promising sources and factoring diverse kinds of information into nuanced judgments about the state of the economy and monetary policy. But in the matter of financial regulation, he broke with the pragmatism that marked his leadership of the Federal Reserve to stake out a position that was extraordinarily rigid and doctrinaire. In this matter, his thinking was very much in line with mainstream economic thought, which advocated the efficient market hypothesis (EMH) with striking unanimity despite the recurrence of economic events that should have called that hypothesis into question.

Paul Krugman has been particularly caustic in his assessment of the profession's failures leading up to the crisis. In a cover essay in the *New York Times Sunday Magazine* (Sept. 6, 2010), he blames the profession's fascination with theoretical elegance as the chief cause of its attachment to theoretical constructs that distort rather than elucidate economic events. The EMH, in particular, seduced mainstream financial and macroeconomists over the past several decades. According to the EMH, the market price of an asset at any moment reflects correctly all existing available information regarding its underlying fundamentals. From this perspective, asset price volatility is explained by reference to the arrival of new information that bears on these underlying fundamentals. If some market traders are irrational and fail to value assets properly, the market as a whole will correct for any temporary price distortions that result from irrational investing. Indeed, the presence of irrational investors creates arbitrage opportunities for others—and it is this opportunity to profit from others' mistakes that ensures that the market as whole will arrive at the correct asset price.

The policy implications of the EMH are clear. If the liberalized market discovers the correct price of assets on its own, there is no basis for government to restrict the creation of new assets or regulate their exchange. No matter how complex financial assets become, the market will divine their correct price and risk profile owing to the incentive that market actors have in getting it right.[1] Hence Ben Bernanke could claim as late as 2006 that

> The management of market risk and credit risk has become increasingly sophisticated . . . Banking organizations of all sizes have made substantial strides over the past two decades in their ability to measure and manage risk (Bernanke June 12, 2006).

A consequence of this reasoning is the expectation that asset markets (if not the prices of individual assets) will remain stable over time, in part because new information that bears negatively on one asset might have a negligible or an offsetting effect on other assets. Government regulation that interferes with market price formation can only induce the financial fragility and instability that the regulation is intended to prevent.

The EMH came to inform not just neoclassical financial and macroeconomic theory but also New Keynesian thought. By the 1980s, the New Keynesians had devised micro-founded macro models that took account of price stickiness, asymmetric information, and other market imperfections—and on this basis could justify fiscal and monetary policy to ensure good macroeconomic performance. But their models did not account for systemic financial market instability. We find little attention in New Keynesian theory to asset market bubbles or systemic financial crisis. In Krugman's view, such disturbances were off the economists' radar, owing to the professional fascination with theoretical elegance and parsimony that led the mainstream in the profession to look past the recurring financial crises of the past two decades when crafting their explanatory models. Even in that branch of mainstream macroeconomics that we should have expected to emphasize serious macroeconomic instability—a school of thought derived from the work of Keynes and that bears his name—we find inattention to one of the most important and dangerous features of a capitalist economy (cf. Skousen 2006). In the view of Willem Buiter, former Chief Economist of the European Bank for Reconstruction and Development, these developments "have set back by decades serious investigations of aggregate economic behaviour and economic policy-relevant understanding"; as a consequence, most "'state of the art' academic monetary economics" is, in his view, "useless" (Buiter 2009).

In their advocacy of financial liberalization, then, Greenspan, Summers, Bernanke, and other leading economists were simply giving voice to a general consensus that had long prevailed among mainstream financial and macroeconomists. With the resurgence of neoclassical orthodoxy during the 1970s, Keynesian insights about the potential volatility of unregulated financial markets had been put aside by the profession's most prominent members. As Krugman explains, "A general belief that bubbles just don't happen" had swept the profession, including its New Keynesian wing that had "come to dominate teaching and research." He continues:

> By 1970 or so . . . the study of financial markets seemed to have been taken over by Voltaire's Dr. Pangloss, who insisted that we live in the best of all possible worlds. Discussion of investor irrationality, of bubbles, of destructive speculation had virtually disappeared from academic discourse (Krugman Sept. 6, 2009).[2]

For Buiter, the problem with these misguided models was not just that they "did not allow questions about insolvency and illiquidity to be answered. They did not allow such questions to be asked" (Buiter March 3, 2009; see also Stiglitz 2009a, 2009b, 2009c).

The consensus view on the virtues of financial market self-regulation informed the policy stance of Ben Bernanke, once he took over as Chair of the Federal Reserve—just as it had his predecessor. In the years immediately preceding the crisis, Bernanke worried much more about the instabilities that might arise from the behavior of Freddie Mac and Fannie Mac, owing to their status as government sponsored enterprises (GSEs), than he did about disruptions emanating from unregulated financial institutions. In February 2006 testimony before the Congressional Committee on Financial Services, Bernanke spoke of the need for tighter regulation of the GSEs: ". . . the portfolios of the GSEs are much larger than can be justified in terms of their fundamental housing mission. And these large portfolios represent a risk to financial stability" (Bernanke Feb. 15, 2006). But Bernanke adopted a complacent stance when discussing other financial institutions. In May of 2006, he spoke of the virtues of "financial innovation and improved risk management," including "securitization, improved hedging instruments and strategies, more liquid markets, greater risk-based pricing, and the data collection and management systems needed to implement such innovations." While recognizing risks associated with financial innovation, he argued that

> these developments, on net, have provided significant benefits. Borrowers have more choices and greater access to credit; lenders and investors are better able to measure and manage risk; and, because of the dispersion of financial risks to those more willing and able to bear them, *the economy and financial system are more resilient* (Bernanke May18, 2006; emphasis added).

In July of 2006, Bernanke wrote: "Today, retail lending has become more routinized as banks have become increasingly adept at predicting default risk by applying statistical models to data, such as credit scores" (Bernanke June 12, 2006).[3] In response to a question about whether there was need for increased regulation of hedge funds, Bernanke told Congress on July 20, 2006 that

> the best way to achieve good oversight of hedge funds is through market discipline, through the counterparties, through the investors . . . at this point I think that the market discipline has shown its capability of keeping hedge funds well disciplined . . .

The confidence of the profession in this period reached levels not seen since the heyday of the neoclassical Keynesian synthesis of the postwar era. By the late 1980s, a "great moderation" in macroeconomic fluctuations had set in, and the profession had come to believe (yet again) that it had acquired the expertise necessary to guide the economy on a steady path of economic growth. Speaking of the lessons learned over the previous decades, Christina Romer argued in 2007:

> We have seen the triumph of sensible ideas and have reaped the rewards in terms of macroeconomic performance. . .The costly wrong turn in ideas and macropolicy of the 1960s and 1970s has been righted, and the future of stabilization looks bright (cited in Postrel 2009).

Under these conditions, those who continued to harp on the risks of serious economic turmoil were easy to ignore. And ignored they were. Among others, the list includes Chicago's Raghuram G. Rajan (2005) who presented a paper at a 2005 Kansas City Federal Reserve Bank gathering at Jackson Hole to celebrate the work of Federal Reserve Chair Alan Greenspan. Rajan argued that financial developments during Greenspan's tenure had made the world far riskier and that financial crisis could be in the offing. In response Lawrence Summers said that he found "the basic, slightly lead-eyed premise of [Mr. Rajan's] paper to be misguided" (Lahart Jan. 2, 2009), while Federal Reserve Governor Donald Kohn "said that for central bankers to enact policies aimed at stemming risk-taking would 'be at odds with the tradition of policy excellence of the person whose era we are examining at this conference'" (Lahart Jan. 1, 2009). The list also includes Yale's Robert Shiller, whose warnings about the pending housing crisis were ignored by Federal Reserve and other economists despite the rich empirical work he had done to cement the case, and despite the fact the he had been among the small minority of economists who had correctly identified the bubble in high-tech stocks in the late 1990s; Andrew M. Lo, the director of the MIT Laboratory for Financial Engineering, who presented a paper in 2004 at a National Bureau of Economic Research conference that "warned of the rising systematic risk to financial markets and particularly focused on the potential liquidity, leverage and counterparty risk from hedge funds" (cited in Lohr 2008, 5); Dean Baker, co-director of the Washington-based Center for Economic and Policy Research, who argued consistently from 2004 onward that the housing market was in a bubble; Morgan Stanley's Stephen Roach, who identified a housing bubble as early as 2002 and who in 2004 criticized the Federal Reserve for having become a "cheerleader when financial markets are going to excess" and having pursued "the ultimate moral hazard play that has turned the world into one gigantic hedge fund" (2004); and New York University's Nouriel Roubini, who argued from 2004 onward that a deep recession and financial crisis were imminent. All of these warnings were summarily dismissed by the vast majority of economists in academia, government, and beyond.

GROUP THINK, INTELLECTUAL BUBBLES, AND THE CRISIS

Economics has had at its disposal for over a century the resources necessary to think carefully about the risks posed by unregulated financial markets (Galbraith 2009). The Marxian tradition features systemic capitalist crisis as one of its central insights and has produced theoretically plausible and empirically rich accounts of the major crises of the twentieth century. At the same time, post-Keynesian thought (including the work of Hyman Minsky and those whose work appears in the *Journal of Post-Keynesian Economics*) has examined at length the crisis tendencies of liberalized financial markets and the need for close government oversight. Moreover, there is by now a well-established historical record of recurring financial bubbles and crises extending back many centuries that has been explored carefully by economic historians and other scholars (Kindleberger 2000; Shiller 2005).[4] Add to this the compelling recent insights from behavioral finance, information economics, and agency theory for which several Nobel Prizes have been awarded in recent years (Eichengreen 2009) and which gives good reason to worry about liberalized financial markets, and the dire warnings offered by respected economists in the years preceding the crisis, and one must conclude that the mainstream in financial and macroeconomics exhibited extraordinary closed mindedness in matters where nothing less than open and critical inquiry would pass professional and ethical muster.

In Eichengreen's view, shared by Simon Johnson (2009), the profession was led astray by financial and other inducements to provide powerful market actors with biased analyses that told them what they wanted to hear. Other explanations focus on the substantial "psychic costs of non-conformity" which induced economists to join rather than buck the intellectual herd that was pronouncing the efficiency and stability of financial markets (Eichengreen 2009). Shiller writes of his own insecurity in raising the idea that housing prices had become unstable during his tenure on the economic advisory panel of the Federal Reserve Bank of New York from 1990 until 2004. He warned about the bubble "very gently and felt vulnerable expressing such quirky views. Deviating too far from consensus leaves one feeling potentially ostracized from the group, with the risk that one may be terminated" (Shiller 2008, 5).[5]

In contrast, Krugman lays much of the blame for conformance across the profession on the advocates of the EMH who resembled "fervent political activists—or members of a cult." "In this sense," he continues,

> efficient-market acolytes were like any other academic movement. But unlike, say, deconstructionist literary theorists, finance professors had an enormous impact on the business world—and not incidentally, some of them made a lot of money (Krugman Aug. 9, 2009, 11).

Eichengreen concludes that the complicity of the economics profession in the crisis lay not in its failure of imagination but in its failure of fortitude and independent mindedness. For Dean Baker, the problem lay in the incentive structure operating within the profession that rewarded conformance and punished dissent:

> Taking issue with the prevailing views in the profession carries enormous risks. Economists who warned of the bubble and the threat it posed to the economy risked ridicule and jeopardized their careers. . .On the other hand, when the consensus within the profession is wrong, there are no obvious consequences. None of [the economists who denied the existence of the bubble] are losing their jobs. In fact, it is unlikely that many are even missing out on a scheduled promotion as a result of having failed to see the largest financial bubble in the history of the world (Baker 2009a, 72; see also Baker 2009b).

Other economists point to particular features of the economics profession as cause for its recent failures. Colander et al. (2009) cite a "misallocation of research efforts" in economics that directed economists away from addressing "the most prevalent needs of society." This view of the culpability of the economics profession is shared by Wall Street insiders.[6] Jeremy Grantham of the institutional asset management company GMO lays much of the blame for the crisis on the doorstep of the economics profession:

> In their desire for mathematical order and elegant models, the economic establishment played down the role of bad behavior . . . The incredibly inaccurate efficient market theory was believed in totality by many of our financial leaders and believed in part by almost all. It left our government establishment sitting by confidently, even as a lethally dangerous combination of asset bubbles, lax controls, pernicious incentives, and wickedly

complicated instruments led to our current plight (cited in Nocera June 6, 2009, B1, 5).

These arguments and insights yield the conclusion that the economic crisis is a joint product of the imprudent behavior of two groups of influential actors—financial market participants and economists—which spawned twin reinforcing bubbles. The profession generated an intellectual bubble that overvalued the virtues of liberalized financial markets and discounted credible theory and evidence that challenged the euphoria. This intellectual frenzy contributed to and helped to sustain an even more dangerous financial and housing market bubble. In turn, rising asset prices in the context of economic growth and rising prosperity substantially increased the professional and psychic costs of intellectual nonconformance among economists. Over the course of the past decade, then, the two herds came to feed off each other's success, sustain each other's optimism, and trample each other's critics. In so doing, they sowed the seeds of their mutual crisis—one borne of short-sightedness and, ultimately, hubris.

PROFESSIONAL ERROR AND PROFESSIONAL ETHICS

That many economists got it wrong in the years leading up to the crisis is not in itself ethically indictable. Professional judgment is always prone to error; if it were not, the field of professional ethics would be much simpler than it is. What is ethically troublesome is why and how it got it so wrong. The profession ignored readily available evidence and theory that should have given it reason to suspect that the EMH could be leading not just the profession but market actors and policy makers into dangerous waters. The group think that Krugman, Shiller (Cohen 2009), and others explore reflects a disturbing refusal of the profession to value intellectual pluralism. More than the other social sciences, economics coalesced during the latter half of the twentieth century around a predominant approach that posits a particular notion of human behavior and a restricted set of methods.[7] Economists who reject this approach are relegated to the professional periphery in terms of where they are likely to be hired, where they can publish, and what influence they can have on public affairs. Economics resembles an intellectual planetary system in which heterodox approaches orbit the mainstream at some distance or other depending on just how much of the mainstream view they reject. In this intellectual constellation, communication is strictly one way. The mainstream broadcasts and the heterodoxies receive, digest, and dispute, but there is little reverse flow of communication.

Closed mindedness also contributed to the profession's failure to recognize its own limitations.[8] It lost sight of the fact that it could commit error that induces substantial harm. As in the case of market liberalization in the South and transition economies, the profession suppressed concerns about the risk of failure of its preferred policy regime. It therefore failed to present for the consideration of policy makers alternative regimes that might have had more congenial risk profiles.

If economics is prone to error that causes severe harm and if, despite this fact, the profession has not established adequate mechanisms to ensure critical self-reflection and humility, intellectual breadth and openness, then the profession is in crisis. It has an obligation to scrutinize its institutional practices, to see how they might induce group think and hubris and thereby discourage independent thinking. Above all else, it must consider ways to encourage among its practitioners the virtues of humility and open mindedness regarding views that contradict their own, and to modulate advocacy of the interventions that they propose. The profession faces the related obligation to sustain pluralism. We return to these matters in the next chapter, where we explore the content of professional economic ethics.

ECONOMIC THEORY AND ECONOMIC REALITY

The contribution of economists to the crisis reminds us that economic theory does not just describe the world it confronts; it seeks to and does influence that world in powerful ways. The pathways of economists' influence are direct and indirect. First, economists at the top of the profession move back and forth between academic and nonacademic institutions. When they take the helm of government agencies, the IFIs, and the like, they set the course for those institutions and their economists. Naturally, their applied work reflects the core insights that predominate in their respective fields. Second, prominent academic economists have an outsized influence on the work of applied economists who make their livelihoods permanently outside of academia. In seeking authority and influence for their work, applied economists may look for patrons among elite academic economists (see Chapter 3). Moreover, applied economists bring to their work the training they received in academia and put to use at least some of the central assumptions and methods from academic economics. This training involves a set of tools but also a worldview that shapes economists' judgments over the course of their careers. Third, economic theory permeates economic institutions and affects the common sense and behavior of private economic actors and public policy makers. A theory that suggests that things cannot go very wrong in financial markets, for instance, may induce behaviors that bring about adverse outcomes. We should recall in this context the famous remark with which Keynes concludes *The General Theory*, which speaks directly to the matter of the academic's influence over public affairs:

> Practical men, who believe themselves to be quite exempt from any intellectual influence, are usually the slaves of some defunct economist. Madmen

in authority, who hear voices in the air, are distilling their frenzy from some academic scribbler of a few years back (Keynes 1964, 383).

In the instant case, the influence of economists was powerful. "Faith in free financial markets grew into conventional wisdom—trumpeted on the editorial pages of the *Wall Street Journal* and on the floor of Congress" (Johnson 2009).

The influence of academic economists on the world implies an ethical burden that they might prefer to ignore. The greater the influence, the more difficult it is to argue that those who restrict themselves to pure theory are spared ethical difficulties. Academic economists might need to attend to the unanticipated effects that their work may induce. I do not mean to suggest, of course, that scholars should be dissuaded from pursuing the work that they find compelling. I am suggesting that the profession faces an obligation to take account of all the pathways of its influence—those that are direct and intended and those that are indirect and unintended—when thinking through its responsibilities. The profession may face an obligation to emphasize the limits of what it has to offer even and especially in the face of high demand for its services. It may face an obligation to take steps to make it more difficult for the consumers of economic theory—be they market actors or policy makers—to pick and choose just those theoretical insights from economic theory that best square with their objectives while ignoring the rest, to bet everything on this selective reading, and to invoke the authority of the economics profession when they do so.

The last point raises important and difficult questions about the extent and legitimacy of consumer sovereignty in the vital transaction between the provider and consumer of economic theory and advice. Rather than produce research without regard to how it might be used, the academic economist may have an obligation to follow her work out into the world, to do what she can to ensure that the limitations of her work are understood, and that it is not employed in ways that cause serious harm to its users and to others. In the view of Colander et al. (2009, 6):

> Researchers have an ethical responsibility to point out to the public when the tool that they developed is misused. It is the responsibility of the researcher to make clear from the outset the limitations and underlying assumptions of his model and warn of the dangers of their mechanic application.

Neither the individual economist nor the profession may be able to control how its work is used, of course, any more than can the producer of consumer goods. But just as in the case of consumer goods, the profession can provide warning labels that instruct the users of its products about appropriate and inappropriate uses and about how best to avoid serious injury when engaging the motor and putting the product to use. Advising competently on such matters requires economists to pay greater attention to the robustness of their models and the "external consistency" of their findings, by which is meant the correlation of its assumptions with evidence and insights gleaned from observations conducted by economists and other researchers (Colander et al. 2009).[9]

CONCLUSION

In the case before us, concerning the culpability of the economics profession in the current global economic crisis, we find none of this. We find instead a herd mentality about the right way to think about financial markets and financial regulation; a dismissal of theory, evidence, and argument about the dangers associated with unregulated asset markets; and perhaps most important, a severe overconfidence among the most influential economists about the extent of economic expertise. The economics profession failed to meet its obligations to society by failing to promote and sustain a diversity of views among its members over matters that are terribly complex and important—and by failing to provide market actors, policy makers, and citizens with a careful assessment of the potential risks of financial deregulation and the reward-risk profiles of alternative policy regimes. These mistakes were avoidable. The failure of the profession to do so is therefore indictable, especially in light of the extraordinary costs that have been imposed on vulnerable communities the world over in the wake of a crisis which a blind faith in efficient markets helped to induce.

The findings of this and the preceding chapter suggest that we should not presume that well-meaning economists, acting on their own and guided by good intentions, will fulfill their professional responsibilities. The challenges associated with professional economic ethics can be daunting; hence the need for sustained attention to the field. The next chapter begins to explore the content of professional economic ethics by drawing on insights that we have encountered along the way.

Notes

1 Just as the EMH yielded overconfidence about the stability of financial markets, the Capital Asset Pricing Model (CAP-M) and Value at Risk (VaR) were taken to be dependable means for pricing obscure assets and measuring a firm's exposure to potential losses (respectively). Faith in these measures provided the illusion of security regarding investment strategies and risk management. Overreliance on VaR assessments became the norm on Wall Street despite the fact that few of its devotees understood its limitations. In the words of David Einhorn, founder of hedge fund Greenlight Capital, VaR is "relatively useless as a risk-management tool and potentially catastrophic when its use creates a false sense of security among senior managers and watchdogs" (cited in Nocera 1/4/2009, 26–27). This, of course, is precisely what happened in the run-up to the current crisis.

2 It is more accurate to say that the discussion of instability continued within minority traditions in economics, ranging from post-Keynesian to Marxian theory, which the mainstream simply ignored.

3 These themes recur in Bernanke's public statements and Congressional testimony well into 2007 (see Bernanke March 6, 2007; April 11, 2007). Even in late spring of 2007, as the subprime mortgage crisis was deepening, Bernanke continued to cite the advantages of market discipline over that of government regulators (Bernanke May 17, 2007).

4 The regularity of such crises has if anything increased since the 1970s (Stiglitz 2009b). The early 1980s witnessed the debt crisis across much of the developing world; this was followed by the Mexican crisis of 1994 and the Asian financial crisis in 1997, which contributed to crises in Russia (1998) and Argentina (1999). The private sector also was implicated in a series of crises in the United States (including the "savings and loan" crisis of the mid-1980s and the implosion of Long-Term Capital Management in 1998). None of these was predicted by the economics profession or caused reconsideration of thinking in macro- or financial economics. The crises were dismissed as anomalous (e.g., "the events that brought down L.T.C.M. were [viewed as] one in a million"; Nocera 1/4/2009, 33) or attributed to misguided government interference in the market.

5 Kuran's theory (1995) of "preference falsification" which occurs when individuals express views or attitudes that they believe to be false may be relevant to the conformity that prevailed within the economics profession in the years leading up to the crisis. See Davis (2004) on the relevance of preference falsification to the economics profession.

6 And, it should be added, by many business and economics correspondents, such as *Time Magazine*'s Justin Fox (2009); *The Times's* Anatole Kaletsky (2009); the *New York Times's* Joe Nocera (1/4/2009 and 6/6/2009); and Roger Lowenstein (2008). Says Lowenstein (2008, B1),

> The Long-Term Capital Management fiasco momentarily shocked Wall Street out of its complacent trust in financial models, and was replete with lessons, for Washington as well as for Wall Street. But the lessons were ignored, and in this decade, the mistakes were repeated with far more harmful consequences.

And an editorial comment that concludes a *Financial Times* symposium (5/12/2009, 39) on the crisis ends with this indictment: "This is not the bankruptcy of a social system, but the intellectual and moral failure of those who were in charge of it: a failure for which there is no excuse."

7 A point raised in the previous chapter bears repeating here. I do not mean to deny that the profession has begun to pursue a range of new approaches over the past several decades. But in the instant case, the leading financial and macroeconomists relied on traditional neoclassical insights (such as the EMH) in the period leading up to the crisis, as Krugman rightly asserts.

8 In the case of economics, these limitations remain considerable, especially in regard to the most important questions concerning economic affairs. For instance, Mankiw argues that "despite many advances in the tools of economic analysis, modern economists armed with the data from [the period preceding the Great Depression] would not have forecast much better" than the economists of the 1920s who failed to anticipate the looming crisis (Mankiw 2008, B6).

9 The essay by Colander et al. (2009) represents one of the best discussions by economists to date of the ways in which the practices of academic economists contributed to the current crisis. In their view, economists had the means available

to do better: they could and should have warned the public about the dangers associated with the use of economic models for pricing complex financial assets and hedging against market risk. For Colander et al., economists' failure to do so amounts to a violation of their ethical responsibility: the economics profession "failed in its duty to society to provide as much insight as possible into the workings of the economy and in providing warnings about the tools it created" (14). These considerations lead the authors to argue that there is a need for "an ethical code for professional economic scientists" (4).

Chapter 11

On Sleeping Too Well

In Search of Professional Economic Ethics

A major problem of our time is that people have come to expect policies to produce results that they are incapable of producing. … we economists in recent years have done vast harm—to society at large and to our profession—by claiming more than we can deliver.

Milton Friedman (cited in William R. Allen 1977, 48)

But it is an ethical vice to pretend you know more than you do; it is an epistemic vice to believe that you know more than you do.

John Hardwig (1994, 92)

Ignorance, arrogance, narrowness of mind, incomplete knowledge, and counterfeit knowledge are of concern to us because they are dangerous; they cause destruction. When united with great power, they cause great destruction.

Wendell Berry (2005, 59)

As economists begin to develop professional economic ethics as a field of inquiry, they can learn much from the insights that have emerged in other professions that have confronted carefully the ethical entailments of their work. But economics certainly cannot import wholesale the professional ethics that have arisen in other fields. Not all professional ethical principles or insights apply to all professions or apply to them in identical ways (Goldman 1980). Different kinds of professional intervention entail different ethical substance. Professional ethics must be tailored to these particulars if it is to be of service, even if some principles and insights are reiterated across many professions. There is good reason why there is no "Uniform Code of Ethics for the Professions."

Economists take delight and comfort in parsimony—and in simple decision rules and the discovery of unique solutions to vexing problems. There is something terribly gratifying and aesthetically pleasing in the derivation of a proof of the existence of a unique and stable equilibrium—in the presentation to the uninitiated of the beautifully well behaved and shapely supply and demand curves that cross once and only once in two-space, revealing a point of economic efficiency. Unfortunately, professional ethics does not yield this kind of clarity.

The field of professional ethics is complex and nuanced. It might indeed include certain explicit rules such as "In your scholarly work, you shall not manufacture or misreport data." But it is not reducible to such rules: it is not a simple tool kit to solve the ethical problems that the profession confronts. Instead, to be of value, professional economic ethics needs to convey the view that the ethical universe that the economist confronts is irreducibly complex. It entails norms and aspirations that are uncertain and vague and that contradict each other at critical junctures when the economist might most want to take refuge in an ethical axiom. Moreover, professional economic ethics concerns the virtues that are required of the economist (and of the profession) and not just the rules of economic practice. The profession therefore faces the prospect of cultivating among economists the willingness to live with ethical ambiguity and aperture so that they don't throw up their hands in impatience whenever they confront ethical problems that do not submit to unique resolution. To put it simply, *there is no ethical Pareto optimality—this must be the first lesson of professional economic ethics*. Professional ethics should keep the economist up at night attending to the ethical complexities of her work. *If, instead, professional economic ethics helps the economist sleep too well, it simply isn't doing its job.*

ETHICAL ISSUES IN ECONOMIC RESEARCH

Several empirical branches of economics research raise difficult ethical questions. Practitioners in econometrics, experimental economics, and the related and relatively new field of randomized controlled trials have begun to explore the ethical complexities of their work. Rather than plow new ground here, I will discuss some of the ethical difficulties that have been identified in these areas of economic research and briefly summarize prescriptions that have been offered to address these difficulties.

Econometrics

For many years, Deirdre McCloskey and Stephen Ziliak have tried to convince the profession that much of its empirical work of the past several decades suffers from a most elementary, consequential, and dangerous error. In their empirical work, economists have come to place unwarranted faith in the notion of statistical significance at the expense of economic significance. In an extensive survey of economics and other literature, Ziliak and McCloskey (2008, 2) find that eight to nine of every ten articles makes the "significance" mistake. The typical research paper that appears in the most prominent economic journals—such as in the *American Economic Review* (Ziliak and McCloskey 2004; McCloskey and

Ziliak 1996)—takes pains to demonstrate that its findings are statistically significant (at, say, the 5 percent significance level) without recognition of just what, if anything, that implies about the economics of the finding reported. Ziliak and McCloskey (2008) argue that, in fact, in most cases that economists confront, the finding of statistical significance reveals little to nothing of scientific use or interest. It illuminates (poorly) an "existence" question—whether there exists any effect of X on Y. What the scientist (and those who will be affected by the science) should want to know is whether that effect has what they call "oomph": whether the relationship between the independent and dependent variables that one purports to have discovered *matters* in any meaningful sense.[1]

Unfortunately, statistical significance does not speak to substantive issues. It tells us something only about the joint adequacy of the sample size and the correlation between independent and dependent variables. Moreover, reliance on this test leads to the fallacy of the "transposed conditional" which entails equating "the probability of the data, given the hypothesis" with "the probability of the hypothesis, given the data" (Ziliak and McCloskey 2008, 41). Ignored in this test is the more important question of whether the causal relationship is so substantial as to give us reason to take it seriously in designing economic models that explain the world or in policy to improve it. Answering these questions cannot be done by rote application of a statistical test or any other mechanical calculation; as McCloskey (2005, 23) puts it, "mattering does not inhere in a number." Discerning whether a finding matters, instead, requires careful judgment and wisdom of the sort that is cultivated only gradually and painstakingly.

Just why economists make the mistake of conflating statistical with economic significance—of taking the former as sufficient evidence of the latter—is perplexing, especially when one considers that the purposes and limitations of tests of statistical significance have been understood and emphasized by leading statistical theorists for over a century. Ziliak and McCloskey cite the misplaced hope for mechanical solutions to nonmechanical problems by leading economists and to sociological factors in the professions that induce new researchers to follow the lead of established economists in order to build their careers. Whatever the origin, Ziliak and McCloskey argue that perpetuation of the mistake is unconscionable since it "costs us jobs, justice, and lives" (Ziliak and McCloskey 2008, 2).[2]

Other economists have raised concerns about econometric practice. Edward Leamer (1978) highlights the way in which the practice of "specification search" undermines the quality of and confidence in statistical work (see also Zelder 2008). Leamer emphasizes the "whimsy and fragility" (1983) that is necessarily involved in all statistical inference. Prescriptively, Leamer calls for much greater attention by economic researchers to the need for sensitivity analysis to ascertain just how fragile are the results they report. In a similar vein, Thomas Mayer (2009a; 2009b) calls attention to the inappropriate use of data mining, coupled with the failure of econometricians to report the various tests they run on data before landing on the test that confirms their hypotheses. Unreported data mining leaves the impression that the reported results are more robust than they in fact are. Mayer acknowledges that sometimes it is appropriate and necessary to run diverse tests—for instance, in cases where a theory claims that the money supply is a relevant causal factor but does not specify whether one should rely on M1 or M2 as the independent variable. In such cases, Mayer argues that whenever the sample size is sufficiently large, the researcher should divide the data into two parts and "use one to formulate the appropriate form of the hypothesis and test that on the other part" (2009a, 13). When the sample size does not permit this procedure, "the next best thing is to let the reader know about all the variants that you have fitted and the results thus obtained so that she can decide how much credence to [give] the results" (2009a, 13–14). Mayer laments that economists "tell the world about the importance of transparency, but do not practice it sufficiently" (2009a, 14).

It is noteworthy that some critics place at least as much responsibility for deficient empirical work on the profession as they do on the proclivities of individual economists. In Mayer's view, while economists typically follow the norms that exist in economics, the profession itself is nevertheless indictable for what could be considered "cheating"—for accepting "practices that we would admit are questionable if we were forced to confront this issue outright" (Mayer 2009a, 18). Like Ziliak and McCloskey, Mayer criticizes economic journals for accepting practices that they have good reason to know are deficient, which in turn induces individual economists to conform. Examples include: failing to require authors to test the sensitivity of their results to changes in statistical packages (despite evidence that the leading packages often generate conflicting results with the same data); neglecting to require authors to list all the variants they tested in the course of their research and to supply their data sets and computer programs for future review; tolerating the use of data that are inappropriate for the purposes to which they are put; overlooking the conflation of statistical and economic significance; not requiring fragility tests when those are appropriate; failing to cultivate in the profession the need to attend to the reproducibility of results; and reducing the space that they dedicate to critical comments on published papers. In all these ways, journals undermine professional norms that might otherwise protect scientific integrity (Mayer 2009a; O'Brien 1994; Zelder 2008).

Sandra Peart and David Levy also draw attention to the need for institutional changes that might induce ethical behavior among econometricians in their academic and applied work. In both their historical work on the eugenics movement (Peart and Levy 2007) and their analyses of the incentive structure facing applied econometricians today, they emphasize the need for inducements toward ethically defensible work. Peart and Levy urge recognition of the fact that all agents—those economists theorize about as well as the economists who do the theorizing—"are *all* tempted to the unethical, by whatever tempts any among us" (Peart and Levy 2008, 101). Consistent with the findings reported earlier (Chapter 3), Peart and Levy worry that when econometricians accept as a client an agent with a preference for biased estimates of economic parameters, they may exhibit sympathy with the client's position which leads them to generate biased estimates.

Peart and Levy demonstrate the failure of competition among econometric experts (such as in juridical settings) to eliminate the generation of nontransparent estimates. To correct this problem, they propose simple rule-based procedures that would "serve to attenuate the temptations that experts, those whose advice is sought, face" (Peart and Levy 2008, 101). In the context of juridical proceedings, they advocate for a variant of final offer arbitration in which a court appointed expert "takes each of the contending models and bootstraps them. The winning model has the smaller bootstrap variance" (Levy and Peart 2008, 109).[3] This rule would provide an incentive for the contending econometricians to present transparent estimates. Generalizing from this case, Levy and Peart (2008, 111) argue that "If transparency is not incentive compatible under one institutional regime, perhaps one can find another regime in which it is."[4] Searching for regimes that entail incentives that promote ethical behavior would certainly fall within the purview of professional economic ethics.

Experimental Economics

There is as of yet much less scholarship focused on questions pertaining to appropriate conduct among economists engaged in the relatively new field of experimental economics. The ethical questions that have begun to attract attention among experimental economists involve, *inter alia*, the effects of the use of deception on experimenters and research subjects and on norms regarding the reporting of research results.[5]

Strategic Misrepresentation to Research Subjects, and the Nature of Harm

Deception arises in two ways in experiments that involve human subjects. The first involves strategic misrepresentation by the researcher to research subjects in instances where full disclosure would undermine the experiment. Shane Bonetti (1998) identifies two schools of thought on deception that have emerged within experimental economics: the "prohibitionists" who contend that deception is always inappropriate, and other practitioners who view deception as an essential tool for conducting many kinds of experiments. Prohibitionists emphasize the harm caused by deception to the science of experimental economics, which occurs when suspicion of deception by research subjects alters their behavior during experiments and so invalidates experimental results. Moreover, the use of deception (which is often revealed during the post-experiment "dehoaxing" process) can taint the subject pool (usually a college campus or department), undermining the viability of subsequent experiments. Hence, "honesty is a methodological public good and deception is equivalent to not contributing." (Ledyard 1995, 134, cited in Bonetti 1998, 378). In this perspective, the victims of deception comprise the community of experimental economists whose work might be undermined by the use of deception among their peers. The ethical question that arises in this context relates to whether a researcher is warranted in capturing the private benefits that might become available through deception at the expense of harming the community of experimental economists. As Hertwig and Ortmann (2008, 87) put it, " … other experimenters who do without deception end up paying the public potential costs (e.g., participants' reactions to suspected deception) of others' use of deception, thus violating an implicit 'social contract' between experimenters."

Bonetti explores the extensive empirical research on the question of deception (largely from experimental psychology) and finds little support for prohibitionists' concerns.[6] On the other side of the ledger, he advances several justifications for the use of deception. First, research subjects "will always attend to cues, information and hunches about features of the experimental design." Deception is useful for distracting subjects and "thus ensuring that the behavior which is measured is more natural and spontaneous, and less affected and contrived" (Bonetti 1998, 386). Second, experiments such as those which examine public goods and the free rider problem benefit from seeding the subject pool with fictitious players whose conduct is controlled by the researchers and also by misleading subjects about the number of other participants in the experiment. Both of these serve to confront the actual research subjects with a greater range of conditions under which they are to fashion their own behavior and so generate more useful results to the experimenter. For instance, misleading subjects about the number of other participants allows researchers to study the effect of group size on the likelihood of free rider behavior. Bonetti concludes from the evidence that deception is not only benign to the profession but that its use may enhance the quality of experimental results.

Despite such arguments, experimental economics has by now developed a strong norm against the use of deception (Fiore 2009; Hertwig and Ortmann 2008). The driving impulse in economics is concern about the effects of deception on the profession and not on research subjects, as we have seen. In particular, researchers are concerned about protecting their reputations among potential subjects, which is vital to the success of their future experiments (Fiore 2009; Davis and Holt 1993). In other fields, ethical questions have been raised about deception in regard to its implications for subjects. In the face of widespread use of deception in psychology, many psychologists have raised two concerns in this regard. One is that deception may cause serious harm to participants. We will examine ethical questions surrounding harm momentarily; for now we should note that deception is but one way in which subjects may be harmed during experimentation. A second concern is that deception, by its nature, conflicts directly with the obligation of researchers to secure meaningful prior informed consent from subjects. In the words of Adair, Dushenko and Lindsay (1985, 60), "Clearly, deceived subjects are not 'informed' and informed subjects are not 'deceived.'" Indeed, the consent they give under deception might better be called "misinformed consent" (see Baumrind 1985, 165). This problem arises whenever truthful reporting to subjects prior to their participation would sabotage the experiment.[7] In such cases, there is a tension between the obligation to honor the integrity and autonomy of the research subject, on the one hand, and the interest of the researcher in misleading subjects about research protocols in advance of the experiment, on the other. Unfortunately, informing subjects only that they may be deceived in the experiment (without revealing the nature of the deception) can have the effect of heightening their suspicions and might motivate them to "form hypotheses to guide their behavior," with the effect of altering their conduct and undermining the validity of the experiment (Adair, Dushenko and Lindsay 1985, 60).

A common feature of experimental design involves rewarding deception on the part of research subjects. Dearman and Beard (2009, 51–52) examine the effects of such experiments, like those that require "student participants to make representations about a particular individual characteristic (e.g., ability, cost) as a basis for payment of economic rewards" and that induce "a significant number of participants to intentionally misrepresent the nature of that characteristic in order to receive a greater reward." Dearman and Beard worry that in such experiments researchers often purposely fail to debrief subjects adequately after the experiment so as to avoid contaminating the subject pool. Drawing on Lawrence Kohlberg's model of "cognitive ethical development," Dearman and Beard explore the ways in which this kind of research protocol may harm college student research subjects by "retarding or compromising their ethical development." They conclude that

> Research employing the experimental methods described herein influences the judgment of student participants by providing tacit authorization to engage in the experimental equivalent of fraudulent behavior, reinforces such behavior through the dispensation of economic rewards, and can lead to regression of the participants' ethical development (Dearman and Beard 2009, 56).

Consideration of this matter requires an adequate appreciation of the complexity of the concept of harm (see Thompson 1987). Harm comprises physical pain, discomfort, and deterioration of physical health, of course, but it can also entail effects that are more subjective (such as the inducement of anxiety or shame). Confounding matters further, it can take forms that cause no unpleasant sensations within subjects and that indeed are not experienced by the subjects as harm at all. The type of harm cited by Dearman and Beard falls into this category. Research subjects who have been rewarded for fraudulent behavior might leave the experiment feeling that they've learned important life lessons rather than recognize that their participation may have undermined their ethical development. This requires of researchers acute attentiveness to both obvious and subtle forms of harm and the direct and indirect ways in which a line of experimentation might induce them. This challenge is complicated by the variability of the effects of a research design on research subjects. The variability of harm is more extensive when the harm is subjective rather than physical—and harm is especially unpredictable when it threatens subjects' moral development rather than their physical integrity.

Variability of harm makes it difficult to anticipate not only how deception will affect participants but also how they will respond to the "dehoaxing" process at the end of the experiment, when they learn that they have been deceived. Some subjects who believe during an experiment (such as the famed Milgram experiment) that they caused harm to others (by dutifully following instructions of an authority figure to do so) might find consolation from a debriefing where they learn that, in fact, they did not harm anyone—that the person they believed they had harmed was an accomplice of the researcher who experienced no discomfort or loss.[8] But others subjects may instead experience an intensification of shame once they realize that the harm they believed themselves to have inflicted was so egregious in the minds of the researchers that it had to be simulated through trickery rather than actually induced. Even researchers who are adept at desensitizing subjects after the fact may fail to alleviate their shame. Complicating matters further, strategies that are likely to help the subjects overcome shame might induce other kinds of harm. A desensitization strategy that is commonly advocated in such cases is to assure the research subject that this behavior "had been completely normal and many other participants had performed similarly" (Holmes 1976, cited in Dearman and Beard 2009, 57). But Dearman and Beard (2009, 58) warn that if we take a broad view of harm which includes lasting effects on subjects' moral development, this strategy might be counterproductive: "Desensitizing the student participant should not at the same time reinforce the unethical behavior, because doing so would constitute harm."

Severe harm of various sorts can and does attend all sorts of economic practice beyond the laboratory. Unfortunately, economics has done little to engage questions pertaining to what constitutes harm, how its presence and degree are to be assessed adequately, by whose lights these questions are to be answered, and related matters. For instance, economic theory typically takes increasing inequality to constitute no harm to those with least resources, provided they do not themselves suffer absolute losses, since an actor's utility is most often taken to be a function merely of his own consumption.[9] While this assumption may make modeling and policy assessment more tractable, it is far too narrow when judged by the prudential principle that has emerged across the professions. Increasing inequality can result in the loss of substantive freedoms for those whose relative income falls; in Amartya Sen's (1992) terms, relative deprivation can generate absolute capabilities failures. Professional economic ethics would open up an overdue inquiry into the nature of the diverse harms that attend economic practice and the means necessary to avoid or minimize them.

On Norms Concerning the Reporting of Research Results

Alvin Roth has raised concerns about the practices that have emerged among experimental economists that govern "how and in what detail we report experimental procedures, what data is reported, how it is aggregated for reporting purposes, and how it is analyzed" (Roth 1994, 280). Roth worries, in particular, about the use of "pilot experiments" that are used to help the researcher design the experiments that will form the basis of the research. This practice has a proper place within experimental economics: pilot experiments can help the researcher to identify and improve upon misleading or overly complex instructions to research subjects. But problems arise when the researcher consciously or unconsciously uses the procedure to discover just that design that confirms his anticipated results and then uses it to produce those results. Here we have a problem similar to specification search in econometrics:

> when pilot experiments are used to search through alternative experimental procedures and parameters, and to decide which experimental investigations shall proceed to the reporting stage, then, if this is not fully reported, it is easy to misinterpret the significance and robustness of the reported results (Roth 1994, 280).

A second problem concerns research design in which every trial within an experiment is considered by the researcher to be an independent experiment. This procedure, too, can have legitimate purposes: treating each trial as an experiment might be appropriate when the goal is to disprove a universal claim because just one disconfirmation out of a large number of trials is scientifically relevant evidence about the status of the claim. But it is far less legitimate if one is instead attempting to confirm a hypothesis. Here, the risk that the bias of the researcher will influence the reporting of results (such as treating all disconfirming trials as pilot experiments) is particularly great. As a consequence, there is a need for research norms that require researchers to report fully on the results of all trials that they undertake. Doing otherwise, claims Roth, undermines the progress of experimental economic science—not least because incomplete disclosure of research protocols makes it far more difficult for other researchers to test the robustness of experimental results. The use of inadequate reporting procedures is also professionally unethical since it may enhance a researcher's professional success at the expense of the profession.

As with econometrics, solutions involve cultivating professional ethical norms that induce trust by encouraging researchers to recognize and refuse to engage in deceptive reporting practices, to "adopt the simplest design that can address [a researcher's] hypothesis" combined with policies by journals to require full reporting "of all published data and procedures" (such as "the experiment's instructions") so as to facilitate replication of research results by other experimenters (Houser 2008, 33). Disclosure should also describe the steps taken by researchers to ensure ethical treatment of research subjects in part because there is extensive evidence from the field of social psychology that procedures which secure informed consent and ensure the right of the subject to withdraw from the experiment at any time can influence subject behavior during experiments (Adair, Dushenko and Lindsay 1985).

Randomized Controlled Trials (RCTs)

One other research practice deserves attention here, owing to its growing presence in academic and applied economic research. While most economic experiments recruit college students as research subjects, economists have now begun to conduct research in target communities using "randomized controlled trials" (RCTs) of the sort that have long been common in medical research. RCTs often seek to assess the effectiveness of public policy options for addressing social and economic problems; as a consequence, RCTs are often conducted among those populations that are characterized by deprivation and vulnerability. Unsurprisingly, then, much of this research has occurred in the developing world. Economic RCTs date to the early 1970s; they have increased in frequency and sophistication only during the past decade. Today, the leading center for such research is the Abdul Jameel Latif Poverty Action Laboratory, or J-PAL, at MIT (http://www.povertyactionlab.org).

To date, proponents of the use of economic RCTs have produced very little scholarship on the ethical aspects of the approach, despite the extensive literature that examines ethical matters in other fields where field trials are commonly used.[10] A brief list of such issues will have to suffice for present purposes. The first is the complexity surrounding the pursuit of trials within vulnerable communities (Nama and Swartz 2002). Vulnerability raises questions about what counts as meaningful prior informed consent by research subjects. Second, there is the imperative to consider the effects of the experiment on those assigned to the control group (who receive a reduced level of treatment as compared with those who receive the treatment that the experiment seeks to investigate)—and on those excluded entirely from the trial. Third, there are the complications associated with the obligation of the researcher to anticipate potential short-term and long-term harms associated with the experiment and to ensure that this information, too, is shared fully with research subjects (and others who might suffer its effects), in a context where potential harms at best can be known only approximately. Fourth, there are questions surrounding the obligation of the researcher to provide compensation when research subjects (or others) are harmed by experimental research. Fifth, the question arises as to when and under what conditions an experiment must be curtailed prematurely, either because it becomes apparent during the trial that it is proving to be too risky or is inducing harm, or conversely, that it is yielding findings that show unequivocally the benefits of the intervention being studied (in which case, there might be an obligation to terminate the study and provide this intervention to all in the trial or in the targeted community). Sixth, there are questions about the obligation of researchers to the targeted community in the event that an experiment must be terminated prematurely, owing to any of the above reasons or due to flaws in the research design that become apparent only after the research has begun (Thompson 1987). Seventh, experimental research involves difficult questions of justice, including an obligation to ensure that the community that serves as the site of the experiment (and therefore bears its risks) will benefit from the results of the experiment (or that the wider population of which the target community is taken to be representative will do so). Eighth, when research has an international dimension (i.e., when researchers or the funding agency are foreign to the research site), there are additional complexities concerning whose values, norms, and rules should govern research protocols (Ulrich 2003; CIOMS 2002). Finally, there is the important question of whether the costs and risks that the experiment imposes on the targeted community will be more than offset by the potential benefits to that community—which depends in part on researchers' presumptions about whether the intervention is scalable under realistic assumptions—and whether the same knowledge could be gained through other research methods that do not impose such risks and costs.

None of these questions is easy to answer, either in the abstract or particular cases, as longstanding controversies in bioethics attest (CIOMS 2002).[11] It is understandable that advocates of RCTs might be hesitant to engage all of these difficulties, especially during the earliest stages of the use of this method when there is a desire not to overburden the technique prematurely with daunting ethical concerns. But the desire to get on with things cannot be tolerated by the profession as a whole, given the nature of experimental interventions and their diverse impacts.

At present, many researchers conducing RCTs are left to police themselves to ensure ethical conduct. For instance, World Bank researchers face no official ethical approval procedure when conducting economic RCTs. While the Bank has guidelines that direct its researchers to follow the procedures of the World Health Organization, these have the status of recommendations that are not enforced by the Bank. The Bank's researchers consult among themselves in pursuit of ethical protocols, and in many trials Bank economists partner with researchers from universities or government ministries that impose regulation (especially when medical researchers are involved). But these regulations vary in scope, intensity, and enforcement from context to context (especially in developing countries).

The foregoing suggests that the economics profession may have a role to play in regulating economic RCTs, just as the medical profession regulates medical trials. Fortunately, researchers in other fields have generated useful insight into how best to conduct ethical RCTs. In this area, professional economic ethics need not recreate the wheel; it would do better to investigate what it can import from traditions with a comparative advantage in the ethics of RCT research. One experienced RCT practitioner suggested to me that the economics profession might require researchers to register their studies in advance of execution in order to prevent the repression of unfavorable results—such as those that are contrary to the preferences of the funder or of the researcher—as is required in biomedical research. Economic journals might play an important role in this regard by requiring researchers to demonstrate ethical conduct in RCTs as a condition of publishing research findings.

ETHICAL ISSUES THAT SPAN ACADEMIC AND APPLIED ECONOMICS[12]

There is extensive overlap between academic and applied economics, owing to the fact that economists, economic theories and methods, and professional norms migrate back and forth between the two sectors. This suggests that it is mistaken to try to segregate those ethical principles that are appropriate for one sector from those that are appropriate for the other. While we have just explored some particular challenges that arise in economic research, we should be aware that these issues arise in the work of applied economics as well, since so many applied economists undertake economic research. Moreover, the questions that we will now examine also arise in both areas of economics even if some of them appear to be particularly salient within the world of applied economics.

Beyond the Prudential Principle

The prudential principle deserves the attention it receives across the professions. When some act on others, they must attend to the potential harm that they can cause. They must take care to put the interests of those served above their own; and they must take care not to impose avoidable risks in hopes of bringing about favorable outcomes.

Since economics is a field that involves risk of substantial and often unpredictable harm, it too must find a place for the prudential principle within its professional ethics. It must be more attentive to and be clearer to all audiences about those cases that involve Knightian uncertainty rather than probabilistically knowable risk (Knight 1921); and in these cases, it must take particular pains to engage the ethical challenges associated with acting when we simply do not know what the future holds. Economics certainly must jettison its attachment to the maxi-max principle in favor of an approach that takes better care of the communities it purports to serve. This is not to say that maxi-max should always be replaced by some alternative care-taking decision rule, such as minimax (e.g., choosing the policy approach that minimizes harm in the event of policy failure), though in cases of true uncertainty where the potential for catastrophe is present, that approach might be appropriate (see Woodward and Bishop 1997). It is to say that there must be greater concern for the risks associated with policy making in the context of fundamental uncertainty.[13]

Sustained attention to the prudential principle in economics would go some distance toward improving professional economic practice. It would encourage the profession to jettison utopian maxi-max interventions for more moderate and safer strategies. It would also open up to careful scrutiny the complexities of the notion of harm. But it bears repeating that the prudential principle is not a decision rule for several reasons. We examined one in Chapter 8, where we found that the medical nonmaleficence principle conflicts with respect for the autonomy and integrity of those whom the physician serves. Other reasons stem from the inherent complexity, uncertainty, and contestation that surround economic interventions.

One troublesome deficiency of the prudential principle as a decision rule in the economic context is its deep conservatism. It is biased in favor of the status quo even when the situation entails extraordinary suffering or injustice. Indeed, that is part of its intent—it reminds the practitioner that the status quo may be better than the proposed alternative, and so she should consider defaulting to the status quo unless there is good reason to believe the proposed alternative is decidedly better and will not leave those targeted by the intervention worse off. But this cannot generally be shown in advance. An intervention that is otherwise desirable might entail "adjustment costs," as economists remind us, and these might be substantial and enduring. Strict application of the prudential principle would therefore seem to rule out most innovation—even in those cases where innovation is warranted by the circumstances, and when the targeted community would itself choose innovation were it empowered to do so. In such cases, application of the prudential principle as a decision rule would prevent a community from seizing opportunities that it would choose to seize, and from facing risks that it would choose to face. For these reasons, it might preclude the achievement of realizable improvements in human well-being.[14] In these respects, the prudential principle is paternalistic and also infantilizing. In applying it rigidly, the economist may conspire unintentionally to keep poor communities poor.

A second problem with the application of this principle as a decision rule in economic affairs follows: it may perpetuate and deepen economic injustice and oppression. Overcoming oppressive arrangements might require social dislocation for the unfairly privileged and enormous risk for the most oppressed. It might require projects whose outcomes are most uncertain, not least because of the resistance they engender among the entrenched. Land reform in grossly unequal societies comes to mind in this connection. In oppressive situations, then, the idea of prudence might have less normative purchase. In the words of Sharon Welch (2000, 24),

> The purity and absoluteness of this guideline to "do no harm" is a recipe for illusion and paralysis. Doing nothing *does harm*: our neutrality helps the oppressors more than the victims of oppression (emphasis in original).

When taken literally and applied stringently, the prudential principle also reproduces a critical shortcoming of the maxi-max decision rule. Like maxi-max, the prudential principle has an extraordinarily narrow information base. While the maxi-max decision rule considers only the potential benefits from policy success and selects the policy that promises greatest reward, the prudential principle considers only the potential harm from policy failure and selects the policy that promises the least danger. Both fail to consider the magnitude of the difference in potential benefits and harms, the probability of policy success and failure, the distribution of benefits and harms (and other justice concerns), and many other salient aspects of the available policy options. Both restrict severely the relevant information base in order to generate unambiguous decision rules—which is, in fact, their chief defect.

An additional perplexing problem precludes the application of the prudential principle as a decision rule. The same epistemic unease that calls forth the prudential principle—an unease that follows from recognition that we do not know what will be the effects of any particular action—also complicates its application. How can we know how *not* to harm if we do not know with certainty what will be the consequences of our actions? This ignorance pertains as well to the perpetuation of the status quo: if we cannot be certain about the effects of doing that, how can we be certain about the effects of courses of action that entail breaking with the status quo? I raise this conundrum to emphasize that recourse to the prudential principle does not solve the problem of uncertainty, and it is dangerously naive to think that it does. It is best to think of it as a means to manage ethically but imperfectly a problem that cannot be eradicated. It bears repeating that application of this or any other principle must induce at least some anxiety in the ethical economist, especially in a world of immense economic hardship.

Anxiety, but not paralysis. For Welch, acting ethically in a world which defeats our desire for certainty and control requires humility, careful attention, and a commitment to learning. Drawing on the work of Mary Daly she writes,

> "Not harming," is something we learn, a continual task that expands as our ability to affect the lives of others expands. We will always need to learn

innocence. As our social worlds change and our individual responsibilities change, there will be more opportunities for harm, thus the necessity of learning again how to respect and honor the life around us (Welch 2000, 174).

The Ethical Imperative of Economic Democracy

We are left with an unhappy result: the prudential principle is both vitally necessary and deeply inadequate. Certainly it cannot provide economists with what, by virtue of their training, they are likely to want—an ethical decision rule to replace the ethically suspect maxi-max principle. The prudential principle is prone to paternalism, it is too conservative, it too easily tolerates oppression, it ignores too many salient and relevant factors in policy assessment and selection, and its application as a decision rule depends on a kind of knowing that it explicitly rejects. Provided we keep in view what the prudential principle is and is not—it is an ethical signpost but not a decision rule—we can and must find an appropriate place for it within professional economic ethics even as we contest its range and applicability (see May 1980).

Just as medical ethics has taken steps over the past several decades to temper its nonmaleficence principle via recognition of the autonomy of the patient, so must professional economic ethics place emphasis on the right of the targeted community to direct its own economic affairs. Respect for the autonomy of the targeted community requires the economist to secure its prior informed consent to proposed economic interventions of consequence, especially those that entail substantial risk. This implies that means must be established to ensure effective participation of targeted communities in the economic decisions that will affect them. In short, we find ethical justification for economic democracy. To the degree practical and achievable, a community the economist serves ought to be recognized as empowered to chart its own economic course (Crocker 1998).

From the perspective of professional economic ethics, economic democracy is not just a platitude: a strong commitment to economic self-determination could alter the behavior of practicing economists (and the institutions that employ them) in important ways. At a minimum, it places into ethical doubt the practice whereby an economist advises an autocrat who obstructs the economic empowerment of those over whom he exerts his authority. Professional economic ethics should have much to say about whether an economist should ever advise a dictator, and if so, under what circumstances and in what ways. It must confront the "many hands" problem (see Chapter 8) by addressing the obligations of a development economist who is assigned to a project that places her in service of an autocratic government. More generally, it should speak to the practices of the diverse institutions that employ economists, and it should provide means by which economists can call on their profession for support when these institutions violate their obligation to secure prior informed consent of those who will bear the consequences of their actions.

What might prior informed consent require of economists? What form might legitimate consent take? Who would give it in situations where an economic intervention will affect the lives of many? In Chapter 8, we encountered recent initiatives that require prior informed consent in the trading of hazardous material. The new treaties might point the way toward implementation of prior informed consent in the area of economic policy interventions. In cases where significant economic reform is proposed, legitimate representatives of the targeted community might have to certify that they understand the goals and the anticipated harms of the proposed intervention and that they are willing to accept the range of unanticipated effects and harms of the intervention prior to its implementation. In cases where the targeted community lacks the requisite knowledge to make these judgments, a multilateral informational clearinghouse (such as that provided for under the Convention on Biological Diversity) could provide the necessary training, information, and other support so that the community is able to engage the relevant issues effectively. Since these representatives would have to be competent to make these judgments, they very likely might have to include among them economists. To the degree possible, the economists would have to take responsibility for promoting the economic literacy of the community on whose behalf they act so that the community could understand and participate meaningfully in the decisions that will affect it (see May 1980). Economists might be obligated to integrate themselves deeply into the community they represent so that they understand the opportunities for and obstacles to the success of economic reform, the values and aspirations of the community's members, the needs and vulnerabilities of those who are most dispossessed, and other factors that bear on the choice of policy intervention. The goal would be to narrow the expertise gap separating the economist from those she serves, in full recognition of the fact that this gap will persist despite these efforts. This case reminds us that professional ethics is pragmatic: it is about managing tensions that inevitably attend professional practice, not about eliminating them through formulas or decision rules.

The Ethical Imperative to Build Capacity

We have seen that professional economic ethics is both inconceivable without and yet inadequately served by the prudential principle. So it is with prior informed consent and economic democracy. An economist who took prior informed consent to be an adequate decision rule might fly in from afar; place before the legitimate representatives of the targeted community a range of possible policy options; lay out for them the likely, anticipated harms; emphasize the possibilities for unanticipated, unknowable harms; and provide them with the opportunity to choose the option that best accords with their community's needs and aspirations. She might then do what she can to ensure the success of the policy option that the representatives have chosen. Having ticked all these boxes, she might feel herself to epitomize the ethical economist who has demonstrated adequate care and respect for the integrity of those she seeks to help.

The problem with self-satisfaction in this kind of case is that in order to thrive, the community she serves might need much more from her and from her profession than what she has offered. Vulnerable communities generally are not able to take on the risk associated with badly needed economic reform. By definition, vulnerable communities lack the reserves necessary to pull them through difficult times. For them, economic disruptions cannot be trivialized as mere "adjustment costs": they represent instead crises of cataclysmic proportions (Kanbur 2001). If empowered to make their own decisions, communities in peril will often be forced by circumstances to choose prudential strategies that are too conservative since they lack the resources and capacities necessary to risk the costs associated with policy failure. Applied economists understand this and often have used the institutional power at their disposal to enact policy initiatives that they took to be for the best when targeted communities were not prepared on their own to adopt them. But in cases of vulnerable communities, such paternalism is not only wrong headed, it is also extraordinarily dangerous.

Ethical economic interventions must do more than provide for informed consent: they must enhance the capacity of vulnerable communities so that they can choose to risk policy reform.[15] At a minimum, economic interventions must target three capacities: the capacity to innovate successfully, so that any desired initiative has a higher probability of success; the capacity to reduce the likelihood and intensity of harm in the event of policy failure (or success); and the capacity to bear, absorb, and manage the harm that occurs nevertheless. In the absence of these capacities, a vulnerable community will likely choose the stagnation associated with the status quo rather than take on the risks associated with innovation. In this context, the economist cannot take refuge in prior informed consent if she has done nothing to enhance the agency of the community. Economic interventions must cultivate these capacities as preconditions for (but also components of) economic reform projects.

Historically, the economics profession has embraced freedom of a limited sort: an agent's freedom to choose from among the possibilities afforded to her by her budget set. For Milton Friedman and the legions of economists whom he influenced, emphasis was placed on "negative freedom" which entails the absence of artificial government-imposed constraints on choice. The respect for the integrity of agents that appears in professional ethics weighs toward a different, more demanding conceptualization of freedom—the "positive" freedom that appears, for instance, in Amartya Sen's "capabilities approach" to human development (Sen 1992). For Sen, freedom refers to a person's capabilities set: those confronting a more extensive range of actual possibilities are decidedly freer than those who face a relatively impoverished opportunity set. He therefore defines "development as freedom" where freedom refers to an expanding terrain of available opportunities, especially for those who are most deprived of capabilities (Sen 1999).

The capabilities approach bears on and illuminates the application of the principle of respect for the autonomy and integrity of those whom the economist serves. In this account, the ethical economist must do more than provide communities with freedom to choose from among the policy options available since, in the absence of the capacity to endure the risks that reform entails, that kind of freedom is largely empty. She must attend first to that capacity—she must envision, advocate for, and work to implement successful interventions that enhance the capability of the community to live the life that it values. In so doing, she expresses the value she places on the rights of others to chart the chief contours of their own lives.

The enhancement of a community's ability to undertake and survive reform is a complex task, to be sure. It invites all sorts of new controversies that economics is only now beginning to face. For instance, does "social capital" theory provide valuable new insights that address capacity building, and does it provide a means by which reformers can envision new development strategies that take serious account of cultural norms as means for economic success (Bebbington 2002)? Or is it of limited use in practice, owing to its inherent vagueness and unsuitability to empirical evaluation (Durlauf 2002); is it apt to be misused to insulate flawed economic policy making and its institutional purveyors from critique, while blaming the targeted communities for their failures; and/or does it overlook institutionalized inequalities of power that solidify exploitation of women and other marginalized groups (Rankin 2002)? What other theoretical and policy approaches might address capacity building in communities where it is most badly needed? Influenced by professional economic ethics, one can imagine a substantial increase in attention to the interdisciplinary field of economic reform management—the study of the prerequisites for and means to implement successful economic interventions. The field would also explore practical mechanisms for ensuring prior informed consent. Combining methods and insights from economics, sociology, anthropology, and other fields, it would place greatest urgency on uncovering the determinants of the capacity of impoverished communities to undertake and survive badly needed economic reform.

It should be clear from this cursory discussion that the pursuit of professional economic ethics would not eliminate controversy or failures in the policy-making domain. But it might help to prevent or reduce the severity of economic reform disasters of the sort that have become familiar over the past several decades across the developing world and in the transition economies.

The Ethical Imperative to Humility

By this point in the exposition, I hope I can risk a question that would have been terribly off-putting at the outset: *how many lives have been harmed or even lost to economists' overconfidence?* Economists have undertaken extraordinary risks with the lives of others, certain of their understanding of economic dynamics and the effects of their interventions.[16] From interventions in Latin America in the 1970s and 1980s to Russia in the early 1990s, economists have made staggering promises of the likely effects of the policies that they recommended, about which only an economist sitting with Plato at the "rim of heaven" (Nussbaum and Sen 1989) could have been confident. Leading economists have pronounced publicly on the effects of policy initiatives, large and small, and have spoken of these matters as if they possessed a degree of knowledge that their science simply did not afford them—and this despite the fact that surveys demonstrate a widespread conviction among economists (and especially nonacademic economists) that over time economics has not improved its performance significantly in explaining behavior or events (Davis 2007). They have dismissed those who raised cautions or questioned the science upon which they drew as self-interested opportunists or economic illiterates who had no rightful place in the policy arena.[17]

It is by now clear that the pathways which channel economic interventions into economic outcomes are far too complex to be captured fully in even the most sophisticated models. Moreover, the background conditions against which these pathways operate and bear on the course of economic events are vast, variable, and largely unknowable. We know now that human motivation is far more complicated than economists tend to presume. This implies that we cannot be nearly as confident as were most economists over the past century about how human actors will respond to any particular economic stimulus, opportunity, or event. All of this argues for an honest and public recognition by economists of the limits of their science, recognition that emphasizes what we do not yet know today, and what we will never know about our field of expertise. Given what is at stake, honest recognition of and engagement with our ignorance is an ethical imperative. Humility must be among the most highly prized virtues in a profession where dependable knowledge is so elusive and where error is so consequential.

What might recognition of uncertainty and the (sometimes incalculable) risk of harm imply for economists? Concluding his consideration of the imponderables of climate change, Martin Weitzman makes an argument of much wider relevance:

> Perhaps in the end the climate-change economist can help most by *not* presenting a cost-benefit estimate for what is inherently a fat-tailed situation with potentially unlimited downside exposure as if it is accurate

and objective—and perhaps not even presenting the analysis as if it is an approximation to something that is accurate and objective—but instead by stressing somewhat more openly the fact that such an estimate might conceivably be arbitrarily inaccurate depending upon what is subjectively assumed about the high-temperature damages function along with assumptions about the fatness of the tails and/or where thy heave been cut off (Weitzman 2009, 18; emphasis in original).

This view on the need for professional reticence is echoed by Thomas Mayer in his consideration of the need for reform in econometric practice:

> An obvious answer is to foster in our day-to-day activities a climate of greater humility, to admit that our methods are imperfect and our results less compelling than they seem. This would make us more willing to admit that some of our procedures are open to doubt, and more willing to challenge prevailing practices. It should also make us less prone to group-think (2009a, 20).

The ethical imperative of humility must be cultivated through deep examination within professional ethics; it is not something that can be legislated effectively in a code. It requires, paradoxically, the cultivation of a degree of professional confidence that would allow practitioners to admit what they don't know when pressed for answers that competent economists cannot give.

Inducements to Hubris

Various features of economics may interfere with the achievement of the kind of humility that Weitzman and Mayer call for here. Philip Tetlock has undertaken the most extensive research in the field of expert judgment, error, and overconfidence. His findings are stunning: over a wide range of professions, experts do little better than nonexperts in forming judgments that pertain directly to the subject matter of their fields.

> When we pit experts against minimalist performance algorithms—dilettantes, dart-throwing chimps, and assorted extrapolation algorithms—we find few signs that expertise translates into greater ability to make either "well-calibrated" or "discriminating" forecasts (Tetlock 2005, 20).

Not all experts perform equally poorly, however. While professional background, status, fame, and ideological commitments make no difference to expert performance, *how experts think* is decisive. Tetlock finds that Isaiah Berlin's description of "foxes" and "hedgehogs" provides the key insight into good expert performance. In Tetlock's studies, hedgehogs were identified as "intellectually aggressive" actors who "knew one big thing and sought, under the banner of parsimony, to expand the explanatory power of that big thing to 'cover' new cases." In contrast, "the more eclectic foxes knew many little things," they "[drew] from an eclectic array of traditions, and accept[ed] the ambiguity and contradiction as inevitable features of life." Foxes were also "content to improvise ad hoc solutions to keep pace with a rapidly changing world" (Tetlock 2005, 20–21; 2). Tetlock's studies reveal that foxes consistently do much better than hedgehogs in their professional judgments.

Mainstream economics as it evolved through the twentieth century came to prize just those features that Tetlock finds undermine expert judgment: the field produces and rewards hedgehogs rather than foxes. During this period, economics came to base its analysis and policy prescriptions on "one big thing"—on what it viewed to be essential features of human and physical nature, and a universal logic and method. In comparison with anthropology, sociology, and political science, mainstream economics came to prize severe reductionism and parsimony in explanation and prediction. It has been far more ready than other social sciences to abstract from complicating factors, and as a consequence, it draws infrequently on insights from other disciplines.[18] The typical graduate level syllabus in economics includes no literature at all from fields other than economics. Indeed, the awarding of the 2009 Nobel Memorial Prize in economics to *political scientist* Elinor Ostrom shocked many economists—-not because they had qualms about the quality of her work but because they had never heard of it (Levitt 2009).

Unfortunately for the field, these attributes undermine economic expertise. In Tetlock's words, there is a

> perversely inverse relationship between my prime exhibit indicators of good judgment ... and the qualities science prizes in scientists—the tenacity required to reduce superficial complexity to underlying simplicity (Tetlock 2006, 203).

Economists also may be led to overconfidence by the pressures they face to provide expertise beyond that afforded by their science—to solve problems that they are insufficiently equipped to fix. This idea is implicit in the Friedman quotation with which this chapter began, and it is one that should be seen to have merit even by those who do not share Friedman's ideological conservatism. Economists are pressed regularly to do more than they, in fact, can do. Wesley C. Mitchell identified this problem in the early-twentieth century:

> Now [economists] are frequently called upon to advise about matters of which their knowledge is slight. They do not always decline the over-flattering invitations with the firmness which befits a scientific conscience (cited in Dorfman 1959, 210).

Social and economic crises can also tempt the economist to exceed his competence. Reflecting on his experience as a World Bank consultant in Sierra Leone and other crisis situations, Griffiths (2003) speaks of the exhilaration of decision making in which hundreds of thousands of lives are at stake. Speaking of advice during crisis Griffiths writes:

> Making the decision does give you a kick, though. It is a big decision, an important decision, a decision that will kill many people and save many

people … The fact that you make the decision, on your own judgment rather than on hard fact and theory, makes you feel important, powerful. I recognize that the power is addictive (Griffiths 2003, 175).

Lee Hamilton, a former Vice Chairman of the Joint Economic Committee of the U.S. Congress, addresses the pressures facing economists in this way:

> Every politician understands the impatience that led Harry Truman to wish for a one-armed economist. But the nation is not well served with economic advice that conceals scientific disagreement or genuine uncertainty about the economic consequences of particular actions.

Hamilton urges the economist to resist these pressures. He asks that economic advisors present a "list of options" rather than a "legal brief," and that they report honestly on "what is known and with what degree of certainty, where there is important disagreement and why, and the pros and cons of particular courses of action" (Hamilton 1992, 64).

Unfortunately, the expectations of Truman rather than Hamilton exemplify what is asked of economists in the public and private sectors. In William Allen's view, this leads to an institutional dynamic which yields a "persistent 'disequilibrium'" in the sense that as economists grow more competent in dealing with policy problems, the questions asked are made broader in scope and more complex." Paraphrasing the words of Harry G. Johnson, Allen writes that government "presses its economists to levels of incompetence. Frustratingly and disconcertingly, more is demanded at any time than can be delivered" (Allen 1977, 87). Hayek concurs:

> [E]ven if the true scientists should all recognize the limitations of what they can do in the field of human affairs, so long as the public expects more there will always be some who will pretend, and perhaps honestly believe, that they can do more to meet popular demands than is really in their power (Hayek 1978, 31).

How might the pressures on economists to overreach be offset? Hardwig (1994) emphasizes an ethical duty of individual practitioners to emphasize the limits of their knowledge, as the epigraph to this chapter suggests. "Refuse to give opinions," he admonishes, "when you are being asked for opinions that are beyond the range of your expertise" (1994, 92). But the strength of these pressures suggests the need for institutional reform as well.

In a discussion of the IFIs, Mark Weisbrot and Dean Baker (2004) offer proposals that are directly on point. The proposals entail installing mechanisms to ensure accountability of economic institutions and the economists they employ when they pursue economic interventions. First, the institution's program goals should be clearly defined *ex ante*. Second, progress during and after implementation should be closely monitored. When the program fails to achieve its announced objectives (or causes other harms), the monitors should indicate whether the failure was due to inadequate implementation, unforeseen confounding circumstances, or poor program design. Third, the economists involved in the program should be publicly identified, as should the others who populate the chain of command that is responsible for the program. This will spread the risk of the policy intervention beyond the targeted community to the architects of the program. Weisbrot and Baker hope that risk sharing will create incentives for economists to design more realistic and more robust policy interventions and to identify more quickly substandard policies (and inept economists).[19]

Weisbrot and Baker's proposals are consistent with new findings from research on the fallibility of expert judgment that we reviewed a moment ago. Drawing on this research, Angner (2006) argues that economists are particularly apt to suffer from overconfidence. This is due in part to the conformity in thought across economics (as compared with other social sciences), the tendency of economic prediction to be imprecise in critical respects, and the consequent absence of adequate feedback mechanisms from which economists can learn quickly whether their predictions and expectations were fulfilled. Imprecision in prediction invites subsequent "confirmation bias" (the claim that unfolding events confirms one's prior predictions, even when the evidence is ambiguous) and "hindsight bias" (the overestimation of one's prediction of past events), both of which preclude learning over time. The evidence from overconfidence studies demonstrates that experts in fields that provide regular and unambiguous feedback are far less likely to exhibit overconfidence. Angner concludes that the failures of economic experts

> seem to stem in part from a lack of effective social or institutional constraints. Economists acting as experts do not appear to face effective social sanctions that encourage them to minimize the ambiguity and vagueness of their predictions. Less vague and ambiguous predictions would make it easier to learn from experience, and should to some extent mitigate the effects of the confirmation and hindsight biases. Similarly, economists-as-experts do not appear to suffer noticeable penalties for expressing extreme confidence in their judgment (Angner 2006, 17).

The faith placed in economics takes other forms that compound the problem of hubris. There is a pronounced tendency to lionize leading economists, by the press and other institutions. The attention paid to central bankers, such as Alan Greenspan, who are portrayed as having an encyclopedic knowledge of economic affairs and super-human judgment about monetary policy; the awarding of a Nobel Memorial Prize in economics (but not in political science, history or other social sciences); the high salaries paid to both applied and academic economists as compared with their colleagues in the other social sciences and humanities; and the impenetrability of the mathematical language in which modern economics is expressed: all these conspire to induce a sense of professional confidence and authority that is unwarranted, dangerous, and therefore, unethical. Economics remains today as much art as science; its grasp of its area of expertise remains tenuous; and its ability to bring about the results it seeks is, at best, limited. The economics profession, therefore, faces an ethical obligation to cultivate a sense of humility among its practitioners (Henderson 1977). It must take greater care to emphasize to its practitioners and the broader community that professional humility is a virtue, not a weakness, even if it doesn't pay as well as hubris. It must emphasize (especially when its individual practitioners do not) what is not known and what cannot be known, so that economists and the public they serve are better situated to understand the risks associated with economic practice.

For a profession that has succeeded in achieving influence by exaggerating what it knows rather than admitting candidly what it does not (and cannot) know, recognition of the limits of our expertise might be unsettling, unsatisfying, and disheartening. How are we to sustain our morale and justify our interventions once we give up the illusion of knowledge and control upon which those interventions are based? How are we to advocate and otherwise intervene once we surrender what Sharon Welch calls the "ethic of control"—"a construction of agency, responsibility and goodness which assumes that it is possible to guarantee the efficacy of one's actions" (Welch 2000, 14)? Welch argues that we must confront the despair that accompanies recognition of what we do not and cannot control; we must learn to live with and act despite our ignorance and impotence. She advocates an "ethic of risk" that accepts the responsibility to act to promote the social good even when the outcome is by no means assured, and she explores what this ethic requires of us as we work with those we intend to assist.

Other theorists have recently begun to explore similar themes in the context of a general appreciation of the limits of expertise. Wendell Berry has called attention to the dangers of intellectual arrogance—of presuming to know what cannot be known. He urges in its place the "way of ignorance," which is "to be careful, to know the limits and the efficacy of our knowledge" (Berry 2005, ix–x). Awareness of the limits of our knowledge directs us to consider carefully the scale on which we ought to work:

> By propriety of scale we limit the possible damages of the risks we take. If we cannot control scale so as to limit the effects, then we should not take the risk. From this, it is clear that some risks simply should not be taken. Some experiments should not be made (2005, 66).

In a similar vein, Wes Jackson (2005) advocates for the adoption of an "ignorance-based worldview," one that requires of us constant attention to what we do not and cannot know. He captures the unknown and unknowable in the concept of mystery, and argues that

> if we are up against mystery, then knowledge is relatively small, and the ancient program is the right one: Act on the basis of ignorance. Acting on

the basis of ignorance, paradoxically, requires one to know things, remember things—for instance, that failure is possible, that error is possible, that second chances are desirable (so don't risk everything on the first chance), and so on (2005, 15).

The way of ignorance that Berry presses upon us is foreign to economists, to be sure, and it invites a reflexive dismissal since it seems to call into question the foundations of our intellectual and practical missions. But this worldview is not hostile to science or practical interventions; nor is it biased toward the political left or right. Its import is to prevent the harm that arises from scientifically unwarranted overconfidence combined with the authority that flows to the professions on account of their expertise and institutional positions. Though the critique originates in epistemic claims (about what we cannot possibly know), it is essentially ethical. It is intended to remind the ethical professional that she fulfills her professional covenant by keeping ever in view the limitations of her craft as she nevertheless intervenes in ways that are designed to promote the welfare of others. She works ethically when she takes careful account of the scale on which she can and should efficaciously act and when she designs interventions that embrace the existence of, rather than deny, the complexities that exceed her science.

Recognition of the ignorance surrounding economic matters implies that all economic interventions have an *experimental* quality: we act based on our best judgments, but we presume always that the full consequences of our acts are unknowable (*ex ante* and *ex post*). This strengthens substantially the normative demand for prior informed consent since those who are targeted by economic interventions are always, in part, research subjects. This is not to say that economic interventions are generally intended as experiments: to the contrary, they are intended to benefit directly the participants rather than simply to learn from their experiences so as to promote the welfare of others. But these benefits may or may not materialize, other benefits may arise instead, and unanticipated harms may attend and overwhelm them. It is this aspect of uncertainty that lends to economic interventions an experimental quality with strong normative entailments.

The Imperative to Promote Pluralism

Fundamental to the ethical demand for humility is the obligation of the field to learn to cultivate (rather than simply tolerate) theoretical pluralism and dissent (McCloskey 1990; Garnett 2009b; Garnett and Butler 2009; Freeman 2009; Ross 2009).[20] For the past half-century, economics has been monopolized theoretically and methodologically to a much greater degree than are the other social sciences. The consensus around the neoclassical approach (and the language of mathematics) has been taken to be a sign of the theoretical maturity of economics. And so it is that most economics graduate students today will never be exposed to any of the various heterodox traditions in economics: they will have no coursework in post-Keynesian, social, feminist, Marxist, Austrian, or original institutionalist theory at any point along the way to their degrees.

The promotion of theoretical pluralism is good professional practice since distinct approaches yield novel insights, owing to their differences in initial assumptions, logic, and method. Pluralism is also warranted by a professional ethical commitment to humility. It is irresponsible for the profession to presume that any one approach to economics or one set of methods is best for understanding economic affairs or designing economic interventions. McCloskey speaks regularly on this point, such as in this passage where she quotes Wayne Booth:

> "The serious ethical disasters produced by narratives occur when people sink themselves into an unrelieved hot bath of one kind of narrative" (237). Dogmatic Marxists, dogmatic neoclassicals, dogmatic Austrian economists, dogmatic institutionalists, who have put the other's writings on an index of forbidden books, are ethically dangerous, all of them (McCloskey 1990, 146).

Certainly, individual economists are ethically warranted in committing to and advocating whichever approach they find most compelling—and a vital professional economic ethics must insist upon their freedom to do so. But there are ethical obligations facing the profession as a whole that do not apply (at all or in the same way) to its individual members. Theoretical pluralism is one of those obligations: the profession must cultivate an environment in which alternative approaches to economics can flourish so that individual economists working in minority traditions can find the kind of support and sustenance upon which professional survival depends. The profession must work to instill the view that no one approach to economic theory or policy has a monopoly on the truth. It must work in concert with economic journals and funding agencies to enact an intellectual opening up to minority traditions and with research departments at major universities to alter hiring practices, curriculum, and pedagogical approaches in order to ensure greater intellectual breadth among those who will enter the profession. I will take up this matter in detail in the next chapter.

Institutionalizing Professional Economic Ethics

The adoption of professional economic ethics may require various kinds of institutional reform in academic economics: new curriculum and training, perhaps, along with new texts and journals, the creation of faculty positions in economic ethics, etc. It might also call forth new institutions to promote ethical conduct among applied economists and to review and evaluate economic practice. One can imagine a range of new institutions that together promote ethical economics. One such institution might be economic practice review boards.

Review boards exist in many professions where they perform a diverse array of functions.[21] For instance, the National Society of Professional

Engineers established a Board of Ethical Review (BER) in 1954. It is "a panel of engineering ethics experts that has served as the profession's guide through ethical dilemmas ... The purpose of the BER is to render impartial opinions pertaining to the interpretation of the NSPE Code of Ethics, develop materials, and conduct studies relating to ethics of the engineering profession." Since its inception, "the BER's nearly 500 advisory opinions have helped bring clarity to the ethical issues engineers face daily" (see http://www.nspe.org/Ethics/BoardofEthicalReview/index.html).[22]

In like manner, economic practice review boards could be charged with providing ethical direction to the economics profession and assessing its performance in meeting its obligations to those it serves. They could also advise and evaluate the conduct of the public, private, and multilateral institutions that provide economic services. For instance, the boards might be charged with thinking through and proposing practical means for securing prior informed consent in cases where economic interventions are apt to affect the lives of many people all at once. They might institute procedures for reviewing proposed economic interventions in advance of their implementation. The boards might advise economists who are undertaking sensitive research and other interventions to ensure that they have taken sufficient care to ascertain and augment the capability of a targeted community to bear the associated risk, secured appropriate prior informed consent, and taken steps to identify and ameliorate potential harms. The boards might also be authorized to review any potential conflicts of interest in which economists might find themselves; pass judgment on and provide guidance in situations where economists are invited to provide consultation to autocratic or otherwise illegitimate governments or when they confront rampant corruption; and perhaps most importantly, provide a sounding board for and advice to economists who confront these and other ethically challenging circumstances.

Since I am not advocating a binding code of conduct for the economics profession, I will not explore how economic practice review boards would enforce it. The mission of the boards would be quite different: it would be to enhance the profession's performance in meeting its diverse obligations through investigation and education rather than through legislation. Moreover, like professional ethics more generally, the mission would not be to prevent misguided economists from doing wrong; instead, it would be to assist virtuous economists in doing good.

CONCLUSION

Drawing on insights from the professional ethics that have emerged in other professions and taking into account the particular exigencies of economic practice, there are good reasons to think that professional economic ethics will encompass reform to ensure transparency, replicability, and robustness in economic research; much greater attention to the potential harm to experimental subjects in the laboratory and in RCTs, where there are also risks of exploitation of the particularly vulnerable and an unjust distribution of risks and rewards; the prudential principle; respect for the autonomy of those whom the economist serves; the need to augment the capacity of communities to undertake economic reform; professional humility in the face of the uncertainty of economic practice; and theoretical pluralism. It is also possible that the profession will come to recognize the need for new institutions to ensure that its ethics reach down to the day-to-day practice of its members, and that those members undertake their work in ways that reflect the highest ethical aspirations of the profession. One important implication of these reforms is that the institutions which employ economists and provide economic services would come to live under the ethical scrutiny of their economist employees and the economics profession more generally.

That said, I should emphasize that the discussion of this chapter is tentative and speculative. It comprises many more questions than answers. The actual content of professional economic ethics and decisions about the kinds of institutions that are necessary to inculcate ethical sensibilities and advance ethical behavior must arise out of careful deliberation among the community of economists, informed by instruction from the best professional ethicists and influenced by voices from the communities that economists seek to serve. While we do not know precisely where such an endeavor will lead, there is good reason to expect that both the profession and those it targets stand to gain much from the encounter.

The inauguration of a field of professional economic ethics would require a rethinking of economics training at the undergraduate and graduate levels. What might this rethinking entail, and where might it lead with regard to pedagogical reform? We turn now to this topic.

Notes

1 Take, for example, the authors' Oomph versus Precision diet pill example (Ziliak and McCloskey 2008, Ch. 2), where they demonstrate how reliance on statistical significance leads to poor judgment.

2 As this discussion suggests, ethical matters are intertwined with matters of professional competence. There is an ethical obligation to competence and to knowing the limits of one's capacities. We return to this matter below.

3 "The basic idea of the [bootstrap] procedure involves sampling with replacement to produce random samples of size n from the original data; each of these is known as a bootstrap sample and each provides an estimate of the parameter of interest. Repeating the process a large number of times provides the required information on the variability of the estimator . . ." (Everitt 2002, 51).

4 Other work confirms the need to alter the incentives facing empirical researchers. Dewald, Thursby and Anderson (1986) present the results of an extraordinary effort to replicate the findings of papers that were published in the *Journal of Money, Credit and Banking* during the early 1980s. They conclude

that "inadvertent errors in published empirical articles are a commonplace" (587). They call on economics departments to emphasize replicability and on journals to "require the submission of programs and data" with all empirical papers (601). Zelder (2008) demonstrates that the interaction between econometricians, economic journals, and their readers is apt to lead to the proliferation of published articles with "distorted" t statistics (i.e., that arise from unreported specification search).

5 Stodder (1998) raises other ethical issues that arise in experimental economics such as those surrounding the use of grades as incentives in experiments involving students.

6 Though, see Hertwig and Ortmann (2008) for contrary evidence from the field of social psychology.

7 Concerns about the use of deception in psychology include

charges that deception violates the individual's right to voluntarily choose to participate, abuses the basic interpersonal relationship between the experimenter and subject, contributes to deception as a societal value and practice, is a questionable base for development of the discipline, is contrary to our professional roles as teachers or scientists, and will ultimately lead to a loss of trust in the profession and science of psychology (Adair, Dushenko and Lindsay 1985, 61).

8 In the Milgram experiment, researchers instructed experimental subjects to apply electrical shocks to "learners" when the learners failed to answer correctly the questions put to them. As the experiment proceeded, the subjects were instructed to increase the intensity of the shocks as the learners cried out in pain. Unbeknownst to the subjects, the learners were actors who were, in fact, not harmed.

9 But see Sen (1992) for an important dissent from the mainstream view.

10 At present, the J-PAL Web site provides little evidence of sustained engagement by these researchers with the ethical issues attending RCTs. For instance, an essay by Duflo, Glennerster and Kremer (2006) featured on the J-PAL Web site that offers a "toolkit" for the conduct of RCTs mentions ethics in passing just once in its 88 pages. Research that explores ethical issues that arise in RCTs include Ravallion (2009a; 2009b), Deaton (2009), Nathan (2008), Oakley et al. (2003), Nama and Swartz (2002), Gueron (2002), Boruch et al. (2002), Cook (2002), Thompson (1987), and Heckman and Smith (1995). The discussions found in these articles range from a mere listing of ethical issues to more substantial treatment.

11 See the *International Ethical Guidelines for Biomedical Research Involving Human Subjects* of the Council for International Organizations of Medical Sciences (CIOMS), updated in 2002, for a detailed examination of the ethical aspects of experimentation on human subjects, with particular focus on the developing country context. The document explores all of the following: respect for the autonomy of research subjects in research that "involves individuals who are not capable of giving informed consent"; the choice of control in clinical trials (a particularly contentious issue in biomedical research); issues that arise in research among vulnerable groups or persons (such as "equitable distribution of burdens and benefits in the selection of groups of subjects"); confidentiality; and the right of those who are harmed during experimentation to treatment and compensation.

It is clear that many of these issues also arise in economic RCTs. Yet, unlike bio-medical research, which is governed by the profession (and by institutions such as ethical review committees), economic RCTs as of yet are largely ungoverned by the profession.

12 A comprehensive treatment of the content of professional economic ethics would require discussion of many issues that I will not explore here. One warrants mention: the role of economists in war making. Influential economists such as Thomas Schelling (see Kaplan 2005; Mirowski 2002) have contributed to military strategy, drawing on the insights gleaned from economic theory (especially game theory). Whether, when, under what circumstances, and with what restrictions economists should contribute to war efforts are very difficult questions that deserve a subfield within professional economic ethics. The issue has been debated within anthropology and psychology owing to initiatives which involve social scientists and psychologists in intelligence work (Price 1998), military operations in Iraq and Afghanistan (including interrogations of prisoners), and also the Pentagon's new "Minerva" program that seeks to recruit social scientists in its efforts to combat security threats (see Cohen 2008; Carey 2008).

13 There is increasing attention today in economics and beyond to the matter of policy making under conditions of uncertainty. Examples include Brock, Durlauf and West (2006), which analyzes strategies to take account of "model uncertainty" in macroeconomic policy making; Orphanides and Williams (2002), which examines the robustness of alternative monetary policy rules; Morgan and Henrion (1990), which presents a detailed examination of public policy and presents "ten commandments for good public policy" in the context of uncertainty; Brainard (1967), which explores optimal policy in a world of uncertainty and which concludes that the policy maker often should not shoot precisely for the optimal value of the target variable and, indeed, that sometimes the optimal policy might require moving in the "wrong" direction. To date, the contributions to this literature are very abstract, stylized, and technical; and it is doubtful that they have any bearing at all on actual policy making or on the work of most applied economists. This is most unfortunate. While a division of labor in economics is inevitable and desirable, of course, the disconnection of the theory of policy making under uncertainty from actual economic policy making is not. What is needed is a bridging that allows for the application of practical insights gleaned "at the theoretical frontier" to "the policy coal face," to borrow a useful phrase from Ravi Kanbur (2009a, 2).

14 Hahn and Sunstein (2005) present a thoroughgoing rejection of the precautionary principle as a decision rule that makes similar points.

15 In this connection, work of the Social Protection Unit of the World Bank that features risk and vulnerability analysis and capacity enhancement of vulnerable groups is noteworthy.

16 And, it should be added, of their motives. Recent research by social psychologists finds that individuals tend to overestimate their propensity to act righteously; indeed, self-inflating bias may be stronger when it comes to moral as opposed to other judgments (see Carey 2009). This implies the need for humility and self-scrutiny not only about one's professional competence but also about one's motivations and character.

17 I will permit myself just one example. Throughout the 1990s, Paul Krugman consistently ridiculed all advocates of "fair trade" (the tying of trade concessions to labor and environmental standards) as economic incompetents and deceitful,

self-interested protectionists (1997; 2001). Only in 2007 did he reverse position, based on evidence of the widespread harm in the United States caused by trade liberalization with China, and begin to advocate fair trade proposals (Krugman 2007).

18 Several heterodox traditions in political economy, including social, institutionalist, and some contributions to Marxian theory eschew reductionism. See Resnick and Wolff (1987) for an extended discussion of anti-reductionism in social theory and economics.

19 Pritchett (2008) argues that there is often a powerful disincentive facing advocates of a project to submit it to evaluation since an unfavorable result might imperil future donor funding. Ravallion (2009b) identifies various problems with project evaluation that need to be addressed in any serious program of evaluation, including a bias toward evaluating policies with short- as opposed to long-term effects and narrow as opposed to widespread benefits. Evaluations also tend to focus on "internal validity" at the expense of evaluations of "external validity" (Ravallion 2009b, 32).

20 The International Confederation of Associations for Pluralism in Economics (ICAPE) is particularly important in this regard (see http://www.icape.org/).

21 Some of these boards have jurisdiction over economic policy. Norway's Petroleum Fund, established in 1990 to invest income generated from oil royalties for the benefit of future generations, today includes an Advisory Council on Ethics that is charged with ensuring "moral" investments by the Fund. Specifically, the Fund's provisions bar any investments "which constitute an unacceptable risk that the Fund may contribute to unethical acts or omissions" (http://www.regjeringen.no/en/sub/Styrer-rad-utvalg/ethics_council/Ethical-Guidelines.html?id=425277). An ethical philosopher and a group of economists manage this initiative.

22 Ethical boards are contentious. Some medical researchers argue that ethics committees obstruct useful projects through unwarranted paternalism (see Garrard and Dawson 2005).

Chapter 12

Training the "Ethical Economist"

If man is not to do more harm than good in his efforts to improve
the social order, he will have to learn that in this, as in all other
fields where essential complexity of an organized kind prevails, he
cannot acquire the full knowledge which would make mastery of
the events possible . . . The recognition of the insuperable limits
to his knowledge ought indeed to teach the student of society a
lesson in humility which should guard him against becoming an
accomplice in men's fatal striving to control society . . .
Friedrich Hayek (1978, 34)

THE AEA AND ECONOMIC TRAINING

PhD training in economics has not changed substantially since the mid-
twentieth century. The curriculum comprises a set of "core" courses that
range over the material that those who earn the degree are expected to
master: microeconomics, macroeconomics, and econometrics. The core is
followed by comprehensive exams and field courses in areas that reflect
the expertise of the faculty at the institution where the student happens
to be enrolled. Typically, field courses include offerings in labor market
economics, industrial organization, environmental economics, economic
development and/or growth, international trade, and the like. In the past,
economic history and the history of economic thought routinely appeared
as options; today, they have been replaced by offerings in behavioral and
experimental economics and advanced quantitative techniques. Training
concludes with the dissertation, which today frequently takes the form of
three essays that demonstrate technical competence rather than an inte-
grated book-length exposition of an economic phenomenon.

Consistency in PhD training should not be taken as satisfaction on the
part of the profession with the curriculum, however. Over the past century, the AEA has expressed concern about economics instruction at all
levels. The AEA Executive Committee has established special and standing committees to investigate whether reform in economic training might
be necessary to achieve the goal of "diffusing light." The matter received
greatest attention at the turn of the twentieth century, during the 1940s,

and then from the 1970s onward (Hinshaw and Siegfried 1991). In 1944, the Executive Committee initiated a comprehensive effort that established the Committee on Undergraduate Teaching in Economics and Training of Economists, an initiative that ultimately spawned 11 subcommittees and involved "56 association members (including two future Nobel Prize winners—Stigler and Schultze) and 22 consultants" (Hinshaw and Siegfried 1991, 376). This effort generated hardly a ripple: the committee produced just one report on undergraduate economics training which precipitated no formal action by the AEA. Soon thereafter, the AEA commissioned Howard R. Bowen to study graduate economics training. Bowen's sweeping report identified many areas of concern which were examined by prominent economists during a roundtable discussion at the annual meetings of the AEA in 1954. Reporting on the discussion, John Perry Miller expressed a sentiment that would recur later on:

> There seemed to be a feeling that we have been more successful in putting out men of high technical skill than in developing men who have a broad and judicious view of social problems and are effective in communicating with decision-makers concerning these problems (1954, 681).

Bowen worried about this tendency. Already by this time, pressure in the curriculum to enhance technical training had been relieved by "reducing or eliminating the time devoted to more scholarly, historical and philosophical inputs" (Coats 1992, 344). Bowen highlighted what he saw as the profession's social obligations:

> It is vital to the future of our society that successive generations of economists be trained who will have the technical skills, the broad perspective, the judgment, the leadership, and the sense of social responsibility necessary to advance the frontiers of knowledge in the field and to translate this knowledge into practicable solutions for social problems (Bowen 1953, 34, cited in Coats 1992, 351).

Despite the subsequent establishment of a standing AEA education committee in 1955, frequent AEA panels on economic training, and the establishment of the *Journal of Economic Education* in 1969, graduate economics training throughout the latter half of the twentieth century remained impervious to change. Throughout this period, the AEA declined to attempt to "enforce a system of accreditation or otherwise seek to enforce standards of any kind" (Miller 1954, 681). In the late 1980s, the AEA again engaged the matter of graduate training through the establishment of another high-profile committee. The immediate catalyst was the publication in 1987 of the results of a survey of economics graduate students in leading programs by David Colander and Arjo Klamer. Colander and Klamer's work (1987; 1990) rightly attracted much attention in the profession. They discovered a profound skepticism among students about the nature of economic training and the orientation of their professors toward what counted as professional success. While students typically entered graduate school with a commitment to apply economic tools and analysis to pressing policy issues, they reported that such work was given no value in their training. They spoke of being "socialized" to understand that abstract theory for theory's sake was the key to professional success where success was defined, in turn, as tenure at leading research universities. In the words of one student who expressed a common sentiment,

> It is very hard [to go into a public policy job] when a lot of friends, and certainly the faculty, are judging you by how good a job you get. When you want to succeed in their eyes you get a job at a major university. It is very hard to chuck all this and be a failure in the eyes of all those people who have been very important in the last four years (Colander and Klamer 1987, 97).

Perhaps most disturbing of the study's findings were student reports about the kinds of knowledge that would place them on the "fast track" for professional success:

> Knowledge of the economy and knowledge of economic literature do not make an economist successful. . .Forty-three percent believed that a knowledge of economic literature was unimportant while only 10 percent felt that it was very important. Sixty-eight percent believed that a thorough knowledge of the economy was unimportant; only 3.4 percent believed that it was very important (1987, 99).

Reflecting on these findings, Colander and Klamer argue that

> There was a strong sense that economics was a game and that hard work in devising relevant models that demonstrated a deep understanding of institutions would have a lower payoff than devising models that were analytically neat; the façade, not the depth of knowledge, was important (1987, 100).

The bias toward demonstration of technical skills devoid of economic depth was reinforced by the core curriculum that initiated students to graduate training. Colander and Klamer found that students quickly identified and conformed to the incentives to master the curriculum's "formal modeling techniques" rather than focus on institutions or "real world problems" (1987, 108). By the time they reached graduation, students had come to internalize the norms of a profession that values mathematical wizardry over economic relevance and employment at research universities over positions at very good liberal arts colleges or nonacademic institutions.

The AEA Response: The COGEE and Related Reports

The Colander-Klamer study touched a nerve: in part, because its findings confirmed what many economists had already come to believe. In 1986, prominent participants in a symposium on the state of economics sponsored by the National Science Foundation

> put forth the view that economics as taught in graduate school had become too divorced from real-world questions. This viewpoint seemed to be shared

by a sufficiently large number of people inside and outside the profession that it merited careful scrutiny (Krueger 1991, 1035).

In 1988, AEA President Robert Eisner established a committee to undertake an examination of graduate economics training. The Commission on Graduate Education in Economics (COGEE) surveyed graduate students, economists, department chairs, and academic and nonacademic employers of new PhDs. It also examined economists' compensation as compared with other professions, reviewed hiring practices and curriculum of universities and colleges at all levels, and explored the relationship between the economics PhD and other related degrees.

The COGEE findings confirmed many of the concerns identified by Bowen and later by Colander and Klamer. COGEE emphasized that graduate economic training had "become too removed from real economic problems" (Krueger 1991, 1039). The report highlights a widely held sentiment that the training overvalued technical expertise at the expense of creativity, relevance to real-world problem solving, and emphasis on real-world institutions and practices. "The Commission's fear is that graduate programs may be turning out a generation with too many *idiot savants*, skilled in technique but innocent of real economic issues" (Krueger 1991, 1044–45).

A survey of nonacademic employers commissioned by COGEE substantiated these concerns. Respondents from the public and private sectors laid bare their frustrations regarding the training and inclinations of new economics PhDs. "We're headed for the same route as the classics," remarked one respondent while discussing the growing irrelevance of economics training; "The economics profession should be asking itself where the hell it thinks it's going," said another. Laurie Bassi, the report's author, summarized the consensus view in more measured terms: "They see a profession that produces far less value for society than could reasonably be expected given the tremendous intellectual power of its members. They see a profession in decline" (Bassi 1989, 7). Several respondents identified the profession's perverse incentive structure as the culprit: students were encouraged to apply themselves to the mastery of puzzle solving and technique rather than economic analysis, creativity, and communication skills. Respondents emphasized the ignorance of new PhDs regarding the sources of and weaknesses in the data that economists use and a related inability to interpret data effectively. A disturbing trend confirmed the complaints: six of the eighteen organizations represented in the survey reported that they had begun to hire noneconomists in positions that in the past would have been filled by economists. Seventy-seven percent of nonacademic employers cited the need for changes in the structure and content of PhD-level training (Hansen 1991).

COGEE's recommendations were rather tepid, especially when compared with those of the Bowen report (Coats 1992). Among other things,

COGEE called for "reasonable" prerequisites for entry into the graduate core and remedial training for those needing it before entering graduate school (something many programs already provided); a better balance between breadth and depth and between abstract theory and real world applications in core training; greater attention to empirical work in field courses; more opportunities for writing and the cultivation of communication skills; greater support during the transition from coursework to dissertation; and greater differentiation across PhD programs, based on the expertise of their respective faculties (Krueger 1991, 1052–53).

Despite the status of the economists who served on the Commission a follow-up study by Colander in 1998 found that the COGEE report was ignored in departmental decision making and failed to provoke any major changes in graduate study (Colander 1998; 2005a). Moreover, a second round of surveys of graduate students reported by Colander in 2005 (2005a; see also Colander 2007) found that, despite some improvement, several of the causes for concern identified in the earlier study remained. For instance, the number of respondents who felt that a thorough knowledge of the economy was very important for professional success had risen from the first survey: from 3 percent to 9 percent. Moreover, interest in empirical work rose from 16 percent to 30 percent. But as Colander notes, these numbers are still very low. Indeed, he finds that "51% still see a thorough knowledge of the economy as unimportant, and 35 percent still see a broad knowledge of the literature as unimportant" (Colander 2005a, 181).[1] Most important for present purposes, Colander finds that the socialization processes in graduate school still devalued these two areas of knowledge. Indeed, only 1 percent of fourth and fifth year students believed that knowledge of the economy was very important (Colander 2005a, 182). The core continued to serve as "a kind of mathematical hazing" that severs completely abstract theory from practical work, with the effect of decreasing "the diversity of thought processes and approaches in the pool of economists" (Colander 2007, 240). This emphasis also induced self-selection among potential economics PhD students, eliminating those with other skills and interests (and perhaps with more creativity) from the pool (Colander 2005a). Colander concludes that while economics as a field had improved in certain respects during the interim between his two studies, particularly in the increasing eclecticism of the approaches that economists pursue and the increasing attention given to real world applications, the training of graduate students lags behind developments in the field. Colander argues that students are still inculcated with the inclination to pursue "cleverness for cleverness's sake" at the expense of the cultivation of good judgment and the advancement of knowledge (Colander 2007, 243). This helps to explain the findings of a recent study by Stock and Hansen (2004) which reports a poor match between the skills taught in graduate economic programs and those required in the job market, especially in nonacademic contexts.

PEDAGOGICAL INADEQUACIES AS ETHICAL FAILURES

The deficiencies in graduate economics training are worrisome. It is in the interest of the profession to undertake reform in order to ensure the continuing relevance of economists, especially in the nonacademic environment. But these findings raise another kind of concern—one that appears in the Bowen report but only sporadically thereafter. The pedagogical inadequacies in economics represent an ethical failure on the part of the profession. To the degree that new economists are emerging from graduate school without knowledge of economic affairs or the institutions that are central to economic governance; have little critical understanding of the value (and weaknesses) of the data (and methods) upon which economic study depends and lack training in economic history and the history of economic thought; and to the degree that their profession sustains a reward structure which emphasizes puzzle solving of no particular social relevance over the attainment of the skills, judgment and sensibilities necessary to promote economic well-being and perform well in the institutions where economists work—to this degree, professional training fails to meet its professional responsibilities.

Bowen understood correctly that economic practice matters too much—not just to practitioners, but to society as a whole—for the profession to neglect reform in economic training when there is so much evidence of its inadequacies. Inappropriately trained economists do not possess and cannot provide the kind of expertise and judgment that society requires of them. As a consequence, economists are apt to do substantial harm. That is the heart of the matter. A profession that takes full account of its ethical responsibilities would be troubled by this state of affairs. It would take pains to understand just where and how it is failing to produce economists who are prepared for the diverse challenges they will face in their work, and it would take decisive steps to put its pedagogical house in order.

How might economics training be amended were the profession to embrace professional economic ethics? Two questions require attention. First, what would ethical economics training entail for nonspecialists? Second, what reforms would be required to train the specialist—those seeking the MA or PhD in economics—to equip the "ethical economist" for the challenges she will face?

ECONOMIC TRAINING FOR DEMOCRATIC CITIZENS

Those economists who stand before lecture halls filled with hundreds of undergraduates taking the requisite introductory economics course are in a position to affect how these students will view economic expertise for the rest of their lives. The audience comprises future "clients" of economic services: from political and business leaders to voters. Their world will be affected in diverse ways by the exercise of economic expertise. As a consequence, economics professors face a set of fascinating and difficult ethical questions. What kind of economic awareness will they try to cultivate in these students? What will be the chief take-away for students who will hardly remember the definition of income elasticity or the significance of an indifference curve? What will the professors try to impart to this constituency about their profession?

Economics professors can instill a sense of awe regarding the economist's knowledge and capacities, and indeed, many do just that. They can cultivate in their students the sense that economic knowledge has achieved a status on par with the natural sciences, with a comparable ability to map the world. They can present benefit-cost analysis, macroeconomic modeling, and econometric testing as dispassionate means for arriving at optimal policy. They can present the historic controversies among rival economic paradigms as settled in favor of the approach that now appears in the textbooks. In these ways, they can do much to persuade students that policy disputes are amenable to objective scientific application of the economic tools which economists have in hand; that economists therefore know best about such matters; and that society does best when it defers to their judgments.

Alternatively, economic instructors can convey to their students a sense of wonder at the complexity of economic affairs. They can affirm the existence of the as-of-yet unknown and the forever unknowable in their field. They can explore the hidden value judgments that appear in all economic theories and methods and encourage their students to consider whether this or that set of values represents a better foundation for economic theory and policy. Economists can introduce and explore with their students the diverse criticisms of economic methods that have arisen within economics, philosophy, and beyond. They can expose their students to the controversies that have arisen in the past and exist now in economics—not just over particular policy matters but over what theoretical approaches to economics are most useful for thinking about these issues. They can ensure the presence of these themes in the curriculum by including diverse theoretical approaches—including neoclassical, Austrian, post-Keynesian, institutionalist, behavioral, social, feminist, steady-state, Marxist, and others—so that students can come to see how these distinct schools of thought produce their insights about the economy and economic policy.[2] In all these ways, they can develop their students' capacity for critical reflection about economic matters and the expertise of the economics profession.

Economists who specialize in pedagogy have had much to say about these choices. Rob Garnett and Michael Butler (2009, 150) explore the ethical imperative of the economics profession to promote intellectual freedom by cultivating "students' 'capacity for critical

judgment' (AAUP 1967)," which incorporates the "art of crafting rea-
soned arguments and conclusions in the face of analytical, empirical
or normative uncertainties" (2009, 149). Garnett and Butler reject the
idea of economics training as the conveyance of received methods and
prepackaged policy prescriptions and the related representation of the
economist as final authority on economic matters. They tie the virtue of
intellectual freedom to the liberal impulses of the economics tradition,
citing in particular complimentary thinking in the work of Smith, Mill,
Shackle, Hayek and Sen. Fortunately, a commitment to cultivating these
capacities is now thriving (see also Garnett 2009a).

David Colander has drawn attention to a distinction within contemporary economic theory that relates to the matter before us. The economics
taught in the undergraduate curriculum, to this day, emphasizes a "simple system" model of the economy that yields an "economics of control"
approach to policy, even though in Colander's view this model has been
substantially displaced in advanced economic thought. The simple system
approach to theory presumes what Colander calls the "holy trinity" of
rationality, greed, and equilibrium which allows the economist to deduce
agent behavior and the outcome of their interactions from first principles. As a consequence, this approach generates parsimonious and elegant
theoretical models. These features imply that economists have at their
disposal sufficient knowledge to generate effective policy. The economics
of control approach to policy presents the economist as capacious—as a
social engineer that can turn this dial or pull that lever in order to ensure
good economic outcomes.

Colander traces the economics of control approach to policy to Abba
Lerner for whom

> applied policy economics was the application of a scientific set of rules
> determined by economic theory to be followed by policy makers and by
> agents in the economy. . .In the economics of control, economic analysis
> became *the* decision criterion, not an input into a broader decision process
> (Colander 2003, 201–02; emphasis in original).

This story remains the centerpiece of the economics curriculum today.
"It is a control story in which there is a knowable social optimum that
government policy is designed to achieve" (Colander 2005b, 254).

Contemporary mainstream economic theory has joined various heterodox traditions in moving away from this simple model of the economy
to an understanding of the economy as an irreducibly "complex" system
more closely associated with the vision of Hayek than Lerner or postwar
Keynesians. The complex system approach of mainstream economics is
predicated on an alternative and less determinant trinity of purposeful
behavior, enlightened self-interest, and sustainability (2005b, 251). The
complexity view understands the economy to encompass emergent prop-
erties at the macro level, path dependencies, discontinuities, multiple
equilibriums, and the like. In this view, one does not presume and then

bet everything on the stability of well-behaved economic relationships; nor does one seek to generate a full economic mapping that can yield definitive conclusions about optimal policy interventions. In place of the illusion of control, the complex system view yields a "muddling through" policy approach in which the economist works as an inductive social mechanic—trying this, then trying that, always watching, evaluating and adjusting, and always attentive to surprise and anomalies—rather than as a deductive social engineer who infers what is right and best from the elegant diagrams that appear in the textbook. In Colander's words,

> Each of the changes currently occurring in the holy trinity can be seen as a movement away from a search for the blueprints of the economic system, and toward a search for understanding a system in which the blueprints are missing, nonexistent, or so far beyond our analytic capabilities that we might as well forget about them (2003, 206–07).

The effect of these methodological innovations on economists' self-conception as policy designers is profound. Rather than imagine themselves to be *"infinitely bright . . . with full knowledge of the system design,"* they now recognize themselves as *"reasonably bright. . .with limited knowledge of the system"* (Colander 2005b, 251; emphasis in original).

These insights resonate naturally with heterodox economists of various sorts who challenge the tendency within the profession to reduce economic complexities for the sake of analytical tractability (see Resnick and Wolff 1987; Gibson-Graham 1996; Ruccio and Amariglio 2003; Bergeron 2006; Burczak 2006). Drawing on insights from feminist economics, for instance, Julie Nelson problematizes conceptions that rely on the metaphor of the economy as a machine. She argues that this metaphor is based on a "seventeenth-century Newtonian" understanding of "a clocklike world" that privileges "observability, predictability and control" (2004, 394; 384) and that hives off ethical considerations as irrelevant to the scientific enterprise. But this conception, Nelson explains, has by now been abandoned in the natural sciences. In contemporary physics, for example, we find attention to

> quantum theory, the theory of relativity, and most recently the study of chaos and complexity [that] reveals that the universe has non-mechanical, unpredictable, non-linear, seemingly incommensurable, surprising and even "spooky" behaviors. More generally, disequilibrium, effects of the observer on the observed, impossibility of prediction and control, jumpy or chaotic processes, emergence and systems that are more than just the sum of their parts demand non-mechanistic and non-reductionist approaches (394).

For Nelson, the application of these lessons to economics implies that there is "no blueprint for economic behavior." Instead, there is a need for context-sensitive economic analysis that probes the specifics of particular cases. It follows that policy making becomes much more laborious and uncertain.

Drawing on Austrian and post-structuralist insights, Deirdre McCloskey also inveighs against the notion of the economist as seated at the command center of economic affairs. In her view, many economists

> have fallen under the modernist spell, articulated, for example, by Wesley Clair Mitchell in 1924: "In economics as in other sciences we desire knowledge mainly as an instrument of control. Control means the alluring possibility of shaping the evolution of economic life to fit the developing purposes of the human race." More than any other economist, our Hayek was out of step with such erotic fascism of prediction and control (McCloskey 2000, 35–36).

We found in Chapter 4 that over the course of its history, the economics profession has been much more concerned with extending its influence than with examining the harm that it might do were it to achieve that influence. There is an ethical need to change this aspiration—to temper substantially the pursuit of influence in concert with a much more candid accounting to students and the public of what the profession does not and cannot know. In McCloskey's view (1990), the profession has cultivated a public that believes it has wares it does not have—magic elixirs to fix what needs fixing—and it then responds to the flattering (and enriching) requests for this "snake oil" by providing it (for a fee or a camera op). If she is correct, then we confront a dangerous application of Say's Law to the market for economic expertise. This state of affairs is untenable. The profession faces an acute obligation to correct this conceit and to deflate its students' and the public's mistaken presumptions about what economists can know and do.

The foregoing suggests the need for reform of undergraduate economic training on ethical grounds in order to enhance the capacities of students: to make informed economic judgments; to understand their obligation as democratic citizens to engage critically economists' claims and policy prescriptions; to know what to ask and not ask of economists and to know how to interpret what economists offer in response; and to hold economists accountable for their work. The economics of control approach should be abandoned in the curriculum just as it is being abandoned in research since it promotes a reassuring but dangerous fiction concerning the profession's knowledge and abilities. The fiction threatens to enhance the authority of economists to unwarranted levels and legitimize irresponsible economic interventions.

This agenda can't be accomplished in full in Econ 101, of course, but neither is the "economics of control" approach that is currently taught there adequately rendered. Teaching requires selection among possible emphases, trade-offs between breadth and depth, and many other judgments. What can be done is what should be done: to awaken students to the enormous importance and value of economic knowledge and study; to explore some of the approaches and methods by which economists attempt to make sense of and influence the world; to balance this with an emphasis on what is not and cannot be known; and to warn them against expecting too much from a profession that faces a subject matter that does not yield to ultimate control or simple blackboard solutions to the world's most pressing social problems. What can and should be done is to explore the opportunities for and obstacles to good economic practice that is informed by Wendell Berry's (2005, ix–x) "way of ignorance," which fixes our attention always on the unknown and unknowable (see Chapter 11).

One additional issue deserves mention here—one that we touched upon in Chapter 11 in connection with the ethics of experimental economics. Economists can affect the sensibilities of their students, including their moral judgments, for better or worse as they teach economic theory. Research has demonstrated that by teaching the neoclassical assumption of rationality as narrow, self-interested behavior, economists might unwittingly cultivate that personality trait in their students (see Frank, Gilovich and Regan 1993; Bowie 1991). In the context of graduate business education, for instance, Gintis and Khurana (2008, 300) conclude from an extensive literature on business education that the domination of neoclassical economic theory in the curriculum

> fosters a corporate culture that . . . encourages an ethic of greedy materialism where managers are expected to care only about personal financial reward, and where human character virtues such as honesty and decency are deployed only contingently in the interests of personal material reward.

In their view, business education therefore is "deeply complicit" in the "high level of managerial misconduct witnessed in recent years" (see also Dobson 2003).

This research is open to dispute, of course—especially on the grounds that it claims too much. Not all students who are trained in the principles of neoclassical theory become the egoistic agents that neoclassical theory posits as its model of human behavior; indeed, some may find their other-regarding moral bearings strengthened by an encounter with the unattractive model of human nature that appears in economics. But the research does suggest that economists may play an unintended role in the character formation of their students by legitimating an impulse to self-interest—including free-riding and the substitution of cost-benefit analysis for moral reasoning when faced with an opportunity to violate the law or important social norms. Recognizing this influence, Bowen (2003) contends that the profession has an obligation to present students with a fuller account of human behavior which exposes them to new research that calls into question the egoism of *homo economicus* and demonstrates that moral conduct (reflecting respect for others and fairness) is prevalent and can be economically rational. Gintis and Khurana (2008, 301) emphasize the need to instruct students in the prevalence of honesty and integrity "for their own sake," even when acting in accordance with such principles entails personal sacrifice. They argue that business schools should craft and teach a professional code of conduct for business managers that cultivates and legitimates students' commitment to other-regarding motives.

Training the Ethical Economist

Professional ethics of the sort envisioned here involves a tradition of sustained inquiry, controversy, and debate. It is not reducible to a list of simple commandments that can be invoked in ethically challenging moments. While engaging principles and rules, it pays equal attention to the virtues that are conducive to ethical economic practice (May 1980). Professional ethics of this sort requires the cultivation of the capacity for critical reflection and self-awareness. An economics profession that embraces professional ethics would encourage its graduate programs to take steps to ensure that students are immersed in the ethical questions that arise in professional economic work.

All of the tools now in use to advance economic knowledge would be of service in the training of economic ethics. Textbooks would emerge that present and contest first principles and take the student through increasingly complex material. Bulletins and journals would appear that provide space for the new professional economic ethicists to think through the content of the field. Conferences would bring economic ethicists together to examine matters of significance. Courses would make their way into the graduate curriculum where students encounter various kinds of material and pedagogical methods. In this regard, economics could learn much from fields like law that have struggled with how best to incorporate ethical training into a professional curriculum. Like law, economics might very well have to pass through various stages of cynicism about ethical training, failure in approach, and frustrations with results on its way to devising successful programs which achieve wide respect among economists and economics students alike. Fortunately, we can draw on the experience of other professions and the broad literature that now examines effective pedagogies of ethical practice (e.g., Rhode 1992; Daly, Green and Pearce 1995; Luban and Millemann 1995).

Training the ethical economist requires something more than exposure to ethical principles and problems, of course. It requires a rethinking of the manner in which the profession conceptualizes what it is that is to be taught and learned, and how. The ethical economist needs technical sophistication, to be sure. But she also needs a kind of knowledge that is altogether lacking in graduate economics training. She needs to acquire *phronesis*, or practical wisdom, so that she can translate her technical competence into interventions that are apt to hit the mark—to help those she seeks to serve. Practical wisdom also entails attending to the limits of one's science and one's own expertise. It involves self-awareness, the ability to recognize external pressures to compromise one's principles, such as by conforming to the judgments of those in authority when one has good reason to dissent (Kuran 1995); and the fortitude to resist such pressures, especially when others will bear the consequences of one's moral lapses. An emphasis on practical wisdom places the *student* and not just the *subject matter* at the center of the educational enterprise. It recognizes that we are training not detached automatons that will process information and render technical judgments but human beings in their fullness who will, of necessity, draw on the full arsenal of human resources in doing their work.

The acquisition of practical wisdom can begin in the classroom, provided curriculum and pedagogy target this goal. Economics training might comprise case studies of actual complex situations in which economists have found themselves. This approach is used widely in ethical training in law and business. Courses might also revolve around well-designed policy simulations that raise difficult technical, practical, and ethical questions of the very sort that economists might face in their careers. Moreover, practitioner-led seminars could draw on the experiences of established economists who have made their careers outside of academia. Indeed, several respondents in the nonacademic employers' survey that was commissioned by COGEE argued for bringing accomplished applied economists into the classroom to share in the instruction of economic graduate students. This proposal makes particular sense in the context of professional economic ethics that recognizes the multiplicity of skills and competencies that the ethical economist must have at her command. It might also help to begin to reduce the hierarchy in economics that places leading academics far above applied economists in status and influence; it might thereby validate the kinds of expertise that applied economists are far more apt than their academic counterparts to have mastered.

Internships, Residencies, and Immersions

Adequate training in practical and ethical wisdom requires something other than classroom training, however—not least since the university tends to emphasize what Schön (1991, vii) identifies as "a *particular* epistemology, a view of knowledge that fosters selective inattention to practical competence and professional artistry" (italics in original; see also Schön 1987). It requires directed exposure to the field of applied economics under the guidance of a trained specialist who can help the student to grasp the complexities of the milieu she enters. Achieving this goal might require student immersion in both the "supply" and "demand" sides of the market for economic practice.

The economist in training needs to acquire the craft of economic application. Developing one's craft comprises experience in the institutions that supply economic expertise—the places where applied economists work and in which economic interventions are contemplated, drafted, and pursued. The student needs to learn firsthand what kinds of challenges well-meaning economists face in the bureaucracies and politicized arenas where they struggle to make a difference. How do routine office politics affect the economist's ability to do her work? In the public sector, how do partisan politics interfere as she attempts to forecast, advise, counsel, and prescribe? How do veteran economists in such environments maintain (or sacrifice) their integrity in the face of the various opportunities, pressures and constraints that they face? What do they do when asked post-haste for a complicated report or forecast that would require days or weeks of work, were it to be done properly? What do they do when the only data available are unreliable for the kind of study that is required of them? And what do they do when they find that some of their peers are cutting corners for the sake of expediency? These things can be discussed in the classroom, and perhaps in the company of a skilled teacher, students can acquire awareness and skills that will allow them to deal effectively with these kinds of situations when they arise later on. But it is certainly the case that witnessing these problems firsthand in the context of the workplace is apt to capture the student's attention and motivate her to find a resolution to a degree that classroom exercises cannot replicate (Luban and Millemann 1995; Venter 1996).

The economist in training also needs to be immersed in the kinds of communities that need and will be served by economic expertise. She needs to identify and cultivate the skills and sensitivity that will enable her to learn about the specific economic, cultural, political, and social institutions that bear on economic affairs in these communities. She needs to decipher the amorphous but consequential norms and conventions (such as conceptions of fairness) that community members share and that affect how they respond to incentives and constraints. She needs to gain access, even if imperfectly, to the community's aspirations, anxieties, and mores; their human and physical resources; and other characteristics that enable and/or inhibit economic practices and bear directly on the possibility and prospects for the success of economic reform. What are the most pressing social problems, and what risks and sacrifices are appropriate in addressing them—not in the eyes of a detached, dispassionate professional economist but in the eyes of the community itself?

These arguments call for protracted immersion of the economist-in-training in the communities that she hopes to serve, to allow for direct observation and extensive dialogue. Certainly, an immersion should promote the ability to translate abstract economic concepts into practice. But it must also engender practical wisdom that allows the student to understand the limits of economic theory and the wisdom of pragmatic adjustment and compromise when situations on the ground contradict blackboard schematics. The immersion must be structured to inculcate cultural sensitivity and ethical sensibilities. The new initiates to the profession need to develop the ethnographic skills of the anthropologist, regardless of whether they are placed in a K Street consulting firm or across town in a poor Southeast DC neighborhood. For economics departments, this proposal would require the implementation of strategies to continue training and guidance during student placements. Placements must be treated as fundamental to the training of the economist as is the core curriculum. Otherwise, they would come to be viewed as a period in which students mark time awaiting their freedom when they can move on to more important activities.

Many professions that require technical skill, practical wisdom, and ethical judgment have adopted various forms of "apprenticeship" as a normal part of professional training. Medical students must complete internships and residencies under the supervision of experienced doctors before they can become full members of the profession; architects, engineers, and other professionals must serve extended apprenticeships before licensing that allows them to work independently; school teachers must serve as interns under the observation of an experienced mentor before completing their degrees. Economics, too, needs such an instrument in order to impart the kinds of wisdom and judgment that are essential to ethical economic practice but that are virtually ignored today in graduate economic training. Under this scenario, graduate programs would create linkages with the providers and users of economic services that place their students in guided internships and apprenticeships. Institutions ranging from public sector, development, and multilateral agencies to economic consulting firms and nongovernmental organizations in developed and developing countries would create opportunities for placements that provide economists in training with a kind of exposure that the classroom, at its best, cannot offer. Indeed, some institutions provide internships for economists already. What is missing is any meaningful coordination with the intern's graduate program, curriculum, or training.

Over the years, several economists have made suggestions of this sort. In his comprehensive study, Bowen (1953) cited the need for internships for economists. Coats (1992, 349) echoed this sentiment:

> [The] best way to develop creativity, tacit knowledge, and connoisseurship is through learning by doing, and, to this end, internships in business, banking, and government during graduate education, possibly as a requirement, would help to narrow the perceived gap between what is and what should be taught and learned.

In a similar vein, Jeffrey Sachs expresses concern about the failure of the profession to prepare its members for the "clinical" challenges they will face, especially in the field of development:

> Economists are not trained to think like clinicians, and are rarely afforded clinical experience in their advanced training. A graduate student in an American Ph.D. program in economics may very well study the development crisis in Africa without ever setting foot in the country or countries under study (2005, 78).

Other economists have called for consideration of the creation of two tracks in economic training: one for those who intend to make their careers in the research university and another for those who seek to apply their expertise in other venues (see Colander 1998). The dual tracks proposal deserves careful attention. Were programs to embrace this approach, students' immersions would be targeted toward their intended careers in order to equip them to face the professional challenges that likely await them in their work.

The Exposure and Dialogue Program: Cornell-SEWA-WIEGO and Beyond

A promising indicator of the value of placements has emerged in the work of various NGOs that have created opportunities for economists and other development experts to participate in immersions in the communities they target in their work. The most important of these to date is the "Exposure and Dialogue Program," or EDP. The EDP was the brainchild of Karl Osner in the 1980s when he was an official with Germany's Federal Ministry for Economic Cooperation and Development. Osner created an exposure project for his colleagues at the Ministry; in 1987, he augmented the immersion component of the program with structured dialogues between the development officials and members of the host communities. In recent years, the EDP has blossomed into an ambitious set of initiatives and institutions such as the German Association for Exposure and Dialogue Programmes (Chen et al. 2004, 10; see also the "Epilogue" to that report, written by Osner).

The goal of the EDP is to break down the barriers between those who provide and those who are targeted by economic development initiatives; to personalize as "subjects" in their own right those who are the intended beneficiaries of these interventions. The program entails three components: exposure, reflection, and dialogue. Each component is taken to be vital to achieving EDP's goals, which are defined as *transferring the know how* of innovative people-based self-help-organisations *from the South to the North* for fighting poverty in the South by shaping pro-poor policies in the institutions of development cooperation in the North" (Chen et al. 2004, 87; emphasis in original).

A particularly important EDP began in 2003 in India (see Chen et al. 2004). The "Cornell-SEWA-WIEGO EDP" involves two women's organizations and several economists from Cornell University. The Self Employed Women's Association (SEWA) of India is a 700,000 member organization that organizes self-employed women in India to secure full employment, self-reliance, and independence. The organization's members are among the poorest of the poor owing in part to the obligations they face to perform household labor while also seeking outside remuneration (often in the informal sector). SEWA began conducting EDPs in 1991; this work is organized by SEWA's technical branch, the SEWA Academy (SEWA World Bank 2006). SEWA conducted its first EDP with the World Bank in 2003 when it placed 10 development expert "guests" in homes of its members.

A second partner in this EDP is Women in Informal Employment: Globalizing and Organizing (WIEGO). WIEGO is an international policy network of researchers, activists, and practitioners working on issues facing the working poor in the informal economy. At present, WIEGO's secretariat is located at Harvard University, and its work is coordinated by Dr. Marty Chen, a specialist in South Asia regional studies. Cornell University provided a natural partner for this EDP, owing to the presence on its faculty of economist Ravi Kanbur. Kanbur had helped to initiate and also participated in a SEWA EDP when he served as the Director of the World Development Report team that authored the *World Development Report 2000/2001*, subtitled "Attacking Poverty." The three parties structured the Cornell-SEWA-WIEGO EDP in order to establish understanding and dialogue between neoclassical labor market economists and the poor. In its words,

> The basic objective of the Cornell-SEWA-WIEGO EDP at SEWA is to start a dialogue between mainstream economists, SEWA activists, and WIEGO researchers around key assumptions of neo-classical economics—and neo-liberal economic policies—which "trouble" ground-level activists and researchers working on issues of employment and labor (Chen et al. 2004, 96).

Like other EDPs, the program involves placing development experts with host members of SEWA for very short visits. In this case, six SEWA members opened up their homes to participants for two nights. Researchers from WIEGO and economists from Cornell worked, ate, and slept alongside host family members. The immersion was followed by two days of dialogue at the SEWA Academy, one half-day of which involved discussion with the host women, while the remainder involved SEWA facilitators and officials, the founder of SEWA (Ela Bhatt), the Cornell economists, and the WIEGO researchers (Chen et al. 2004, 11).

One might be forgiven for skepticism. How could such a short visit have an appreciable effect on the participants?[3] It is therefore striking to read the personal and technical reflections of the economists who have participated. Labor economist Gary Fields reports that his immersion changed his understanding of the minimum wage in the context of the community he visited. During his visit, SEWA representatives met with officials at the Gujarat Commissioner of Labor's Office "to establish a minimum wage for kite-makers" and "to establish a Provident Fund for bedi workers" [tobacco rollers] (Chen et al. 2004, 36). Fields sat in on the meetings and was profoundly affected:

> Because of what I saw on the ground, my professional judgment about minimum wages and supplementary benefits changed. With the standard labor economics model in mind, I had worried that the minimum wage might hurt the very women it was meant to help, because of job losses. In this context, though, the minimum wage does not act as a wage floor. It acts as an aspirational target. . . Set in this way by negotiators who take full

account of possible job losses as well as earnings gains, the minimum wage and Provident Fund are meant to help all of the women in their respective occupations, and not, as is often the case in other contexts, insiders at the expense of outsiders. This kind of "wage" increase is something that I favor. Without this experience on the ground, that is not something I would have said two days earlier (Chen et al. 2004, 36).

For Marty Chen, insights like these represent the most important outcome of the EDP. The EDP is crucial for enabling economists to begin to understand that the abstract, deductive modeling, and statistical testing upon which their science depends is insufficient to grasp the nature of the problems facing the poor. The worlds that the poor inhabit are marked by complexities that economists tend to suppress in the pursuit of explanatory simplicity, universality, and tractability. They often ignore features of social life that do not lend themselves to quantification. This impulse comes to economists naturally by virtue of their training.

Participation in the EDP creates opportunities for economists to face up to the limitations of this kind of knowledge. It alerts them to the value of the ways of knowing of anthropologists who revel in the particularities of the contexts they encounter. In Chen's view, the natural antipathy of economists to such ways of knowing can lead to consequential error. For instance, it leads economists to neglect questions pertaining to the quality of data. Economists often employ data gathered for one purpose in other contexts where they are inappropriate, without awareness of what is at stake. In contrast, anthropologists understand how hard it is to gather good reliable data. They are therefore much less willing than economists to invest any particular data set with the authority to settle theoretical questions or determine policy interventions (author interview with Chen Nov. 13, 2008).

The work of Ravi Kanbur reveals the transformative power of the EDP immersions. In a series of papers written over the years that he has been involved in EDPs, he has explored in a respectful way the distinct worldviews that economists and community advocates and activists bring to bear on matters pertaining to economic policy. Kanbur (2001) argues that the two groups disagree on three fundamental issues: aggregation, time horizons, and market structure and power. Economists tend to what Kanbur calls the "Ministry of Finance" view of economic affairs. This perspective takes a bird's eye view of the economy that involves extensive aggregation, reflected in the importance placed on measures such as GDP/capita. Economists tend to take a long-term view of the effects of economic policy which encourages them to tolerate substantial short-run adjustment costs. Finally, economists tend to presume a competitive model when analyzing an economy—one that discounts the presence of economic power. In contrast, community advocates impose what Kanbur calls the "Civil Society" perspective. This is a "worm's eye" view that emphasizes the disaggregated impact of economic interventions and pays particular attention to inequality by gender, ethnicity, race, and region in assessing policy. The Civil Society view emphasizes the salience of short-run rather than long-run policy effects because vulnerable communities often cannot weather economic dislocation of any duration in hopes of subsequent improvements. Finally, this perspective recognizes that markets often are the site of local monopoly power—indeed, this perspective is attuned to the presence of power in social relationships at all levels of analysis, and so it finds the economist's emphasis on perfect competition to be extraordinarily naive (Kanbur 2001; also see Kanbur 2007; 2009c).

The EDP experience has promoted a mutually beneficial dialogue between development economists and the communities they target in their work—one that for the economists has resulted in greater understanding; respect for the poor; and especially, humility. Kanbur argues that the EDP has encouraged him to realize that "the greatest weakness of economics is that it doesn't recognize or understand its own weaknesses." One learns from the EDP that "one needs both kinds of knowing: the deductive and the attention to particulars, and to context. The experience changes the way you relate to other economists and other professionals; you become more careful about your models, about what they capture and what they miss" (author interview with Kanbur May 18, 2009). Kanbur emphasizes the enduring effects of the EDP; he and his colleagues are now less apt to presume and to impose the competitive market model in their policy work. They are also less apt to default to high levels of aggregation at the expense of disaggregated analyses and to overlook the short run in policy assessment.

The transformative effect of the EDP suggests the pedagogical value of longer immersions for students who are placed in targeted communities during their graduate training. The EDP format is certainly too demanding of host families to permit long stays. The challenge for the economics profession is to explore and establish institutional means for placements that are manageable for communities but also pedagogically useful for students. The world of NGOs represents one possible avenue for institutional collaboration that could create such immersion opportunities.[4] One can also imagine the creation of new organizations—"Economists without Borders," for instance—that seek to achieve the dual purpose of serving communities' economic needs while also providing on-the-job training for economics graduate students. Such programs would not necessarily require students to travel far or even leave home, since many universities today have established "service learning" programs that seek to contribute to the well-being of their host communities.

CONCLUSION

Embracing professional economic ethics requires critical reflection on pedagogy at the undergraduate and graduate levels. Current debates over undergraduate pedagogy would expand to investigate how economic training for majors and for those who will take just a few economics cours-es should be amended to ensure that the profession achieves its ethical responsibilities to these students. The questions that arise in this context are fascinating and difficult and would, no doubt, yield divergent answers. Different departments and faculty members would form distinct judg-ments about what is appropriate at this level of instruction, keeping in mind the ethical obligations that the profession faces to society at large.

At the graduate level, one hopes that a serious engagement with pro-fessional ethics induces substantial changes in the content and structure of economics training. Might there be two tracks, as Bowen and others have suggested? Would a course on professional economic ethics be inserted into the core curriculum? Would applied economists be invited to teach case study-focused curriculum that exposes students to the exigencies and complexities of the milieus that they will inhabit in their profes-sional life? Would programs establish internships and apprenticeships on both sides of the market for economic expertise that create opportunities for investigation of the ethical quandaries associated with the applica-tion of economic expertise? And in the event of any of these changes, what would become of the traditional curriculum? Might the dissertation be supplemented (or replaced altogether) by other forms of training, at least for those students who will leave academia upon graduation? Ideally, answers to all of these questions would emerge through a wide range of pedagogical experiments that enliven economics training for faculty and students and that are consistent with the profession's ethical obligations to all those whom it serves.

Notes

1 Also see Klamer's interpretation of the findings. Speaking of the interim between the two reports he says: "If anything, the discipline has become more homogeneous, more single-minded, more hard-nosed about the science of eco-nomics and hence less heterogeneous and arguably less intellectually exciting" (in Colander 2007, 230).

2 Barone (1991) describes the contending economic perspectives approach that is in place in undergraduate economics curriculum at Dickinson College. See also the upcoming symposium in the *International Journal of Pluralism and Economics Education* on "Contending Perspectives as Pluralism: What Have Our Students Learned?"

3 Participants in this EDP have continued up to the present to undertake immersions in other developing countries and to sustain a dialogue on their respective and changing views of economics and development. This may help to explain the EDP's enduring effects, and may point to the value of repeated par-ticipation in immersions throughout an economist's career.

4 Other organizations have created various kinds of placements for econo-mists-in-training to enhance their awareness and cultivate their professional devel-opment. One is the Economics for Equity and the Environment Network (E3), an environmental advocacy organization that places economics graduate students in summer internships with various environmental organizations.

Chapter 13

The Economist's Oath

But I would argue that decisions about public policies inevitably need to speak both to the heart and the head, that it is important to think deep and hard about the moral dimensions of our economic decisions, and that one can, and indeed one should combine this kind of moral analysis with a hard headed analysis of the consequences and risks associated with alternative policies.

Joseph Stiglitz (2000, 16)

Over the long sweep of its history, the American economics profession has been far more ambitious about achieving influence than it has been attentive to the harm that it might do or the ethical questions that might arise were it to achieve the influence it sought. This is most unfortunate: it is irresponsible for a profession to seek more influence than it is prepared to bear, given the maturity of its expertise and the extent of knowledge (and ignorance) that marks its subject matter. Rather than rush to influence with an unwarranted level of confidence, the profession would have done better to modulate its influence with a steadfast honest and open appreciation of the limits of what it can offer.

It is time to correct this situation through a serious engagement with professional economic ethics. As I have argued throughout, professional ethics is something other than a code of conduct. It encompasses a tradition of serious and sustained inquiry into economic practice that emphasizes the ambiguities, tensions, and conundrums facing the economist and the profession. The emergence of professional economic ethics would promote new venues (including textbooks, journals, and the like) to debate and educate economists and others in matters pertaining to professional economic practice; economic practice review boards to assist individual economists in their work and to help the profession think through the myriad ethical issues that economic practice entails; and a new conceptualization of undergraduate and graduate economic training. Emphasis would most certainly be placed on the ethical virtues of humility and open mindedness when confronting a world that defies control and manipulation by the economic practitioner.

CHANGING SENTIMENTS

Fortunately, there are scattered signs of changing sentiments today across the profession. In their survey of economics journal editors, for instance, Enders and Hoover (2004) asked respondents about plagiarism—about its definition, frequency, and the policies their journals employed in response to actual cases of plagiarized work (see also Laband and Piette 2000). Surprisingly, given the long-standing antipathy of the profession to professional ethics, they report that

> The question eliciting the strongest opinions asked editors if they favored a code of ethics for the economics profession. . . Of the 111 editors responding to this question, 73 (65.8 percent) reported that the economics profession would benefit from such a code. Dissenting editors indicated that "a code of ethics is a good idea but would do nothing to curb plagiarism because it would be 'pro forma' and unenforceable" (491).

Reacting to the tendency toward professional adventurism in economics, economists such as Joseph Stiglitz (2000), Dani Rodrik (1998), Richard B. Freeman (1994), William Easterly (2006), and many others have called attention to the need for greater professional care to avoid harm, especially when an economist targets vulnerable communities. For his part, Jeffrey Sachs has begun to advance the argument that development economics "needs an overhaul in order to be much more like modern medicine, a profession of rigor, insight, and practicality" (2005, 74). Indeed, Sachs advocates the transformation of "development economics" into "clinical economics." Given his long-standing proclivity toward grand social engineering projects in the South and transition economies, this reversal in stance is particularly notable and welcome. The "lessons" that he believes clinical economics should take from medicine include the idea that "*medicine is a profession,* and as a profession requires strong norms, ethics, and codes of conduct. The Hippocratic Oath is not a mere curiosity to remind doctors of the ancient lineage of their profession" (2005, 78; emphasis in original). He continues as follows:

> [The] development community lacks the requisite ethical and professional standards. I am not suggesting that development practitioners are corrupt or unethical; such cases are rare. Rather, the development economics community does not take on its work with the sense of responsibility that the tasks require. Providing economic advice to others requires a profound commitment to search for the right answers, not to settle for superficial approaches. It requires a commitment to be thoroughly steeped in the history, ethnography, politics, and economy of any place where the professional adviser is working. It also requires a commitment to give honest advice, not only to the country in question, but to the agency that has hired and sent the adviser. . . Any IMF or World Bank official, as well as any academic development practitioner, has the responsibility to speak truth not only to the

policy makers within the impoverished country, but to the policy makers of the rich and powerful countries as well (2005, 80–81).

Joseph Stiglitz has also subjected development economists to ethical evaluation. In "Ethics, Economic Advice, and Economic Policy," for instance, he inquires into the ethical performance of IMF advisors during the 1980s and 1990s. He asks whether "In [providing economic advice], do [advisors] behave ethically" (2000, 2)? Stiglitz assesses economic practice against what he takes to be unobjectionable "ethical precepts"—honesty, fairness, social justice, externalities, and responsibility. Stiglitz's judgment is largely negative: he concludes that the economists under review acted badly. In particular, they were insufficiently attentive to the ethical imperatives that should have driven their work.

What are these imperatives? "To the extent possible," Stiglitz writes, "there is a moral responsibility to think creatively about what kinds of policies might enhance the opportunities for the poor, allowing them to take more responsibility for their own well being (4)." He emphasizes that "Any policy that undermines the sense of community, social norms, a country's culture and pride, can, from this perspective, be viewed as a violation of ethical principles (15)." Stiglitz concludes the essay with the ethical appeal that appears as the epigraph to this chapter.

Evidence of growing ethical awareness is also emerging at the institutional level. In the late 1990s, both the World Bank and the IMF adopted codes of conduct to guide the behavior of their employees. Both call attention to the conflicts of interest, corruption, and other dangers that may arise in their work and instruct their employees in how to manage these matters (Powers 2005; World Bank Group, undated). It is unfortunate but unsurprising, however, that neither institution makes any note of the particular obligations facing the economists who work for these institutions. If anything, the codes confirm what economists have long held—that there is nothing particular to economic practice that warrants a specialized field of professional ethics for economics. That said, the existence of these codes could open the door to an investigation of and training on the particular ethical challenges that IMF and World Bank economists face, especially were a broader conversation about professional economic ethics to emerge across the profession.

In the 1990s, the National Association of Forensic Economists introduced the first and only code of ethics for applied economists in the United States. The code is intended to raise awareness among forensic economists about the ethical quandaries that infuse forensic economics and to cultivate ethical behavior. Like most other codes, it is neither binding nor enforceable. Yet it has attracted substantial attention among forensic economists and generated a new and promising literature on the ethics of professional practice.

In the past few years, two Swedish associations with economist members have also adopted codes. In 2005, Civilekonomerna—a union of economists working in the public and private sectors—adopted ethical guidelines for its members that are intended

> to increase our awareness concerning the importance of ethical questions in our working life. They shall serve as guidance and support in the practice of our trade. The guidelines invite dialog in ethical questions so that we can handle moral conflicts with knowledge and competence. As Economists we shall strive to ensure that ethical perspectives are noticed and handled in one's own working environment.[1]

The guidelines emphasize economists' diverse professional and institutional roles and relationships and the obligations that flow from economists' practice. For instance, economists are encouraged to value knowledge (and competence) acquisition, integrity, and honesty. While the code is not enforceable per se, a union member who exhibits conduct that "severely injures the union's reputation can be expelled from the union." The union has a hotline that members can call for help with any ethical issues that arise in their work.

In 2007, Akademikerförbundet SSR, a Swedish union that represents professional employees (economists and others) adopted *Ethics for Economists: Ethical Code for Economists in the Public and the Non-Profit Sector*.[2] Like the guidelines of Civilekonomerna, the code distinguishes among the various roles that economists play and emphasizes the obligations that are associated with each role. It, too, emphasizes that appropriate professional performance requires humility: "The economist should be aware of the limits of his/her own competence and be open to critical investigation of his/her work." Moreover, the code draws attention to the ethical difficulties that emerge from role conflicts, and it attempts to provide economists with the resources to think through how best to manage such conflicts. But the code does not oversimplify for the sake of ethical closure—there are no formulas here to lead the economist to ethical security. Instead, the document seeks to enhance ethical sensibilities by exposing economists to scenarios that pose difficult ethical challenges, and it concludes with a series of open-ended questions that are intended to provoke further ethical reflection.

Today, there is some evidence of increasing grassroots attention among economists in the United States to the matter of professional economic responsibility. In 2007, the Association for Integrity and Responsible Leadership in Economics and Allied Professions (AIRLEAP) was founded by a group of Washington, DC-based applied economists.[3] The organization now includes applied as well as academic economists; its goal, as the organization's name suggests, is to increase the attention of economists to the ethical questions that economists confront in their day-to-day work. While the organization is far too new to judge the prospects for its success, its existence might promote consideration by economists about subject matter that has been long dismissed: namely, the difficult ethical issues that are associated with the status, influence, and work of the economist.

Just how deep and sustainable are these sentiments for change in economics? To date, the gestures toward professional economic ethics are scattered and terribly tentative. But there are signs that the profession may be approaching the point where it is willing to have a serious conversation about the matters before us. Recognition of the growing influence of economics, owing to the intellectual monopoly and institutional authority that leading economists now enjoy—coupled with evidence of how, sometimes, economic interventions work out very badly—may prove sufficient to awaken the profession to the heavy burdens that it necessarily faces. It is increasingly difficult today to deny that economic practice carries ethical entailments that are complex and demanding.

THE ECONOMIST'S OATH

I began this examination of professional economic ethics by asking that we imagine ourselves in attendance at a graduation ceremony in which those receiving the PhD in economics rise to their feet to recite the *Economist's Oath*—one that expresses principles and virtues that will guide them in their work. I took note then of the skepticism that many economists would harbor about the *Oath* and the field of professional economic ethics that it reflects.

I hope by now that this scenario is somewhat less irksome. *Economic practice matters: this is the heart of the case for professional ethics.* The economics profession has achieved the influence that it sought so strenuously over the past century. But the profession's influence comes with substantial risk of doing harm and violating rights. It is an unfortunate but undeniable fact that the profession has been relatively careless in exercising this influence. This situation cannot be sustained by a profession that commits itself to the service of others.

To what might the *Economist's Oath* commit new initiates to the profession? What might it ask of economists, and how might it protect the communities that these economists will serve? For my part, I would hope that it reads something like what follows. Adapted from a contemporary version of the Hippocratic Oath, it encompasses the most important principles and virtues that we have encountered in this book.

Might taking the *Oath* make a difference? More importantly, might a serious commitment to professional economic ethics improve the conduct of economists and the economics profession, and the legitimacy and quality of our interventions? These things we do not know today and cannot know in advance of our taking the leap into professional economic ethics. What we do know is that it is time to find out.

The Economist's Oath

I do solemnly swear:

That I will be loyal to the Profession of Economics and be just and generous to its members. That I will practice the art of economics in uprightness and honor.

That into whatever community I shall enter, it shall be for the good of the community to the utmost of my power, holding myself aloof from wrong, from corruption, from the tempting of others to vice.

That I will recognize and keep always in view that the community I serve is never a means for my ends, but always an end unto itself. It, and not I, is the rightful architect of its future. I will therefore endeavor to use my expertise to enhance the capabilities of that community to undertake those economic innovations that it deems desirable and achievable. In furtherance of this objective, I will endeavor to introduce for the community's consideration a range of economic perspectives and strategies, even while I advocate for that approach that I deem to be most appropriate. So long as I remain associated with a community as a teacher, advisor or public servant, I will endeavor to establish the conditions for the success of the projects adopted by that community, even when those projects are at odds with my preferred arrangements.

That I will recognize and keep always in view that economics is and will forever be an imperfect science. At its best, it is an art that is shrouded in uncertainty, imprecision, mystery and error. I will approach my work with an honest and open recognition of the imponderables that bear on the success of my work. I will teach those whom I instruct and with whom I work of the vagaries of the practice of economics, alert them to the dangers of economic experimentation, and to the best of my ability, help them to anticipate and prepare for unintended consequences. Whenever I find myself in a position to act on behalf of others, I will act prudently, taking care to minimize harm, especially to those who are most vulnerable.

That I will recognize and keep always in view that economic arrangements are interminably contested and contestable, fraught with conflict, and are often the site of oppression, inequality and injustice. I will recognize and keep always in view that any policy prescription I offer will bear unequally on a community's members, and so may induce tension and social dislocation. I will seek to expose oppression; I will be on guard against the self-serving argument of the privileged; and I will take pains to give voice to the needs and aspirations of the dispossessed.

That I will recognize and keep always in view the virtue of economic pluralism. I will treat respectfully the ideas of those who advocate theoretical perspectives that differ from those I embrace—and I will undertake through my words and deeds to sustain this pluralism in the profession.

These things do I swear. I now bow my head in sign of acquiescence. And now, if I am true to this, my oath, may prosperity and good repute be ever mine; the opposite, if I shall prove myself forsworn.

Notes

1 Translation by Emma Ekdahl; available at: http://www.civilekonomerna.se/portal/page?_pageid=34,3132322&_dad=portal&_schema=PORTAL.

2 Available at: http://www.akademssr.se/portal/page/portal/akademssr/profession/ekonom/Etik%20f%C3%B6r%20ekonomer_0.pdf.

3 The organization's Web site can be found at http://www.airleap.org/. I am a member of the board of this organization.

References

Adair, J.G., T.W. Dushenko and R.C.L. Lindsay. (1985) "Ethical Regulations and their Impact on Research Practice," *American Psychologist* 40(1): 59–72.

Adams, G.B. and D.L. Balfour. (2004) *Unmasking Administrative Evil* (rev. ed.), Armonk, NY: M.E. Sharpe.

Ahuja, A. (3/12/2009) "Warning: Capitalism Can Damage Your Health," *TimesOnline*, available at: http://www.timesonline.co.uk/tol/comment/columnists/guest_contributors/article5891103.ece.

Akademikerförbundet SSR. (Sweden) (2007) *Ethics for economists. Ethical Code for Economists in the Public and the Not for Profit Sector*, available at: http://www.akademssr.se/portal/page/portal/akademssr/profession/ekonom/Etik%20f%C3%B6r%20ekonomer_0.pdf.

Allen, W.R. (1977) "Economics, Economists, and Economic Policy: Modern American Experiences," *History of Political Economy* 9(1): 48–88.

American Anthropological Association. (1998) "Code of Ethics of the American Anthropological Association," available at: http://www.aaanet.org/committees/ethics/ethcode.htm.

American Economic Association. Archives, various years, folders, and files, Duke University.

Amy, D.J. (1984) "Why Policy Analysis and Ethics are Incompatible," *Journal of Policy Analysis and Management* 3(4): 573–91.

Andrews, E.L. (8/26/2005) "The Greenspan Effect: The Doctrine was not to Have One," *New York Times*: C1.

———. (10/24/2008) "Greenspan Concedes Flaws in Deregulatory Approach," *New York Times*: B1.

Angner, E. (2006) "Economists as experts: Overconfidence in theory and practice," *Journal of Economic Methodology* 13(1): 1–24.

Appell, D. (1/18–19/2001) "The new uncertainty principle: For complex environmental issues, science learns to take a backseat to political precaution," *Scientific American* 284: 1.

Applbaum, A.I. (1999) *Ethics for Adversaries: The Morality of Roles in Public and Professional Life*, Princeton, NJ: Princeton University Press.

Arendt, H. (1963) *Eichmann in Jerusalem: A Report on the Banality of Evil*, New York, NY: Viking Press.

Ariely, D. (2009) *Predictably Irrational*, New York, NY: Harper Collins.

Baker, D. (8/9/2004) "Bush's House of Cards," *The Nation*.

———. (2009a) "Creating Political Space for Effective Financial Regulation," *Dialogue on Globalization* 42: 66–72.

———. (2009b) *Plunder and Blunder: The Rise and Fall of the Bubble Economy*, Sausalito, CA: PoliPoint Press.

Barber, W.J. (1995) "Chile con Chicago: A review essay," *Journal of Economic Literature* 33(3): 1941–1949.

Barone, C.A. (1991) "Contending Perspectives: Curricular Reform in Economics," *Journal of Economic Education* 22(1): 15–26.

Bassi, L.J. (1989) "Special Study to Interview Nonacademic Employers of Economists," Prepared for Commission on Graduate Education in Economics: 7.

Baumrind, D. (1985) "Research Using Intentional Deception: Ethical Issues Revisited," *American Psychologist* 40(2): 165–74.

Beauchamp, D.E. and B. Steinbock (eds.). (1999) *New Ethics for the Public's Health*, New York, NY: Oxford University Press.

Beauchamp, T.L. and J. Childress. (1989) *Principles of Biomedical Ethics*, 4th ed., New York, NY: Oxford University Press.

Bebbington, A. (2002) "Sharp Knives and Blunt Instruments: Social Capital in Development Studies," *Antipode* 34(4): 800–03.

Bergeron, S. (2006) *Fragments of Development: Nation, Gender and the Space of Modernity*, Ann Arbor, MI: University of Michigan Press.

Bernanke, B.S. Hearing before the Committee on Financial Services. U.S. House of Representatives. 109th Cong., 2nd Sess., February 15, 2006.

_____. (5/18/2006) "Basel II: Its Promise and its Challenges," speech delivered at the Federal Reserve Bank of Chicago's 42nd Annual Conference on Bank Structure and Competition, Chicago, IL.

_____. (6/12/2006) "Modern Risk Management and Banking Supervision," speech given at the Stonier Graduate School of Banking, Washington, DC.

_____. Hearing before the Committee on Financial Services. U.S. House of Representatives. 109th Cong., 2nd Sess., July 20, 2006.

_____. (3/6/2007) "GSE Portfolios, Systemic Risk, and Affordable Housing," speech delivered at the Independent Community Bankers of America's Annual Convention and Techworld, Honolulu, Hawaii.

_____. (4/11/2007) "Financial Regulation and the Invisible Hand," speech delivered at the New York University Law School, New York.

_____. (5/17/2007) "Regulation and Financial Innovation," speech delivered at the Federal Reserve Bank of Atlanta's 2007 Financial Markets Conference, Sea Island, GA.

Bernstein, M. (2001) *A Perilous Progress*, Princeton, NJ: Princeton University Press.

Berry, W. (2005) *The Way of Ignorance*, Berkeley, CA: Counterpoint Books.

Bhagwati, J. (1994) "Which Way? Free Trade or Protection?" *Challenge* 37(1): 17–24.

Black, W. (2005) *The Best Way to Rob a Bank is to Own One: How Corporate Executives and Politicians Looted the S&L Industry*, Austin, TX: University of Texas Press.

BLS. Occupational Employment and Wages, Estimates, May 2008 (19-3011 Economists). Available at: http://www.bls.gov/oes/2008/may/oes193011.htm.

BLS. Standard Occupation Classification (19-3011). Available at: http://data.bls.gov/oes/datatype.do. Ch. 2.

Bok, S. (1980) "Whistleblowing and Professional Responsibility," *New York University Education Quarterly* 2(4): 2–7.

_____. (1989) *Lying: Moral Choice in Public and Private Life*, New York, NY: Random House.

Bonetti, S. (1998) "Experimental Economics and Deception," *Journal of Economic Psychology* 19(3): 377–95.

Boruch, R. *et al.* (2002) "The Importance of Randomized Field Trials in Education and Related Areas," in F. Mosteller and R. Boruch (eds.) *Evidence Matters: Randomized Trials in Education Research,* Washington, DC: Brookings Institution Press: 50–79.

Bourgois, P. (1990) "Confronting Anthropological Ethics: Ethnographic Lessons from Central America," *Journal of Peach Research* 27(1): 43–54.

Bowen, H.R. (1953) "Graduate education in economics," *American Economic Review Supplement* 43(Part 2) (September): 1–223.

Bowie, N.E. (1991) "Challenging the Egoistic Paradigm," *Business Ethics Quarterly* 1(1): 1–21.

Bowles, S. (1998) "Endogenous preferences: The cultural consequences of markets and other economic institutions," *Journal of Economic Literature* 36(1): 75–111.

_____. (2008) "Policies Designed for Self-Interested Citizens May Undermine the 'Moral Sentiments': Evidence from Economic Experiments," *Science* 320(5883): 1605–09.

Bowles, S. and H. Hwang. (2008) "Social Preferences and Public Economics: Mechanism Design when Social Preferences Depend on Incentives," *Journal of Public Economics* 92(8–9): 1811–20.

Brainard, W.C. (1967) "Uncertainty and the Effectiveness of Policy," *American Economic Review* 57(2): 411–25.

Brock, W.A., S.N. Durlauf and K.D. West. (2007) "Model Uncertainty and Policy Evaluation: Some Theory and Empirics," *Journal of Econometrics* 136(2): 629–64.

Buchanan, A.E. and D.W. Brock. (1989) *Deciding for Others: The Ethics of Surrogate Decision Making,* New York, NY: Cambridge University Press.

Buchanan, J.M. (1964) "What Should Economists Do?" *Southern Economic Journal* (30)3: 213–22.

Buchanan, J.M. (1979) *What Should Economists Do?* Indianapolis, IN: Liberty Press.

Buiter, Willem. (3/3/2009) "The Unfortunate Uselessness of Most 'State of the Art' Academic Monetary Economics," available at: http://blogs.ft.com/maverecon/2009/03/the-unfortunate-uselessness-of-most-state-of-the-art-academic-monetary-economics/more-667.

Burczak, T.A. (2006) *Socialism After Hayek,* Ann Arbor, MI: University of Michigan Press.

Calvo, G.A. and F. Coricelli. (3/1993) "Output Collapses in Eastern Europe," *IMF Staff Papers* 40(1): 32–52.

Cárcamo-Huechante, L.E. (2006) "Milton Friedman: Knowledge, Public Culture, and Market Economy in the Chile of Pinochet," *Public Culture* 18(2): 413–35.

Carey, B. (8/16/2008) "Psychologists Clash on Aiding Interrogations," *New York Times*: A1.

_____. (5/5/2009) "Stumbling Blocks on the Path of Righteousness," *New York Times*: D5.

Chen, M. *et al.* (eds). (4/2004) "Reality and Analysis: Personal and Technical Reflections on the Working Lives of Six women," Cornell-SEWA-WIEGO, available at: http://www.arts.cornell.edu/poverty/kanbur/EDPCompendium.pdf.

Civilekonomerna (Sweden). (11/15/2005) *Work Ethical Guidelines for Economists,* established at delegation meeting, available at: http://www.civilekonomerna.se/portal/page?_pageid=343132322&_dad=portal&_schema=PORTAL.

Coats, A.W. (1960) "The First Two Decades of the American Economic Association," *The American Economic Review* 50(4): 555–74.

———. (1968) "The Origins and Early Development of the Royal Economic Society," *The Economic Journal* 78(310): 349–71.

———. (1985) "The American Economic Association and the Economics Profession," *Journal of Economic Literature* 23(4): 1697–1727.

———. (1991) "Economics as a Profession," in M. Bleaney, D. Greenaway and I. Stewart (eds.) *Companion to Contemporary Economic Thought*, New York, NY: Routledge: 119–42.

———. (1992) "Changing Perceptions of American Graduate Education in Economics, 1953-1991," *Journal of Economic Education* 23(3): 341–52.

Cohen, P. (6/18/2008) "Pentagon to Consult Academics on Security," *New York Times*: E1.

Colander, D. (1998) "The Sounds of Silence: The Profession's Response to the COGEE Report," *American Journal of Agricultural Economics* 80(3): 600–07.

———. (2003) "Muddling Through and Policy Analysis," *New Zealand Economic Papers* 37(2): 197–215.

———. (2005a) "The Making of an Economist Redux," *Journal of Economic Perspectives* 19(1): 175–98.

———. (2005b) "What Economists Teach and What Economists Do," *Journal of Economic Education* 36(3): 249–60.

———. (2005c) "From Muddling Through to the Economics of Control: View of Applied Policy from J.N. Keynes to Abba Lerner," *History of Political Economy* 37(Supplement 1): 277–91.

———. (2007) *The Making of an Economist Redux*, Princeton, NJ: Princeton University Press.

Colander, D. and A. Klamer. (1987) "The Making of an Economist," *The Journal of Economic Perspectives* 1(2): 95–111.

Colander, D. *et al.* (2009) "The Financial Crisis and the Systemic Failure of Academic Economics," *Critical Review* 21(2): 249–67.

Commission on Behavioral and Social Sciences and Education. (1999) *Sowing Seeds of Change: Informing Public Policy in the Economic Research Service of USDA*, available at: http://books.nap.edu/openbook.php?record_id=6320&page=R1.

Cook, T.D. (2002) "Objecting to the Objections to Using Random Assignment in Educational Research," in F. Mosteller and R. Boruch (eds.) *Evidence Matters: Randomized Trials in Education Research*, Washington, DC: Brookings Institution Press: 150–78.

Corrigan, O. (2003) "Empty ethics: the problem with informed consent," *Sociology of Health & Illness* 25(3): 768–92.

Coy, P. and S. Woolley. (9/21/1998) "Failed Wizards of Wall Street," *BusinessWeek* 3596: 114–20.

Coyle, D. (2007) *The Soulful Science: What Economists Really Do and Why it Matters*, Princeton, NJ: Princeton Press.

Crocker, D.A. (1998) "Toward Development Ethics," in C.K. Wilbur (ed.) *Economics, Ethics, and Public Policy*, New York, NY: Rowman and Littlefield: 305–55.

Crunden, R.M. (1982) *Ministers of Reform: The Progressives' Achievement in American Civilization, 1889–1920*, New York, NY: Basic Books.

Daly, M.C., B.A. Green and R.G. Pearce. (1995) "Contextualizing Professional Responsibility: A New Curriculum for a New Century," *Law and Contemporary Problems* 58(3/4): 193–211.

Davis, D.D. and C.A. Holt. (1993) *Experimental Economics*, Princeton: Princeton University Press.

Davis, W.L. (2004) "Preference Falsification in the Economics Profession," *Economic Journal Watch* 1(2): 359–68.

_____. (2007) "Reflections and Self-Reflections on the Economics Profession," *American Journal of Economics and Sociology* 66(2): 267–88.

Dearman, D.T. and J.E. Beard. (2009) "Ethical Issues in Accounting and Economics Experimental Research: Inducing Strategic Misrepresentation," *Ethics & Behavior* 19(1): 51–59.

Deaton, A. (2009) "Instruments of Development: Randomization in the Tropics, and the Search for the Elusive Keys to Economic Development," *NBER Working Paper No. 14690*.

DeMartino, G. (2000) *Global Economy, Global Justice: Theoretical Objections and Policy Alternatives to Neoliberalism*, London, UK: Routledge.

Dewald, W.G., J.G. Thursby and R.G. Anderson. (1986) "Replication in Empirical Economics: The Journal of Money, Credit and Banking Project," *American Economic Review* 76(4): 587–603.

Dobson, J. (2003) "Why Ethics Codes Don't Work," *Financial Analysts Journal* 59(6): 29–34.

Dorfman, J. (1959) *The Economic Mind in American Civilization: Volumes Four and Five, 1918–1933*, New York, NY: Viking Press.

Dorfman, R. (1993) "An Introduction to Benefit-Cost Analysis," in R. Dorfman and N.S. Dorfman (eds.) *Economics of the Environment, 3rd ed.*, New York, NY: W.W. Norton and Co: 297–322.

Drake, P.W. (ed.) (1994) *Money Doctors, Foreign Debts, and Economic Reforms in Latin America from the 1890s to the Present*, Wilmington, DE: Scholarly Resources.

Duflo, E., R.Glennerster and M. Kremer. (2006) "Using Randomization in Development Economics Research: A Toolkit," *NBER Working Paper No. W10008*.

Durlauf, S.N. (2002) "Symposium on Social Capital: Introduction," *The Economic Journal* 112(483): 417–18.

Dworkin, G. (12/20/2005) "Paternalism," *Stanford Encyclopedia of Philosophy*, available at: http://plato.stanford.edu/entries/paternalism/.

Easterly, W. (2006) *The White Man's Burden: Why the West's Effort to Aid the Rest Have Done so Much Ill and so Little Good*, New York, NY: Penguin Press.

Eberstadt, N. (1994) "Demographic Shocks After Communism: Eastern Germany, 1989-93," *Population Development Review* 20(1): 137–52.

Economist. (8/31/2000). "Wall Street dramas: Lesson learned?" Economist.com, from *The Economist* print edition.

Edwards, F.R. (1999) "Hedge Funds and the Collapse of Long-Term Capital Management," *Journal of Economic Perspectives* 13(2): 189–210.

Eichengreen, B. (4/30/2009) "The Last Temptation of Risk," *National Interest online*.

Enders, W. and G.A. Hoover. (2004) "Whose Line is it? Plagiarism in Economics," *Journal of Economic Literature* 42(2): 487–93.

Epstein, R.A. (2008) *In Pursuit of Liberalism: International Institutions in Postcommunist Europe*, Baltimore: Johns Hopkins University Press.

Evans, J.M. (2000) "A Sociological Account of the Growth of Principlism," *Hastings Center Report* 30(5): 31–38.

Everitt, B.S. (2002) *The Cambridge Dictionary of Statistics, 2nd ed.*, Cambridge, UK: Cambridge University Press.

Faden, R.R. and T.L. Beauchamp. (1986) *A History and Theory of Informed Consent*, New York, NY: Oxford University Press.

Fetter, F.A. (1925) "The Economists and the Public," *The American Economic Review* 15(1): 13–26.

Financial Times Editors. (5/12/2009) "The Consequences of Bad Economics," *Financial Times*: 39.

Fiore, A. (January 2009) "Experimental Economics: Some Methodological Notes," Munich Personal RePEc Archive.

Fox, J. (2009) *The Myth of the Rational Market: A History of Risk, Reward, and Delusion on Wall Street*, New York, NY: HarperCollins.

Fox, P. (1991) "The Economic Expert in Wrongful Death/Personal Injury Cases: Workable Competition or Monopoly Power?" *Journal of Forensic Economics* 4(3): 255–62.

Frank, R.H., T. Gilovich and D.T. Regan. (1993) "Does Studying Economics inhibit Cooperation?" *Journal of Economic Perspectives* 7(2): 159–71.

Freeman, A. (2009) "The Economists of Tomorrow," *MPRA Working Paper 15691*, available at: http://mpra.ub.uni-muenchen.de/15691/1/MPRA_paper_15691.pdf.

Freeman, R.B. (1994) "What direction for labor market institutions in Eastern and Central Europe?" in O.J. Blanchard, K.A. Froot and J.D. Sachs (eds.) *The Transition in Eastern Europe*: Vol. 2, Chicago, IL: University of Chicago Press.

Frey, B.S. (1997) "A Constitution for Knaves Crowds out Civic Virtues," *Economic Journal* 107(4): 1043–53.

Friedman, M. (1962) *Capitalism and Freedom*, Chicago: University of Chicago Press.

———. (9/13/1970) "The Social Responsibility of Business is to Increase its Profits," *New York Times Magazine*: 32–33 and 122–26.

Friedman, M. and R.D. Friedman. (1999) *Two Lucky People: Memoirs*, Chicago, IL: Chicago University Press.

Furner, M.O. (1975) *Advocacy and Objectivity: A Crisis in Professionalization of American Social Sciences, 1865–1905*, Lexington, KY: University of Kentucky Press.

Galbraith, J.K. (2009) "Who are these Economists, Anyway?" *Thought and Action* (Fall): 87–97.

Garnett, R.F. (2009a) "Liberal Learning as Freedom: A Capabilities Approach to Undergraduate Education," *Studies in Philosophy & Education* 28(5): 437–47.

———. (2009b) "Rethinking the Pluralist Debate in Economics Education," *International Review of Economic Education* 8(2): 58–71.

Garnett, R.F. and M.R. Butler. (2009) "Should Economics Educators Care About Students' Academic Freedom?" *International Journal of Pluralism and Economics Education* 1(1–2): 148–60.

Garrard, E. and A. Dawson. (2005) "What is the Role of the Research Ethics Committee? Paternalism, Inducements and Harm in Research," *Journal of Medical Ethics* 31(7): 419–23.

Gibson-Graham, J.K. (1996) *The End of Capitalism (as we knew it): A Feminist Critique of Political Economy*, Oxford, UK: Blackwell Publishers.

Gintis, H. and R. Khurana. (2008) "Corporate Honesty and Business Education: A Behavioral Model," in P.J. Zak (ed.) *Moral Markets: The Critical Role of Values in the Economy*, Princeton, NJ: Princeton University Press: 300–27.

Goldman, A.H. (1980) *The Moral Foundations of Professional Ethics*, Totowa, NJ: Rowman and Littlefield.

Goode, W.J. (1960) "Encroachment, Charlatanism, and the Emerging Profession: Psychology, Sociology, and Medicine," *American Sociological Review* 25(6): 902–65.

Goodman, P.S. (10/9/2008) "Taking Hard New Look at the Greenspan Legacy," *New York Times*: A1.

Grabel, I. (1996) "Financial Markets, the State and Economic Development: Controversies within Theory and Policy," *International Papers in Political Economy* 3(1): 1–42.

Greenspan, A. (10/5/2004) *Remarks at the American Bankers Association Annual Convention*. New York, NY.

_____. (5/15/2005) *Commencement address*. Wharton School, University of Pennsylvania, Philadelphia, Pennsylvania, available at: http://www.federalreserve.gov/boarddocs/speeches/2005/20050515/.

Griffiths, P. (2003) *The Economist's Tale: A Consultant Encounters Hunger and the World Bank*, London: Zed Press.

Grusky, D. and R. Kanbur. (2006) "The Conceptual Foundations of Poverty and Inequality Measurement," in D. Grusky and R. Kanbur (eds.) *Poverty and Inequality*, Stanford, CA: Stanford University Press: 1–29.

Gueron, J.M. (2002) "The Politics of Random Assignment: Implementing Studies and Affecting Policy," in F. Mosteller and R. Boruch (eds.) *Evidence Matters: Randomized Trials in Education Research*, Washington, DC: Brookings Institution Press: 15–49.

Hahn, R.W. and C.R. Sunstein. (2005) "The Precautionary Principle as a Basis for Decision Making," *The Economist's Voice* 2(2): Article 8.

Hamilton, L.H. (1992) "Economists as Public Policy Advisers," *Journal of Economics Perspectives* 6(3): 61–64.

Hansen, W.L. (1991) "The Education and Training of Economics Doctorates: Major Findings of the Executive Secretary of the American Economics Association's Committee on Graduate Education in Economics," *Journal of Economic Literature* 29(3): 1054–87.

Hardwig, J. (1994) "Toward and Ethics of Expertise," in D.E. Wueste (ed.) *Professional Ethics and Social Responsibility*, Lanham, MD: Rowman and Littlefield Publishers: 83–101.

Harris, G. (3/27/2009) "3 Researchers at Harvard are Named in Subpoena," *New York Times*, available at: http://www.nytimes.com/2009/03/28/health/policy/28subpoena.html?ref=us).

_____. (11/9/2009) "Academic Researchers' Conflicts of Interest Go Unreported," *New York Times*: A17.

Hayek, F. (1978) *New Studies in Philosophy, Politics, Economics and the History of Ideas*, London: Routledge.

Heckman, J.J and J. A. Smith. (1995) "Assessing the Case for Social Experiments," *The Journal of Economic Perspectives* 9(2): 85–110.

Heermance, E.L. (1924) *Codes of Ethics: A Handbook*, Burlington, VT: Free Press.

Henderson, J.B. (1977) "Professional Standards for the Performance of the Government Economist," *American Economic Review* 67(1): 321–25.

Hertwig, R. and A. Ortmann. (2008) "Deception in Experiments: Revisiting the Arguments in Its Defense," *Ethics & Behavior* 18(1): 59–92.

Hinshaw, C.E. and J.J. Siegfried. (1991) "The Role of the American Economics Association in Economic Education: A Brief History," *Journal of Economic Education* 22(4): 373–81.

Hippocrates. (1995) *Epidemics, Bk. I*, Section 1 (trans.) W.H.S. Jones, Loebs Classic Edition, Cambridge, MA: Harvard University Press.

Hirschman, A.O. (1970) "The Search for Paradigms as a Hindrance to Understanding," *World Politics* 22(3): 329–43.

———. (1980) "The Turn to Authoritarianism in Latin America and the Search for its Economic Determinants," in D. Collier (ed.) *The New Authoritarianism in Latin America*, Princeton, NJ: Princeton University Press: 86–87.

———. (1988) "How Keynes Was Spread from America," *Challenge* 31(8): 4–7.

Holland, K. (3/15/2009) "Is it Time to Retrain B-Schools?" *New York Times*: BU1.

Hont, I. (2005) "Adam Smith and the Political Economy of the 'Unnatural and Retrograde Order,'" in I. Hont *Jealousy of Trade: International Competition and the Nation-State in Historical Perspective*, Cambridge, MA: Harvard University Press: 354–88.

Houser, D. (2008) "A Note on Norms in Experimental Economics," *Eastern Economic Journal* 34(1): 126–28.

International Monetary Fund, Ethics Office. (2007) *Annual Report 2007: Practical Ethics*.

International Statistics Institute. (August 1985) "Declaration on Professional Ethics."

Jackson, W. (2005) "Toward an Ignorance-Based Worldview," *The Land Report* 81(Spring): 14–16.

Johnson, S. (5/2009) "The Quiet Coup," *The Atlantic Online*, available at: http://www.theatlantic.com/doc/print/200905/imf-advice.

Johnson, W.D. (1991) "Qualifications, Ethics and Professional Responsibility in Forensic Economics," *Journal of Forensic Economics* 4(3): 277–85.

———. (1995) "Ethics in Forensic Economics: A Reply to Depperschmidt," *Journal of Forensic Economics* 8(3): 289–91.

Kaletsky, A. (2/5/2009) "Economists are the Forgotten Guilty Men," *TimesOnline*, available at: http://www.timesonline.co.uk/tol/comment/columnists/anatole_kaletsky/article5663091.ece.

Kanbur, R. (2001) "Economic Policy, Distribution and Poverty: The Nature of Disagreements," *World Development* 29(6): 1083–94.

———. (2007) "Development Disagreements and Water Privatization: Bridging the Divide," WP 2007–09, Cornell University, Department of Applied Economics and Management.

———. (2009a) "Why Might History Matter for Development Policy?" WP 2009–02, Cornell University, Department of Applied Economics and Management.

———. (2009b) "The Co-Evolution of the Washington Consensus and the Economic Development Discourse," WP 2009–05, Cornell University, Department of Applied Economics and Management.

———. (2009c) "A Typical Scene: Five Exposures to Poverty," WP 2009–06, Cornell University, Department of Applied Economics and Management.

Kaplan, F. (10/11/2005) "All Pain, No Gain," *Slate Magazine*, available at: http://slate.msn.com/id/2127862/.

Keynes, J.M. (1964) *The General Theory of Employment, Interest, and Money*, New York, NY: Harcourt, Brace, and World.

Kindleberger, C.P. (2000) *Manias, Panics and Crashes, 4th ed.*, Hoboken, NJ: John Wiley & Sons.

Klamer, A. and D. Colander. (1990) *The Making of an Economist*, Boulder, CO: Westview Press.

Klein, N. (2007) *The Shock Doctrine: The Rise of Disaster Capitalism*, New York, NY: Metropolitan Books/Henry Holt.

Kleiner, M.M. (2000) "Occupational Licensing," *The Journal of Economic Perspectives* 14(4): 189–202.

———. (2006) *Licensing Occupations: Ensuring Quality or Restricting Competition?* Kalamazoo, MI: W.W. Upjohn Institute for Employment Research.

Knight, F.H. (1921) *Risk, Uncertainty and Profit*, Boston, MA: Houghton Mifflin Co.

Krueger, A.O. (1991) "Report of the Commission on Graduate Education in Economics," *Journal of Economic Literature* 29(3): 1035–53.

Krugman, P. (3/20/1997) "In Praise of Cheap Labor," *Slate*, available at: http://www.slate.com/id/1918.

———. (4/22/2001) "Hearts and Heads," *New York Times*: 4.

———. (5/14/2007) "Divided Over Trade," *New York Times*: A19.

———. (8/9/2009) "School for Scoundrels," *New York Times Book Review*: 11.

———. (9/6/2009) "How Did Economists Get it so Wrong?" *New York Times Magazine*: 36–43.

Kuran, T. (1995) *Private Truths, Public Lies: The Social Consequences of Preference Falsification*, Cambridge, MA: Harvard University Press.

Kydland, F. and E.C. Prescott. (1977) "Rules Rather than Discretion: The Inconsistency of Optimal Plans," *Journal of Political Economy* 85: 473–91.

Laband, D.N. and M.J. Piette. (2000) "Perceived Conduct and Professional Ethics Among College Economics Faculty," *American Economist* 44(1): 24–33.

Lahart, J. (1/1/2009) "Ignoring the Oracles: You Are With the Free Markets, or Against Them," *Wall Street Journal Blogs: Real Time Economics*, available at: http://blogs.wsj.com/economics/2009/01/01/ignoring-the-oracles/tab/article/.

———. (1/2/2009) "Mr. Rajan Was Unpopular (But Prescient) at Greenspan Party," *Wall Street Journal*: A7.

Larson, M.S. (1977) *The Rise of Professionalism: A Sociological Analysis*, Berkeley, CA: University of California Press.

Law, M.T. and S. Kim. (2005) "Specialization and Regulation: The Rise of Professionals and the Emergence of Occupational Licensing Regulation," *The Journal of Economic History* 65(3): 723–56.

Leamer, E.E. (1978) *Specification Searches: Ad Hoc Inference with Nonexperimental Data*, New York, NY: John Wiley & Sons.

———. (1983) "Let's Take the Con Out of Econometrics," *The American Economic Review* 73(1): 31–43.

Leland, H. E. (1979) "Quacks, Lemons and Licensing: A Theory of Minimum Quality Standards," *The Journal of Political Economy* 87(6): 1328–46.

Letelier, O. (8/28/1976) "The Chicago Boys in Chile: Economic Freedom's Awful Toll," *The Nation*: 137–42.

Levitt, S.D. (10/12/2009) "*What This Year's Nobel Prize in Economics Says about the Nobel Prize in Economics*," New York Times Blog. Available at: http://freakonomics.blogs.nytimes.com/2009/10/12/what-this-years-nobel-prize-in-economics-says-about-the-nobel-prize-in-economics/.

Levy, D.M. and S.J. Peart. (2008) "Inducing Greater Transparency: Towards the Establishment of Ethical Rules for Econometrics," *Eastern Economic Journal* 34(1): 103–14.

Lock, F.P. (2007) "Adam Smith and "the man of system": interpreting The Theory of Moral Sentiments, VI.ii.2.12–18," *The Adam Smith Review* 3: 37–48.

Lohr, S. (11/5/2008) "Wall Street's Extreme Sport," *New York Times*: B1, 5.

Lowenstein, R. (9/7/2008) "Long-Term Capital: It's a Short-Term Memory," *New York Times*: B1, 9.

_____. (2000) *When Genius Failed: The Rise and Fall of Long-Term Capital Management*, New York, NY: Random House.

Luban, D. and M. Millemann. (1995) "Good Judgment: Ethics Teaching in Dark Times," *Georgetown Journal of Legal Ethics* 9(31): 31–87.

Machlup, F. (1965) "Why Economists Disagree," *Proceedings of the Philosophical Society* 109(1): 1–7.

Mandel, M.J. (1999) "Going for the Gold: Economists as Expert Witnesses," *Journal of Economic Perspectives* 13(2): 113–20.

Mankiw, N.G. (2006) "The Macroeconomist as Scientist and Engineer," *Journal of Economic Perspectives* 20(4): 29–46.

_____. (10/26/2008) "But Have We Learned Enough?" *New York Times*: B1, 6.

Maslin, J. (1/25/2009) "Connecting the Dots," *New York Times*: E13.

Matthews, R.C.O. (7/1991) "The Economics of Professional Ethics: Should the Professions be More Like Business?" *The Economic Journal* 101 (407): 737–50.

Mauro, P. (2/1997) "Why Worry about Corruption?" *Economic Issues Publication* 6, IMF.

May, W.F. (1980) "Professional Ethics: Setting, Terrain, and Teacher," in D. Callahan and S. Bok (eds.) *Ethics Teaching in Higher Education*, New York, NY: Plenum Press: 205–41.

_____. (2001) *Beleaguered Rulers: The Public Obligation of the Professional*, Louisville, KY: Westminster John Knox Press.

Mayer, T. (2009a) "Honesty and Integrity in Academic Economics," *UC Davis Working Paper Series, No. 09–2*, University of California at Davis, Department of Economics.

_____. (2009b) "Honesty and Integrity in Academic Economics," *Challenge* 52(4): 16–24.

McClintick, D. (2006) "How Harvard Lost Russia," *Institutional Investor International Edition* 30(12): 66–94.

McCloskey, D.N. (1990) *If You're So Smart: The Narrative of Economic Expertise*, Chicago, IL: University of Chicago Press.

_____. (1996) *The Vices of Economists, the Virtues of the Bourgeoisie*, Amsterdam: Amsterdam University Press.

_____. (2000) *How to be Human, Though an Economist*, Ann Arbor, MI: University of Michigan.

_____. (2005) "The Trouble with Mathematics and Statistics in Economics," *History of Economic Ideas* 13(3): 85–102.

McCloskey, D.N. and S.T. Ziliak. (1996) "The Standard Error of Regressions," *Journal of Economic Literature* 34(March): 97–114.

McMillan, J. (2008) "Avoid Hubris: And Other Lessons for Reformers," in W. Easterly (ed.) *Reinventing Foreign Aid*, Cambridge, MA: MIT Press: 505–13.

Meyer, L.H. (2004) *A Term at the Fed: An Insider's View*, New York, NY: HarperCollins.

Mill, J.S. (1859) *On Liberty*, London, UK: Pelican Books.

Miller, J.P. (5/1954) "Round Table Discussion of the Bowen Report on Graduate Training in Economics," *American Economic Review* 44(2): 680–82, Papers and Proceedings of the Sixty-sixth Annual Meeting of the American Economic Association.

Mirowski, P. (2002) *Machine Dreams: Economics Becomes a Cyborg Science*, Cambridge, UK: Cambridge University Press.

Montague, P. (2/19/1998) "The Precautionary Principle," *Rachel's Environment and Health Weekly* 586.

Morgan, M.G. and M. Henrion. (1990) *Uncertainty: A guide to Dealing with Uncertainty in Quantitative Risk and Policy Analysis*, Cambridge, UK: Cambridge University Press.

Murrell, P. (1995) "The Transition According to Cambridge, Mass.," *Journal of Economic Literature* 33(1): 164–78.

Nama, N. and L. Swartz. (2002) "Ethical and Social Dilemmas in Community-Based Controlled Trials in Situations of Poverty: A View from a South African Project," *Journal of Community and Applied Social Psychology* 12 (4): 286–97.

Nathan, R. P. (2008) "Point/Counterpoint: The Role of Random Assignment in Social Policy Research," *Journal of Policy Analysis and Management* 27 (2): 401–15.

National Association of Forensic Economics. (Undated) "Statement of Ethical Principles and Principles of Professional Practice National Association of Forensic Economics (NAFE)." Available at: http://nafe.net/about-nafe/nafes-ethics-statement.html.

National Opinion Research Center (NORC), University of Chicago. (2006) *Doctorate Recipients from United States Universities, Summary Report 2006*. Sponsored by the NSF, NIH, U.S. Dept. of Education, NEH, USDA and NASA, available at: http://www.norc.org/projects/Survey+of+Earned+Doctorates.htm.

Nelson, J. (2004) "Clocks, Creation and Clarity: Insights on Ethics and Economics from a Feminist Perspective," *Ethical Theory and Moral Practice* 7 (August): 381–98.

Nelson, R.H. (1987) "Economics Profession and the Making of Public Policy," *Journal of Economic Literature* 25 (1): 49–91.

——. (3/22/2003) "What is "Economic Theology"? Speech delivered to the Second Abraham Kuyper Consultation "Theology and Economic Life," Princeton Theological Seminary, Princeton, NJ.

——. (2010) *The New Holy Wars: Economic Religion Versus Environmental Religion in Contemporary America*, University Park, PA: Pennsylvania State Press.

Nocera, J. (1/4/2009) "Risk Mismanagement," *New York Times Magazine*: 24–33, 46, 50–51.

——. (6/6/2009) "Poking Holes in a Theory on Markets," *New York Times*: B1, 5.

Nozick, R. (1974) *Anarchy, State and Utopia*, New York, NY: Basic Books.

Nussbaum, M. and A. Sen. (1989) "Internal Criticism and Indian Rationalist Traditions," in M. Krausz (ed.) *Relativism: Interpretation and Confrontation*, Notre Dame, IN: University of Notre Dame Press: 299–325.

Oakley, A. *et al.* (2003) "Using Random Allocation to Evaluate Social Interventions: Three Recent U.K. Examples," *Annals of the American Academy of Political and Social Science* 589(September): 170–89.

O'Brien, D.P. (1994) *Methodology, Money and the Firm*, Brookfield, VT: Edward Elgar.

Orphanides, A. and J.C. Williams. (2002) "Robust Monetary Policy Rules with Unknown Natural Rates," Federal Reserve Bank of San Francisco Working Paper 2003–01.

Ortmann, A. and R. Hertwig. (2002) "The Costs of Deception: Evidence from Psychology," *Experimental Economics* 5(2): 111–31.

Peart, S.J. and D.M. Levy. (2007) *The "Vanity of the Philosopher": From Equality to Hierarchy in Post-classical Economics*, Ann Arbor, MI: University of Michigan Press.

_____. (2008) "Introduction to the Symposium on Ethics," *Eastern Economic Journal* 34(1): 101–02.

Pilkington, E. (4/5/2008) "How to Save the World," *The Guardian.*

Pollan, M. (12/9/2001) "Precautionary Principle," *New York Times Magazine*: 92, 94.

Postrel, V. (4/2009) "Macroegonomics," *The Atlantic*: 32–35.

Powers, J.S. (2005) "Overview of the Rules on Conduct and Ethics at the IMF," in C. de Cooker (ed.) *Accountability, Investigation and Due Process in International Organizations*, Boston, MA: Martinus Nijhoff Publishers.

Price, D. H. (1998) "Cold War Anthropology: Collaborators and Victims of the National Security State," *Identities* 43(3-4): 389–430.

Pritchett, L. (2008) "It Pays to be Ignorant: A Simple Political Economy of Rigorous Program Evaluation," in W. Easterly (ed.) *Reinventing Foreign Aid*, Cambridge, MA: MIT Press: 121–44.

Rachels, S. (2007) *The Elements of Moral Philosophy, 5th ed.*, Boston, MA: McGraw-Hill.

Radest, H.B. (1997) "First, Do No Harm! Medical Ethics and Moral Education," *Humanism Today* 11.

Rajan, R.G. (11/2005) "Has Financial Development Made the World Riskier?" NBER Working Paper No. *W11728.*

Rankin, K.N. (2002) "Social Capital, Microfinance and the Politics of Development," *Feminist Economics* 8(1): 1–24.

Ransom, D. (1975) "Ford Country: Building an Elite for Indonesia," in S. Weissman (ed.) *The Trojan Horse: A Radical Look at Foreign Aid, (rev. ed.)*, Palo Alto, CA: Ramparts Press: 93–116.

Ravallion, M. (2009a) "Should the Randomistas Rule?" *Economist's Voice* 6(2): article 6, available at: http://www.bepress.com/ev/vol6/iss2/art6/.

_____. (2009b) "Evaluation in the Practice of Development," *The World Bank Observer* 24(1): 29–53.

Rawls, J. (1971) *A Theory of Justice*, Cambridge, MA: Harvard University Press.

Resnick, S.A. and R.D Wolff. (1987) *Knowledge and Class*, Chicago, IL: University of Chicago Press.

Rhode, D.L. (1992) "Ethics by the Pervasive Method," *Journal of Legal Education* 42(1): 31–56.

Rhodes, R. (2005) "Rethinking Research Ethics," *The American Journal of Bioethics* 5(1): 7–28.

Roach, S. (7/19/2004) "The World's Biggest Hedge Fund," *Morgan Stanley Today.*

Rodrik, D. (1998) "Who Needs Capital Account Convertibility?" in P.B. Kenen (ed.) *Should the IMF Pursue Capital Account Convertibility?* Essays in International Economics 207, International Economics Section, Princeton, NJ: Princeton University Press.

_____. (1997) *Has Globalization Gone too Far?* Washington, DC: Institute for International Economics.

Ross, A. (2009) "The Knowledge and Skills Required by the GES," *Royal Economic Society Newsletter* 147: 6–8.

Ross, D. (1991) *The Origins of American Social Science*, Cambridge, UK: Cambridge University Press.

Roth, A.E. (1994) "Let's Keep the Con out of Experimental Econ: A Methodological Note," *Empirical Economics* 19(2): 279–89.

Ruccio, D.F. and J. Amariglio. (2003) *Postmodern Moments in Modern Economics*, Princeton, NJ: Princeton University Press.

Sachs, J. (1991) "Poland and Eastern Europe: What Is To Be Done?" in A. Kovas and P. Marer (eds.) *Foreign Economic Liberalization: Transformations in Socialist and Market Economies*, Boulder, CO: Westview Press: 235–46.

_____. (1993) "Life in the Economic Emergency Room," in J. Williamson (ed.) *The Political Economy of Policy Reform*, Washington D.C.: Institute for International Economics: 501–23.

_____. (2005) *The End of Poverty*, New York, NY: Penguin Press.

Sartre, J.P. (1960) "Dirty Hands," in *No Exit and Three Other Plays*, (trans.) Lionel Abel, New York, NY: Vintage.

Sattler, E.S. (1991) "Economists, Ethics, and the Marketplace," *Journal of Forensic Economics* 4(3): 263–68.

Schön, D.A. (1987) *Educating the Reflective Practitioner*, San Francisco, CA: Jossey-Bass.

_____. (1991) *The Reflective Practitioner: How Professionals Think in Action*, Aldershot, UK: Ashgate Publishing.

Schultze, C.L. (1982) "The Role and Responsibility of the Economist in Government," *American Economic Review* 72(2): 62–66.

Sen, A. (1987) *On Ethics and Economics*, London, UK: Blackwell.

_____. (1992) *Inequality Reexamined*, Cambridge, MA: Harvard University Press.

_____. (1999) *Development as Freedom*, New York, NY: Alfred A. Knopf.

SEWA-World Bank. (2003) *Exposure and Dialogue Programmes: A Grassroots Immersion Tool for Understanding Poverty and Influencing Policy*, Ahmedabad, India: SEWA.

Shapiro, C. (1986) "Investment, Moral Hazard, and Occupational Licensing," *The Review of Economic Studies* 53(5): 843–62.

Shiller, R. (2005) *Irrational Exuberance, 2nd ed.*, Princeton, NJ: Princeton University Press.

_____. (11/2/2008) "Challenging the Crowd in Whispers, Not Shouts," *New York Times*: B5.

_____. (5/12/2009) "The Future of Capitalism: A Failure to Control Animal Spirits," *Financial Times Magazine*: 14–16.

Shuster, E. (November 13, 1997) "Fifty Years Later: The significance of the Nuremberg Code," *The New England Journal of Medicine* 337: 1436–40.

_____. (1998) "The Nuremberg Code: Hippocratic Ethics and Human Rights," *Lancet* 351(9107): 974–77.

Siegfried, J.J. (Undated) "Demographic Profile of Doctoral Recipients in Economics and Econometrics, Selected Years, 1960-2006" (data from NORC).

Siegfried, J.J. and W.A. Stock. (2004) "The Market for New Ph.D. Economists in 2002," *American Economic Review Papers and Proceedings* 94(2): 272–85.

Silk, L.S. (1972) "Truth vs. Partisan Political Purpose," *American Economic Review* 62(1–2): 376–78.

Silva, P. (1991) "Technocrats and Politics in Chile," *Journal of Latin American Studies* 23(2): 385–410.

Skousen, M. (2006) *The Big Three in Economics: Adam Smith, Karl Marx, and John Maynard Keynes*, Armonk, NY: M.E. Sharpe.

Smart, J.J.C. and B. Williams. (1973) *Utilitarianism: For and Against*, London, UK: Cambridge University Press.

Smith, A. (1976) [1759] *The Theory of Moral Sentiments*, Oxford, UK: Clarendon Press.

Stigler, G.J. (1965) "The Economist and the State," Presidential Address to the American Economic Association 1964," *American Economic Review* 60: 1–18.

_____. (1980) *Economics or Ethics?* The Tanner Lectures on Human Values, Cambridge, MA: Harvard University Press.

Stiglitz, J. 2000. "Ethics, Economic Advice, and Economic Policy." Available at: http://www.policyinnovations.org/ideas/policy_library/data/01216.

_____. (2002) *Globalization and its Discontents*, New York, NY: W.W. Norton.

_____. (January 2009a) "Capitalist Fools," *Vanity Fair* 51(1): 48.

_____. (2009b) "The Current Economic Crisis and Lessons for Economic Theory," *Eastern Economic Journal* 35: 281–96.

_____. (2009c) "Wall Street's Toxic Message," *Vanity Fair* 51(7): 82.

Stock, W.A. and W.L. Hansen. (2004) "Ph.D. Program Learning and Job Demands: How Close is the Match?" *AEA Papers and Proceedings* (May): 266–71.

Stodder, J. (1998) "Experimental Moralities: Ethics in Classroom Experiments," *Journal of Economic Education* 29(2): 127–38.

Stuckler, D., L. King and M. McKee. (1/15/2009) "Mass Privatisation and the Post-Communist Mortality Crisis: a Cross-National Analysis," *The Lancet*, Early Online Publication. Original Text.

Sullivan, W.M. (2005) *Work and Integrity: The Crisis and Promise of Professionalism in America, 2nd ed.*, San Francisco, CA: Jossey-Bass.

Svensson, J. (2005) "Eight Questions about Corruption," *The Journal of Economic Perspectives* 19(3): 19–42.

Tetlock, P.E. (2005) *Expert Political Judgment*, Princeton, NJ: Princeton University Press.

Thaler, R.H. and C.R. Sunstein. (2008) *Nudge: Improving Decisions about Health, Wealth and Happiness* (rev. ed.), New York, NY: Penguin Books.

Thompson, D.F. (1983) "Ascribing Responsibility to Advisers in Government," *Ethics* 93(3): 546–60.

_____. (1987) *Political Ethics and Public Office*, Cambridge, MA: Harvard University Press.

Ulrich, G. (2003) "Charges and Counter-charges of Ethical Imperialism: Towards a Situated Approach to Development Ethics," in P. Quarles, V. Ufford and A. Kumar Giri (eds.) *A Moral Critique of Development*, New York, NY: Routledge: 153–68.

United Nations Children's Fund (UNICEF). (11/1993) "Public Policy and Social Conditions," *Regional Monitoring Report No. 1*, Florence: UNICEF Innocenti Research Centre.

U.S. Office of Personnel Management, "Employment-Sept. 2008," available at: http://www.fedscope.opm.gov/.

Venter, C.M. (1996) "Encouraging Personal Responsibility: An Alternative Approach to Teaching Legal Ethics," *Law and Contemporary Problems* 58(3/4): 287–96.

Walzer, M. (1973) "Political Action: The Problem of Dirty Hands," *Philosophy and Public Affairs* 2(2): 160–80.

Wayne, L. (5/29/2009) "A Promise to Be Ethical in an Era of Immorality," *New York Times*: B1.

Wedel, J.R. (2001) *Collision and Collusion: The Strange Case of Western Aid to Eastern Europe*, New York, NY: Palgrave.

Weinstein, J. (1968) *The Corporate Ideal in the Liberal State 1900–1918*, Boston, MA: Beacon Press.

Weinstein, M. (1992) "Economists and the Media," *Journal of Economic Perspectives* 6(3): 73–77.

Welch, S.D. (2000) *A Feminist Theory of Risk* (rev. ed.), Minneapolis, MN: Fortress Press.

Weisbrot, M. and D. Baker. (7/20/2004) "Applying Economics to Economists: Good Governance at the International Financial Institutions," *CEPR Briefing Paper*.

Weitzman, M.L. (2009) "On Modeling and Interpreting the Economics of Catastrophic Climate Change," *The Review of Economics and Statistics* 91(1): 1–19.

Westin, A.F. (ed.). (1981) *Whistle Blowing! Loyalty and Dissent in the Corporation*, New York, NY: McGraw Hill.

Weston, S.C. (1998) "Toward a Better Understanding of the Positive/Normative Distinction in Economics," in C.K. Wilbur (ed.) *Economics, Ethics and Public Policy*, Lanham, MD: Rowman and Littlefield: 33–49.

Wight, J.B. (2007) "The Treatment of Smith's Invisible Hand," *Journal of Economic Education* 38(3): 341–58.

Williams, B. (1973) "A Critique of Utilitarianism," in J.J.C. Smart and B. Williams, *Utilitarianism: For and Against*, London, UK: Cambridge University Press: 77–150.

Wilson, D. (1/3/2010) "Hospitals Connected to Harvard Cap Outside Pay to Top Officials," *New York Times*: 1.

Winston, K.I. (1994) "Necessity and Choice in Political Ethics: Varieties of Dirty Hands," in D.E. Wueste (ed.) *Professional Ethics and Social Responsibility*, Lanham, MD: Rowman and Littlefield: 37–66.

Wolf, A. (2000) "Informed Consent: A Negotiated Formula for Trade in Risky Organisms and Chemicals," *International Negotiation* 5(3): 485–521.

———. (2002) "The Emergence and Implementation of the Advance Informed Agreement Procedure," in P.G. Le Prestre (ed.) *Governing Global Biodiversity: the Evolution and Implementation of the Convention on Biological Diversity*, Burlington, VT: Ashgate: 127–44.

Wolpe, P.R. (1998) "The Triumph of Autonomy in American Bioethics: A Sociological Approach," in R. DeVries and J. Subedi (eds.) *Bioethics and Society*, Upper Saddle River, NJ: Prentice Hall: 38–59.

World Bank. (1995) *World Development Report*, Oxford, UK: Oxford University Press.

World Bank Group. (12/1999) "Living our Values: Code of Professional Ethics," available at: http://www.worldbank.org/ethics.

Woodward, R.T. and R.C. Bishop. (1997) "How to Decide when Experts Disagree: Uncertainty-Based Choice Rules in Environmental Policy," *Land Economics* 73(4): 492–507.

Wueste, D.E. (ed.). (1994) *Professional Ethics and Social Responsibility*, Lanham, MD: Rowman and Littlefield.

Yeager, L.B. (1976) "Economics and Principles," *Southern Economic Journal* 42(4): 559–71.

Zak, P.J. (2008) "Introduction," in P.J. Zak (ed.) *Moral Markets: The Critical Role of Values in the Economy*, Princeton, NJ: Princeton University Press: xi–xxii.

Zelder, M. (2008) "Why the Con Hasn't Been Taken Out of Econometrics," *Eastern Economic Journal* 34(1): 115–25.

Ziliak, S.T. and D.N. McCloskey. (2004) "Size Matters: The Standard Error of Regressions in the *American Economic Review*," *Journal of Socio-Economics* 33(5): 527–46.

_____. (2008) *The Cult of Statistical Significance*, Ann Arbor, MI: University of Michigan Press.

Index

Global economic crisis (*cont.*)
  due to mainstream economic
    thoughts, 162–66
  and economic theory, 169–71
  and efficient market hypothesis
    (EMH), 162–66
  hedge fund crisis, 166
  high-tech stock crisis, 166
  housing market crisis, 166
  lessons from, 159
  and "maxi-max" principle, 160–62
Global financial distress, 7
Good professional conduct, 105
Government-induced monopoly,
  effects of, 78
Government sponsored enterprises
  (GSEs), 164
Grantham, Jeremy, 167
Greenspan, Alan, 7–8, 161, 164–65, 197
Gresham's Law, 42
Griffiths, P., 195
Group think, 47–48
Guru worship, 47–48

H
Hamilton, Lee, 196
Hampshire, Stuart, 108
Harberger, Arnold, 8
Hardwig, J., 196
Haymarket Riot, Chicago, 56
"Heal the patient" directive, 125
Hedgehogs, 194
Heritage Foundation, 33
Hindsight bias, 197
Hinshaw, C. Elton, 63
Hippocratic Oath, 96, 128
Historical perspective, in
  economics, 55–58
  of American Economic Association
    (AEA), 58–66
Holocaust, 133
Hughes, Everett C., 12
Human behavior and professional
  economic ethics, 88–91

I
Inducements, 4
Informed consent, 130–32, 138*n*6, 152
Institutionalized power, 109–11
Intellectual enterprise, 78

Intellectual pluralism, 15
International Financial Institutions
  (IFIs) economists, 29–31

J
Jackson, Wes, 198
Job insecurity, 50
Job pressure, 50
Johnson, Harry G., 196
Johnson, Simon, 148, 166

K
Kanbur, Ravi, 147, 223–25
Kantian principle, 128
Kazakhstan, impact of economic
  errors, 9
Keynesianism, 11–12, 165
Keynesian macro-models, 11
Keynesian managerialism, 149
Khurana, Rakesh, 96
Klamer, Arjo, 208–9
Kohn, Donald, 165
Krugman, Paul, 163, 167

L
Lancet, The, 9
Latvia, impact of economic errors, 9
Laughlin, J. Laurence, 59
Leamer, Edward, 177
Levy, David, 178–79
Liberal-left economists, 12
Licensure, 77–78
Lindsay, R.C.L., 181
Lithuania, impact of economic errors, 9
Lo, Andrew M., 166
Long-Term Capital Management
  (LTCM), 5–6, 110
  debacle, 6

M
Mac, Fannie, 164
Mac, Freddie, 164
Machlup, Fritz, 114
Mainstream economic theory, 111
Mainstream neoclassical economic
  theory, 76
Management, Scientific and Technical
  Consulting Services, 21
Margin rules, 6
Market liberalization, 10